THROUGH RED LENSES

It was the Labour Party which made Britain 'Great'

By Danny Marten and Dermot Rathbone (2011- 2014)

First published 2014 by Searching Finance Ltd, ISBN 978-1-907720-69-7

Typesetting by Randesign UK

During the three years it took to complete this book the authors have had to endure and overcome two life-threatening illnesses; anti-GAD Cerebellar Ataxia and Testicular cancer, spread to lymph nodes and lungs. It is with this in mind that we dedicate this book to the small army of NHS staff that saved our lives.

With thanks for Catherine, Conor, Julia, John and Charlie for their eternal patience in us whilst completing this book.

About the authors -

"Danny Marten is a political graduate of The University of Hull. Since graduation he has run his own business that helps companies become more ethical. He is working towards an MA in Globalisation and Political Economy and has a long-term aim of becoming a teacher. He stood for the Labour Party in 2010 for the constituency of Haltemprice and Howden and hopes to stand again, maybe in a more winnable seat one day."

www.twitter.com/dannymarten

http://dannymarten.tumblr.com/

"On graduation with a degree in History from University of Ulster in 1989, Dermot Rathbone worked in a freight warehouse office at Heathrow Airport before completing teacher training in 1990. He went on to work in three secondary schools. He was diagnosed with the devastating brain degenerative disease Cerebella Ataxia and had to retire on ill health grounds in 2005. Thanks to the pioneering work of Prof. Gavin Giovannoni at the Royal London Hospital, the dedication of the staff at the Therapeutic Apheresis Unit at St. James Hospital, Leeds, and the endless support of his beloved wife and son, life is once again liveable. He has been a member of the Labour Party for 30 years and is also active with UNITE the union and the People's Assembly Against Austerity and the Co Operative Movement."

www.twitter.com/DermotR1968

http://dermotrathbone.wordpress.com/

Danny and Dermot met as a result of Danny's campaign to become an MP. Dermot became his constituency party chairman and together they run a number of local campaigns. In 2012, despite them both being gravely ill they founded Save our NHS (Hull & East Yorkshire). Since then they have organised campaigns against government cuts, NHS reform, the bedroom tax and flooding- amongst others.

Contents Page

It should be noted in the later chapters of this book that the statistics may be out of date. This is due to the fast changing nature of modern politics. As such any statistic should be checked against the latest information available.

Chapter 1 - Introduction

Think of the words "the Labour Party" and what do you think of? Labour remains one of the most divisive words in politics. For some, the Labour Party is the social conscience of Britain; it symbolises what it is to be British. It stands for equality, fairness and the struggle to move Britain from the age of empire to the age of modernity.

However, for many others the words 'Labour Party' stir great emotions of anger and frustration. For these people there is something distinctly un-British about Labour and its values. For a generation of young people, for example, the Labour Party no longer stands for the ideals of fairness and equality but instead it has become synonymous with the Iraq War, university tuition fees and sleaze. They could also argue that Labour is now a by-word for economic mismanagement, benefits, greed, political in-fighting and elitism.

Just how did the name of Labour become synonymous with such bleak terms? The Labour Party was formed not on the values of tyranny and greed, but something quite different. Those values that still exist within the vast majority of the party. For the many members who make up the party, the pursuit of social and economic justice remains the core aim of the party.

We will argue that there has been a great political struggle in Britain taking place since the turn of the 20th century. This was a struggle between the political elite - made up of economically neo-liberal politicians - and those who pursued social and economic justice for the many in Britain. The book begins in 1900 where the Liberal elite then in power believed that Britain was a county in rude health; a country where the sun never set on the Empire and where free trade and invention had made Britain the richest and most powerful country in the world. However, there was a bleak underbelly to Britain that the political elite had ignored. Britain in 1900 was a country where around 80% of people lived on or below the poverty line. A great divide between those who had and those who had not had emerged, and politicians had little or no desire to do anything about it.

Why would they? Although the political system was crude, creating great inequality and poverty, it kept many in work - although on chronically poor wages and with little in the way of protection for the employee. It also made many a man extremely wealthy. The political class believed that Britain's prosperity would continue forever. This system of financial liberalism *(which would later morph into neo-liberalism or modern-day capitalism)* had built a position of great economic strength for Britain, but not for many of the people within it. A low-wage economy left many living in squalor, hunger, extreme poverty and ill health. This period of financial liberalism has been pointed to by many a pro-business politician as a great age for Britain that we should strive to return to. But the fact of the matter is that there have been two great ages of financial liberalism. The first stretched from around the end of the Industrial Revolution in about 1840 until the election of 'progressive' politicians in the 1920s. The second? Well, the second we live in now. This second great period of financial liberalism is a global phenomenon, built by neo-liberal politicians, who reformed our financial and economic systems to have a distinctly capitalist feel. In Britain this started with the election of Margaret Thatcher in 1979, and it continues to this day. Domestically this has seen the breakup of the nationalised utilities, privatisation of key public services, a high unemployment rate and a growing gap between the rich and the poor. In fact, it was the policies of neo-liberalism that caused the financial on going crisis.

This book will argue that is was the first age of financial liberalism that Labour was born into, and it is in its second age that Labour must re-assert itself. Why is this so important? Because financial liberalism follows a clear path and creates the same problems; it destroys basic concepts of a fair society such as social mobility, free education, free health care and the alleviation of poverty.

This books charts what we call, "The Slow Revolution"; the slow march towards social and economic justice that has taken place in Britain since the turn of the 20th century. This book is about the Labour Party, so it is only right that we focus on the role the Labour played in this. But there were others; social campaigners and trade unionists for example. Had it not been for those men and women who fought for a fairer Britain, it is likely that matters would have become so bad that the elite would no longer have keep able to keep order; revolution may well have swept the nation, as it did in many other leading European economies. This preservation of social order in Britain should not be overlooked. 'The Slow Revolution' refers to the idea that those on the side of reform in Britain chose parliament and democratic evolution rather that violent revolution. It means they rolled their sleeves up and had the debate about why it was important for Britain to move away from a greedy financially liberal system, and towards a political system that looked after the many and strived for economic and social justice. 'The Slow Sevolution' plots the path from the People's Budget in 1909, to the housing reforms of the 1920s, the creation of the welfare state in the 1940s, the political side of the social revolution in the 1960s and the enlargement of the welfare state under New Labour between 1997-2007.

This book argues that through its periods in government during the 20th Century, Labour modernised Britain. It dragged it kicking and screaming into modernity. We argue that the only way to run Britain is to strive for social and economic justice. Making Britain a fair place for all of the people within it. That this is the only way to tackle the huge challenges Britain faces today.

It is undeniable that Britain is in a mess. But the ordinary and everyday families and individuals in the UK did not create this mess. It was created primarily by the financial sector, and also by the politicians *(of the financially liberal breed)* who let them get away with murder. There is now little doubt that the long-term economic and political effects of the 2008-2012 financial crisis will have a long-term detrimental effect on this country. It will play a role in every decision politicians make from now on. Or will it? The myth from the financially liberal politicians is that Britain has a debt because of long-term overspend by a Labour government; this is frankly baloney and a distraction from the rotten system that will allow another financial disaster to happen. The reality is that the banks we have our money saved with, mortgages lodged with and investments attached to were always likely to fail. These banks went pop due to the fact that they were under-regulated, because financially liberal politicians think that's the way to run things. We were about to have an economic year zero. But luckily Labour, as the party of government, saved the day. Firstly, they bailed out the banks, then spent billions staving off the threat of mass unemployment by pumping cash into the economy. Yet has the coalition reformed the banking sector, as it promised? No. But who is paying for this government debt? You and me. We are paying for it because the public services our taxes have spent years building up are being slashed, sold off cheaply and even scrapped.

But there are other financial liberal policies that have put Britain in a mess. Take the cost of housing, or the cost of renting. This is creating great gaps between those who have and those who have not. Then there is the privatisation of the rail and energy firms. The private companies (that trade on the assets that many tax pennies bought) now make huge profits and charge us through the nose for using the railways or heating our own homes. This is the same neo-liberal economy that de-industrialised Britain, giving us a narrow economy that is overly reliant upon the service sector and finance for jobs and growth. We don't make anything anymore and these policies have left graduates working in call sectors, several million unemployed and millions more on low pay, or worse still under-employed.

This is the long-term mess Britain finds itself in. But new liberal/financially liberal politicians, (see UKIP, Liberal Democrats, Conservatives and dare we say it New Labour), fail to see the problems. They are wrong. They are failing to identify the challenges facing Britain. They fail to see that the UK economy does not act in the national interest but in the interest of profit making. It's time it stopped; it's time a politician stood up and identified the challenges. It is time Labour re-asserted itself.

The UK is at a crossroads. Do we continue on the path of financial liberalism? Let's be clear; this means indulging in cutthroat capitalism to take part in the global race, leaving the poor behind so a few elites can get super rich. Or instead Labour values can come to the fore. We can develop new policies based on collective aspiration, which see the lot of everyone in Britain increase. Britain is facing a real and serious decline if we fail to take a new path. Social mobility is dying, personal and government debt is out of control and our economy doesn't serve the national interest. People on the street feel frustration. They feel the helplessness of politicians. They know they are not as well off and have less to look forward to. They just can't identify what the problem is - or maybe they just don't want to see it.

In this light, is it understandable that people turn to UKIP, a party who want an end to immigration and EU membership? Despite UKIP essentially representing a turbo version of the capitalist, neo-liberal dogma that got us into this tragic mess in the first place, they at least offer a solution. They are at least radical. That's the problem with modern politics; no one in the mainstream is prepared to be radical. The political class have set the end game as the pursuit of power, and it blurs all other visions and objectives.

12

They no longer want to upset the status quo. They fail to identify the real challenges facing Britain in 2014. This is all such a far cry from the politics from which the Labour Party was formed.

This book is a twin, part one of two. It makes the argument that Britain has been a country ravaged by financial liberalism and that Labour has continually picked up the pieces. It argues that once again, following the financial crash, Labour will have to pick up the pieces. The next book will mark out why the financial crash left Britain in a mess and how Labour, through the pursuit of social and economic justice can take Britain back to former glory.

Chapter 2 How Conservatism and Financial Liberalism made Socialism

Try to capture a picture in time. A time that many Conservative British politicians look back upon as a golden age. An age where Britain led the way in industry and innovation, an age of free trade that had created great wealth for those who held power, and where Britain ruled over so many countries that the sun never set on its Empire. Yet the richest and most powerful country in the world, ruled over by an elite of liberal politicians, had failed to modernise. This short window in time was the Edwardian era. The reality is that Britain was polarised between a minority of the wealthy and middle class and the huge majority of working poor. This was the backdrop to which the Labour Party was born in Britain.

The British economy, like so many of that period, had been built on the premise of conflict and free trade. This was a system propped up by liberal politicians and political elites who ruled over people and took little interest in them. Although crude and rudimental, this system of governance worked. Not only did it keep people wealthy, but it also employed many, although at pitiful wages. The pursuit of power and wealth at whatever cost left Britain with a vast empire and the richest economy in the world. However, on these shores we found a nation where 80% of people lived on or below the poverty line.

This was a time that had two political movements: Conservatism, represented by the same Conservative Party that we see today, and Liberalism, represented by the Liberal Party, the predecessor to the Liberal Democrats of our era. The parties of that age were not dissimilar to today in that they were ruled by elites. The aristocracy and the new Victorian business class who had been at the right place at the right time to embrace the wealth of the industrial revolution dominated politics. These were men who had enjoyed extreme wealth and luxury on the back of the class system, either through inherited wealth or the poverty and suffering of others not born to the same luck. Then there was the newer business class who enjoyed wealth and its trappings through free trade liberalism and an economic structure desperate to supply the empire. If we examine the issues of that time, we will see that many of the failings found in the great age of liberalism and free trade have been repeated time and time again over the subsequent century. But time and time again it is never the wealthy that suffer when the consequences of these failings hit home.

 When we examine this period in time it is not hard to understand that many men and women of the period became obsessed by campaigning against the great social injustices of the time. This was a country where millions starved, wore threadbare clothes and had holes in their shoes. This was a country where democracy, equality and education were mere pipe dreams.

This was a Britain built on a political system that generated great wealth, where the political elites in Parliament had the power to rule half the word, but did little to alleviate the poverty found at home.

This despair, like in so many other countries, made Britain ripe for revolution, as unthinkable as it seems. We will chart how the great social reformers and the Labour Party pushed reform through, however slowly, stalling political revolution.

This evolution rather than revolution, over a period that spanned from around 1900 the present day has seen incremental reforms. These reforms came in short bursts as the political and social conditions allowed. But this "Slow Revolution", transformed the lives of millions in Britain. The Labour Party played a key role in this social reform. But we will begin by looking at some of the early key social reformers. Many were Labour members, but not exclusively. They played a key part by lobbying the political elite or in some cases by joining it to implement change.

Yet this isn't just a battle or Edwardian times; this is a challenge that has passed from that day to this. A battle between the political elite who are mainly liberal of mind and their protection of the establishment, versus those who pursue social and economic reform.

In 1900 Britain was a country that had believed that it was on the right path, and that the wealth and good times would continue in much the same manner for the next 100 years. Britain believed its empire would be a continued source of power and wealth. Little did they know that empire and liberalism were to contribute to what could turn into the descent into mediocrity of Britain and the possible breakup of the United Kingdom. Had it not been for those men and women who fought for social justice and change there is little doubt Britain would have slid into terminal decline and then revolution. For had Britain continued on its pre-war course it is likely there would be no social security, no NHS and no free education post-16. It is likely that the extreme financially liberal system, if unreformed, would have left the UK looking much like America; with vast, extreme poverty, a high prison population, unemployment and under employment, poor health and education rates juxtaposed with extreme wealth. Alternatively this country would have seen socialist revolution, as the 80% of people who live on or below the bread line would have risen up as they realised the great social injustices taking place to them. Have social reformers and their "Slow Revolution" been the one thing that has kept the establishment in place?

That's why this book argues that Labour modernised Britain. We believe that the pursuit of social and economic justice is the only way to contend with the challenges facing Britain. Here is the mistake that many people in modern Britain make: they believe that Labour and what Labour stands for is old, out-dated and stuffy. This is a matter of perception. When placed next to the well-branded and articulated arguments of Liberal Democrats and Conservatives, it is plain to see why people might think this. The, "I agree with Nick" factor, seeing well-polished leaders branded into a cult-like status, has allowed politicians to avoid the real issues of the day for years. This is personality politics. The fact is that this is a ploy that allows the main parties to avoid debating the real issues of the day. The Conservatives for example, haven't taken a serious policy review since Mrs Thatcher was elected leader in 1975, when - under the influence of Sir Keith Joseph - she adopted neo-liberalism. These policies believe in less government, less regulation and more market. You can see this in the way the coalition have reformed the NHS and education. Policies that are failing because they are not fit for our time and the challenges we face. Whilst the Liberal Democrats in government have shown a lack of policy maturity, trying to be all thing to all people. Both coalition parties have one thing in common; a belief in financial liberalism and its modern version, neo-liberalism.

Thatcherism or neo-liberalism, *(with neo-liberalism being the core political ideology of Thatcherism, these terms will be used interchangeably)*, has become the mainstream political ideology of western capitalism. It entered

17

mainstream political theory through the elections of Ronald Reagan and Margaret Thatcher. For the UK this meant a huge departure from the previous social democratic policies of the Conservative and Labour parties, with neo-liberalism becoming the core ideology of the UK Conservative Party until this very day. But what is this neo-liberalism? Its ultimate aim is to produce diverse free markets with the reduction of the state, or government taking a minimal role in every way possible. It has become the dominant economic and political theory across the world because it has been accepted by all the major western capitalist economies, mainly because of global trade agreements signed under the World Trade Organisation and the EU. It has spread into the developing world by organisations such as the International Monetary Fund and the World Bank, who demand developing states adopt neo-liberalism in return for hard cash.

Neo-liberalism believes that free markets are efficient, and as such are more efficient than any action of the government. The market should be left alone by government, and markets should carry out what could be seen as core functions of government. Neo-liberals believe that market-based economic theory produces economic growth, and that the same free markets produce economic stability. The theory dictates that free markets incentivise people to work hard by offering an opportunity for social mobility and the chance for the hard worker to raise their living standards. Because neo-liberalism is efficient, (so the theory goes), it offers the quickest and easiest way to respond to the challenges of globalisation. It is also argued by some that market choice ultimately protects consumers and workers. How has neo-liberalism manifested itself in UK government policy? Firstly, it is exhibited through the increased use of private companies to run government contracts or asking private contractors to take the role of the state. This is part of a conscious reduction in the size and reach of the state. Pursued on the grounds that private providers with their profit motive can provide a higher quality of service than those in the public sector. There has also been a conscious drive towards reductions in taxation, especially on those who earn the most. This has been pursued on the grounds that it will incentivise economic growth. It has seen the government actively rescind certain responsibilities, such as full employment or economic planning, in favour of a market-based or 'by chance' approach. By the same approach, private contractors have been left to run financial investment markets with little or no regulation from the government.

These theories of Liberalism are nothing new or revolutionary. They have evolved from Adam Smith's *The Wealth of Nations.*[1] The 18th Century Liberal political economist and thinker Adam Smith spoke of had many great things: freedom of speech, encouraging innovation, enlightenment and ensuring liberty for the individual. Many of these liberal political theories have been rightly adopted into mainstream socialism *(the traditional ideology of Labour)* and conservatism. But when applied in its most extreme modern day versions, Liberalism creates great inequality and poverty. This leads perfectly back to our point. Many British people believe that the Liberal Democrats and Conservatives are the modern alternative to Labour. Nothing could be further from the truth. As a response to the grinding poverty inflicted by Liberalism in 19th century Europe, an alternative political theory was created. Socialism as an ideology was created to curb the excesses of liberalism and conservatism, by using the state or government to reduce inequality and meet the national interest.

This was the bedrock from which Labour was formed; The pursuit of social and economic justice. This was a movement about equality, fairness and democracy. No longer should the squalor you were born into dictate the direction of your life. European socialism and social democracy have placed social justice as a key priority, along with welfare, full employment, strong economic growth, economic diversity, equality and public ownership. These were the policies used between 1945-1979 in the UK, as an aim of economic growth was met with the need for full employment and the reduction of poverty through the creation of the welfare state. This was a political vision designed to do away with the evils of financial liberalism. Neo-liberalism was the antithesis of this post war consensus. The post-war consensus which saw Labour and more often Conservatives run British government in the national interest.

What we have seen since 1979 is an awkward co-existence of neo-liberalism with the use of the state to promote social justice where affordable. Markets, especially financial and big business have been left to get on with it largely unregulated, causing huge inequality and gaps between the haves and have-nots. Meanwhile governments have chosen to use the welfare system, via a system of benefits and state spending, to provide a safety net for the ever-growing number of people who need it. This system has been seen as the best of both worlds- neo-liberalism, or aggressive economic policies and a socially minded government. The reality, however, is that the govern-

1 *An Inquiry into the Nature and Causes of the Wealth of Nations, Smith A, Re-published by Gutenberg ebook project in 2009*

ment (e.g. the tax payer) is picking up the bill, as neo-liberalism gets more excessive, to the tune of £120 billion for a population of 60 million. Nearly 35 years on we see the strains of neo-liberalism appearing in everyday life. High debt, high unemployment, a weak and absent government, low aspiration for the young who although well educated lack in economic justice.

In global terms, socialism is a mere adolescent in comparison to its older relatives which have been used to order many societies for hundreds of years. This may be the reason why the many strands of socialism have made many mistakes and we return to the old ways of elitism and financial liberalism. Take for example, one of the more extremes of socialism that was used following the Russian revolution. This Marxist Leninist brand of extreme socialism pulled the centre of socialism to the east, leaving the much more moderate versions in mainland Europe, Britain and Scandinavia. There have been many strands of socialism, all with the guiding principle of economic and social justice. All of them a response to political elitism and economic liberalism but they produced differing results. In Russia, it could be argued that socialism did as much damage to democracy, economics and social justice than the preceding system of Tsarist autocracy ever did.

In Britain, thankfully we kept ourselves away from the revolutionary road. But it was close, the political elites pushed the poor to the brink on a number of occasions. This path was avoided by the reforms won by the men and women who pursued social justice and later the ideals of equality for British people. How long post-war would we have stood high poverty rates and such extreme inequality?

The slow revolutionaries

Just who were these founding fathers of the slow revolution? Who were these people who pushed Britain towards social and economic justice? Who were these people that subconsciously formed the modern Labour Party and radicalised the way that Britain is run?

Of course there are too many to name them all in this short passage. But we can identify three broad groups: the advocates of social justice, the trade unions and campaigners for equality like the Suffragettes. These are the creators of Britain's social conscience. They fought for reform in a time of destitution and extreme poverty in Britain created by years of financial liberalism. This was the backdrop to which the Labour Party was born - born to fight for social and economic justice. This is Labour's raison d'être, and anyone who believes this to be otherwise is mistaken.

For too long the consensus view was that the poor only had themselves to blame for their situation. This view was challenged as Liberal Politicians such as David Lloyd George began championing social justice. He began to campaign using Seebohm Rowntree's *Poverty: A Study of Town Life* (1901), which examined day-to-day life for the lower classes in York. The book researched the two-thirds of the York population who could not afford a middle class lifestyle. His team spoke to around 46,000 people and revealed that around 20,000 were living in poverty. He found that 28% of York's total population was living in absolute poverty. This poverty was often created by the man of house being ill, injured, unemployed or dead. A not-uncommon occurrence given the harshness of the late Victorian economy; the Victorians were not known for their love of health and safety. These people were unable to obtain basic clothing or food. Overall, Rowntree predicted that 80% of British people were on or below the bread line. Rowntree's findings concluded that a family needed 20 shillings a week to survive with no luxuries. A skilled, employed man earned an average of 21 shillings a week, but there was no fall back for ill-health and no old age pension. Doctors were expensive and unemployment amongst the non-idle was increasing on the advent of the new century. Rowntree wasn't alone. Take the relatively unknown Christian machinery worker John Galt, who travelled from Scotland to the East End of London. He was mortified by the poverty he witnessed and used the new medium of photography to expose the plight of the poor. His pictures reported unemployment, damp homes with no heat, six people sleeping in a room and starvation. There were people who did what they could to get by; for example, the home industries were a way for a widowed woman to make money when nothing else was available. Matchbox makers and mattress stuffers might make 7 shillings a week. This simply wasn't enough.

David Lloyd George, like many from the Liberal Party, would find themselves on the right side of the social justice debate throughout the 20th century. But as a political movement they failed to deliver a serious commitment to social justice. Ultimately many in the Liberal Party had made their fortunes through financial liberalism and believed that free trade and a smaller state, rather than welfare, represented the best way to keep Britain great. The Liberal Party and the unions courted each other, but it was never to be a happy marriage, as the elite of the party clearly held the workers of the country and their unions in contempt.

Take the Taff Vail Railway Strike of 1900. A small dispute escalated into a full industrial action which bought large parts of Wales to a halt. The workers gained little from the strike other than the promise of re-employment but it was the subsequent legal case bought by the Taff Vale Railway Company against the Amalgamated Society of Railway Servants (ASRS) in which the courts held that a union could be sued for damages caused by the actions of its officials in industrial disputes.[2] The unions were ordered to pay crippling sums. This was the elite holding the workers in contempt, and the union movement realised that they would have to move beyond the Liberal Party and gain representation in parliament to change laws.

The formation of the Labour Representation Committee (LRC) was the move of the trade unionists away from the Liberal Party towards creating their own party. The Labour Party moved matters away from the Liberal tradition of benign regulation of work and poverty, and sought to take a more radical way of alleviating the lot of the working classes. Religion played a huge part in the social conscience of the emerging Labour Party. Christian instincts that were present in the paternalistic Liberal Party could be seen in the emerging Labour Party whose leader was a charismatic religious preacher called Keir Hardie. This led 1950's Party General Secretary Morgan Phillips to reflect that, "*Socialism in Britain owed more to Methodism than Marx*".[3] Christianity is an important influence on radicalism and anti-establishment thought in England. Even recently Tony Blair told Michael Parkinson that he would, "*answer to God*" for his actions in Iraq rather than to Parliament, the Labour Party or, God forbid the British public.[4] This way of thinking had been taken up in the 17th century by a non conformist sect known as the Diggers. Taking their cue from the Act of the Apostles written by St. Luke the Gospel writer, they called for an end to land ownership so that each family could farm as they needed to with their neighbours on land not owned by any landlord. "*The group of believers was one in mind and heart. No one said that any of his belongings was his own, but they all shared with one another everything they had.*"[5]

It was this Christian socialism mixed with British stoicism that pushed

2 http://www.britannica.com/EBchecked/topic/580194/Taff-Vale-case

3 (Note: p.131 The Foundations of the British Labour Party by Matthew Worley ISBN 9780754667315

4 (Note: Independent March 2006 http://www.independent.co.uk/news/uk/politics/blair-god-will-be-my-judge-on-iraq-468512.html)

5 Act of the Apostles Ch4 v32)

the movement away from Marxism to socialism. This disaffiliation from Marxism meant that the fledgling Labour Party was committed to the parliamentary route to implement change to society. All their energies went into achieving the elections of MP's, which was in contrast to other left parties in Europe who became involved in street fighting politics, especially in Germany and Russia where socialists were excluded from the democratic process.

Whilst we have touched on social campaigners and the union movement, there was one other movement that campaigned for equality. Equality for women. We cannot under estimate its importance.

The Suffragette Movement was seared into the history of early 20th Century Britain by the tragically spectacular death of Emily Davidson during the running of the 1913 Derby at the Epsom horse-racing course. Whether or not she intended to die is a disputed issue, but the shocking filmed footage brought the whole issue of what these women were fighting for into stark focus. What the Suffragettes did achieve was to produce a seismic shift in the UK establishment by combining a campaign to change the minds of MPs in partnership with mass agitation outside of Westminster. By making a strong moral argument and producing a narrative that highlighted injustice, they helped develop a template by which the Labour Party achieved real power and ultimately led to the election of a Labour government on a socialist programme in 1945.

John Stuart Mill was a famous 19th Century philosopher and a Liberal Party MP. He was on the progressive wing of the Party and reflected the ideals of using legislation to deaden the worst impacts of capitalism. Mill wrote a book called *'The Subjugation of Women'.*[6] The book had a tremendous impact and pushed the idea of equality for women up the social agenda. The Suffragette Movement came out of this so called "New Liberal Movement" and these female activists challenged the established order via mass public meetings following in the tradition of the Chartists, and this method of agitation was copied by early Labour Party leaders such as Keir Hardie. It was Hardie who was to present the early legislation to give women the vote in 1906. He tabled a Commons resolution in April of that year, *"in the opinion of this House, it is desirable that sex should cease to be*

6 (Note: Mill, John Stuart(1869). The Subjection of Women(1869 first ed.). London: Longmans, Green, Reader & Dyer.)

ar to the exercise of the parliamentary franchise."[7]

The New Liberals included deep thinkers such as John Maynard Keynes and William Beveridge who went on to have such a huge influence on the post-war Labour government, Keynes via economic theory and Beveridge with his 1942 Report which led to the extension of the Welfare State and the foundation of the NHS.

These three sets of campaigners set about changing Britain. Whether they knew it or not these three groups would ensure that Britain took a new and exciting path. However long it took to get there. The suffragettes ensured equality, campaigners ensured social justice and trade unionists ensured fair pay and rights at work. The party the trade unions had formed would be highly influenced by these campaigns.

Socialism

As with most things, it's a case of being in the right place at the right time. This book argues that the only reason that globalisation has taken a distinctly neo-liberal tack in this day and age is because Reagan and Thatcher were touting neo-liberalism at the same time that the mass communication and the jumbo jet were in their element. Had the Internet and computers really been up to modern standards in the 1950s, global social democracy may well have been the order of the day, using the advances of globalisation to promote social and economic justice. In the same manner, socialism and social justice were ending a 200-year birth just as the Labour Party was coming into being. There was clearly a real imbalance in the world; elites and financial liberalism were impoverishing millions and socialism was the antithesis of this.

So just what is socialism? Just what have these people who desired social and economic justice unintentionally cast upon this island of ours? Some would argue that socialism, as a means of pursuing social justice, is rather un-British. Socialism is defined crudely as, *"social and economic doctrine that calls for public rather than private ownership or control of property and natural resources."[8]* However, for the authors, this crude description misses the point. It would be fair to say that this definition encompasses the strategy but not the aim; rather, socialism encompasses the values of those Ed-

7 (Note: *http://www.johndclare.net/Women1_SuffragetteActions_Rosen.htm*

8 *http://www.britannica.com/EBchecked/topic/551569/socialism*

wardian Campaigners. The ideals that those who work hard should have fair pay and good, safe conditions, that all people should be treated as equal, that those in poverty should be assisted by the state, not only to gain a better quality of life but to be given the opportunities to better themselves. But, most importantly, to end the advantage taken by the boss class over the working classes and to put the common good before selfish motives and actions. How else could we have turned a country where 80% of people lived in poverty into the society we see today? It wasn't done through financial liberalism or Thatcherism. No, it was done through the values of equality, redistribution, rights for all and collective aspiration.

John Ball was a priest who was one of the instigators of the English Peasants Revolt in 1381. In 1385 he was recorded as saying: *"We may be all united together, and that the lords be no greater masters than we be. What have we deserved, or why should we be kept thus in servage? We be all come from one father and one mother Adam and Eve whereby can they say or shew that they be greater lords than we be"*[9]

Roughly translated, it seems Ball is wondering that, since we are all born equal, why should some people be masters, and others servants due to an accident of birth regarding their social status? He questions why the masters feel that the underclass somehow are "deserving" of their place.

Suzanne Moore, writing in the Guardian as the coalition cuts began to bite in 2012, picked up on the feeling expressed by John Ball all those centuries ago. Bemoaning the erosion of empathy for those in the poverty trap she said that many people now felt that, *"Poor people are not simply people like us, but with less money: they are an entirely different species. Their poverty is a personal failing"*.[10]

The myth that the poor can be undeserving was dispelled by our Edwardian forefathers and their pursuit of social justice. We dispensed with elite-based politics built on pure financial liberalism for this reason. But when the UK voted to return to this ideology with the election of Mrs Thatcher, the myth returned. This idea of poverty as a personal failing is classic Tory ideology, expressed in political speech and writing, most regularly in the large Tory press. They believe that the state has no role and is trying to equalise inequality, as explained by philosopher Roger Scruton: *"Conserva-*

9 (Note: John Ball, in J Froissart, Froissart's Chronicles (1385) translated by GC Macaulay (1895)

10 (Note: Guardian 16th Feb 2012 http://www.theguardian.com/commentisfree/2012/feb/16/suzanne-moore-disgusted-by-poor)

tives believe that our identities and values are formed through our relations with other people, and not through our relation with the State."[11]

This means that the Tories do not see the point in the equality of opportunity which is at the heart of what Ball was talking about, and that socialism stands for today. A child born during the 1960s in the UK into a family earning on or below the average wage had the opportunity to live in decent housing provided by the state in contrast to their grandparents who, pre the Labour Housing Acts of 1924, 1930 and 1945 were often forced to live in squalor and in fear of the landlord. The sixties child was cared for by the NHS and their survival chances at birth were not determined by whether the family could afford a medically supervised delivery. The 1960s young person was given a free education for as long as they wanted, or needed it. Going to university in the mid 1980s attracted not debt, but a local authority grant of £700 a term. This enabled the sixties child entry into the professions as an adult and opportunity to rise as high as they wished based on ability. This is just one example of where socialist values and the Labour Party pushed things along, life chances provided by the state directly taking a role to balance inequality, a direct contradiction to the politics of conservatism, elitism and financial liberalism.

By Scruton's argument that our lives should develop, *"through our relations with other people"[12]* and that the state can play little or no role in engineering the course of a person's life, what then happens to the child born into poverty, with a lone parent who cannot cope with everyday life? They should be left to rot, be poor and have no chance to better themselves, we assume. Also, by Scruton's argument it is only right and proper that the children of the wealthy should attend the best fee paying schools and get the best internships because of their *"relationships with other people"*. Scruton is, at least honest. We see this nepotism at work in the coalition cabinet today with Cameron's Royal connections landing him a plum job at Conservative Central Office. According to Daily Mail journalists Francis Elliot and James Hanning, a call from the Palace was placed, *"I understand you are to see David Cameron, 'said a man with a grand voice. 'I've tried everything I can to dissuade him from wasting his time on politics but I have failed. I am ringing to tell you that you are about to meet a truly remarkable*

11 (Note: *Roger Scruton: What do Conservatives believe? January 6th 2014 Conservative Home* http://www.conservativehome.com/platform/2014/01/roger-scruton-what-do-conservatives-believe.html

12 (Note: *Roger Scruton: What do Conservatives believe? January 6th 2014 Conservative Home* http://www.conservativehome.com/platform/2014/01/roger-scruton-what-do-conservatives-believe.html

young man." [13] It is fair to say, some men are more equal than others.

If socialism is so great, why did the British people turn their backs on it?

Britain was governed through a socialist agenda from 1945-79, but from 1979 onward we returned to liberalism. Why? Did socialism not work? We will argue strongly in the coming chapters that it did. How can those who the system was designed to help most reject the political system that advocated collective aspiration? In modern times we call this the *working class Tory*. The reality that the mid 1970s had offered little other than industrial strife and neo liberalism offered a new vision, a vision where you could have the rewards for hard work. It was so successful that even John Major managed a record 14 million votes in 1992 and then a stonking 9 million in the year of the Labour landslide.

But just how has financial liberalism, a system that oppressed millions in this country won back the trust of so many? The fact of the matter is popularism. Mrs Thatcher's genius was as a populist politician. She identified the UK's decline at home and on the international stage, which had led to a collective loss of confidence for the British people. The Winter of Discontent set the seal on a decade of appalling industrial relations and by getting rid of Labour, and with a new decade on the horizon the voters felt they were turning a page by voting Tory. They could leave the bad old days of the 1970's behind them and look to a more optimistic future. Thatcher emphasised this on the door step of Number Ten on her first day in office. *'Where there is discord, may we bring harmony. Where there is error, may we bring truth. Where there is doubt, may we bring faith. And where there is despair, may we bring hope".* [14]

The fact is, neo-liberalism is a far easier argument to make than socialism. It offers less interference from these dodgy politicians, lowers taxes promises that those who work the hardest will get the most reward. Whilst socialism is complicated, it's about fairness (just what is fairness anyway?) it involves cooperation and taxation and supporting the needy. It just isn't sexy or simple. Ultimately its not really a ticket to get filthy rich, is it?

Guardian journalist Gary Younge is far more scathing, claiming that Mar-

13 (Note: *The many faces of Mr. Cameron 17/3/07* http://www.dailymail.co.uk/news/article-442913/The-faces-Mr-Cameron.html

14 (Note: http://www.margaretthatcher.org/document/104078)

garet Thatcher appealed to some pretty unpleasant aspects of the British psyche. "*Her petty nationalism in Europe and post-colonial nostalgia played out in the Falklands War; her monocultural racism, expressing sympathy for Britons who "fear rather being swamped by an alien culture"* were the factors that helped her to tune in and be on the same wave length as the voters.[15]

Charles Saatchi, who designed the infamous, "Britain isn't Working" campaign poster for the successful 1979 Tory campaign perhaps sums up Maggie's appeal the best: "*Mrs Thatcher was a romantic. She understood that dreams are important. She knew that in politics, as in law, motive is all. People give credit to someone whose heart is in the right place. She knew that a certain idealism, a certain moral urgency, a marching tune people can respond to, is the essential precondition for electoral success."*[16]

The neo liberal parties have not been able to solve any of the long-term decline questions facing Britain. Mrs Thatcher offered optimism, a vision and courage. She offered neo liberalism as a one-size-fits-all, simple solution. It is now up to those who crave social and economic justice to argue this didn't work.

Britain's slow revolution towards social justice

While other countries did away with their old political orders through revolution, Britain opted for reform. For the sake of short hand we have dubbed this reform the '*slow revolution*': a move away from financial liberalism and extremes of wealth and poverty and towards social justice. This reform was piecemeal; it was hard fought and slow. The aim of this passage is to chart Labour's involvement in the slow revolution, following the reforms under the first Labour governments of the 1920s, the 1945-51 government, the 1960s governments and finally New Labour. We will also examine social justice that came from the Liberal Party and also examine further the conditions that spurred this country into slow revolution.

---

15 (Note: Gary Younge, "*How Did Margaret Thatcher Do It?* April 2013 http://www.thenation.com/article/173732/how-did-margaret-thatcher-do-it)

16 "Note:("*Why Did Mrs. Thatcher Win Three Elections In a Row?*" by Charles Saatchi (2013) for Centre for PolicyStudies http://www.cps.org.uk/about/news/q/date/2013/04/08/why-did-mrs-thatcher-win-three-elections-in-a-row/)

But why was this a slow revolution, and not an all-out revolution, where the people rise up against their oppressors? In Britain we have held a deep mistrust of politicians, spurred on by the fact that Conservatives believe that politicians should do as little as possible. A rotten political class, elitism and a cynical conservative press maintain this view. This meant that change came slowly. Bland politicians are the norm in the UK and we are at best apathetic towards politics. But such was the state of the UK reform was desperately needed.

The first such reforms came from the 1870 Education Act. There was a need to ensure that Britain stayed ahead of its competition, and education was seen as a way of achieving this. All 5-13 year olds were to be educated. This Education Act was passed by a Liberal government headed by William Gladstone and contained cabinet ministers such as William Forster who was responsible for the legislation's passage through Parliament. Forster epitomised Liberal values of the day. He was a wealthy industrialist but as a Quaker he felt a sense of religious duty to help the poor. Such attitudes did a lot for the working classes, but naturally could only ever go a limited way because of core beliefs in free markets. However, there was further reform. Sending children into dangerous workplaces, for example was eliminated. However their parents were still forced to work long hours in factories where industrial accidents were an everyday hazard. It wasn't until 1867 that belonging to a trade union ceased to be a criminal offence, and this move had taken a Royal Commission to sort out, demonstrating just how terrified the capitalists and factory owners were of organised labour. *(They still are!)* Under financial liberalism every worker has their value, and with more supply of workers wages can be squeezed and driven down. This abuse of the worker, taking advantage to maximise profits, forced the beginning of collective bargaining. The idea of collective aspiration is the idea that we are more than just actors prey to economy, that we are all going up or down together. This vision of collective aspiration has seen huge increases in the collective standard of living across the UK. For example we now all get an education, and we all get health care.

The collective spirit of the trade union movement influenced the Liberal Party. David Lloyd George was the Liberal Party Chancellor of the Exchequer in Prime Minister Herbert Asquith's government that came to power in 1908. Lloyd George was a fiery Welshman renowned for his skills of oratory. He was very much inspired by his religious upbringing and as a Baptist he campaigned for the disestablishment of the Church of England.[17] Following in the Victorian tradition of religiously motivated social reformers such as Lord Shaftsbury and William Wilberforce, Lloyd George was appalled by the poverty and squalor present in a country that was the dominant nation on the world stage. His first budget was presented to the House of Commons in April 1909 and sought to declare war on poverty. Introducing what became known as the "People's Budget", Lloyd George told the House:

"It is a war Budget. It is for raising money to wage implacable warfare against poverty and squalidness. I cannot help hoping and believing that before this generation has passed away, we shall have advanced a great step towards that good time, when poverty, and the wretchedness and human degradation which always follows in its camp, will be as remote to the people of this country as the wolves which once infested its forests."[18]

This budget included ideas such as a 20% tax on land, as well as a *"super tax"* on very high incomes. The Tory Establishment were horrified and used their inbuilt Lords majority to reject the Budget, prime minister Asquith toyed with the idea of asking the King to create 500 new Liberal Peers, but to stave off a crisis an election was called that resulted in a hung parliament but with the Liberals as the biggest Party. The Lords grudgingly accepted the Budget but crucially the Land Tax was dropped which curtailed Lloyd George's ability to use wealth redistribution as a means to alleviate poverty and increase pensions.

The Labour Party can take credit for pushing the Liberal's in a more radical direction as they had increased their seat share to 29 in 1906 up 27 from the previous election. By the 1910 election Labour had broken the ½ million vote barrier and won 40 seats. The Liberals would have to look to their left flank and take account of it in the future.

The Great War (1914-18) was fought on the backs of young men, many needlessly sent into the path of machine gun fire. A war fought over an old European elite. Many of the men came from the squalor and poverty from which we refer. Yet did the petrified young British men revolt? No, they were heroic in the face of futility. A futility that saw a four-year war grind through the dreams and aspirations of so many young men. How did the

17 http://www.bbc.co.uk/wales/history/sites/themes/figures/lloyd_george.shtml)

18 (Note: Hansard 29th April 1909)

politicians who arranged this slaughter repay the survivors? With very few reforms, and nothing of the scale seen following World War Two.

The one big change that came about in the 1920s and 1930s was a change in the housing conditions for both the working and middle classes. *Homes for Heroes* was the promise from politicians. It was the Housing acts of 1924 and 1930 that got the ball rolling regarding the status of public housing being elevated as an aspiration for the working class. This was the start of a housing change in Britain, which saw slum clearance and councils providing suitable homes. Away went the private landlords who forced their tenants to live in squalor. This was complemented with a 1930s middle class housing boom, which revolutionised the housing stock in Britain. These acts were in part down to short-lived Labour governments. As a result of the Act nearly ¼ million slum dwellings were cleared and by the outbreak of war in 1939, 700,000 new homes had been constructed.[19] Despite the Labour Prime Minister Ramsay's McDonald ignominious exit from the Labour Party, it is fair to say that a number of radical measures were attempted to improve the conditions for workers. The 1930 Coal Mines Act could have had a tremendous effect on the lives of miners but was not enforced by the pit owners and Labour did not have the clout to ensure compliance due to being a minority administration. The idea was that no man was expected to work more than a 7 ½ hour day, and the government wanted to intervene directly to regulate production as a means to stop owners flogging their men beyond endurance to see off competition from other pits. The second Ramsay MacDonald Labour government was determined to improve everyday life for all, not just the industrial working class. It succeeded in passing the Agricultural Marketing Act in 1931. This was important because it guaranteed minimum market prices for hard-pressed farmers and their workers. This industry was and still is notoriously volatile and the act gave much needed protection to the agricultural sector. The Agriculture Wages Board, founded by Lloyd George as part of his 1909 People's Budget was strengthened by MacDonald and lasted right until 2013 when they it was abolished by Lib Dem Farming Minister David Heath. The message was that government had a key role to play in the conditions that people were forced to live in, and that Labour politicians would actively lead the way in ending poverty.

The American Depression that started with the Wall Street Crash of 1929

---

19 (Note: *http://www.parliament.uk/about/living-heritage/transformingsociety/towncountry/towns/ overview/councilhousing/*)

had an effect on Britain. As the economy contracted, the knock on effects saw factory upon factory closed. It seemed there was little or nothing that governments could or wanted to do. A piece of legislation that could have had a profound effect on the UK had it been passed in full, has disappeared from view. MacDonald's Labour government, responding to the crisis of destitution for many working class people in the wake of the Wall Street Crash proposed a Land Utilisation Act. It allowed the government to buy land where and whenever it wanted and for whatever purpose.[20] This would have meant that if a Labour government wanted to nationalise the land, and embark on a planned economy, there would have existed the legal framework to permit it. Nevertheless that Act, which was passed in 1931, did create the Allotment System which allowed councils to give land to families to grow much needed food. That Labour government fell and the *Hungry 'Thirties* were a disastrous decade for the UK working class.

Britain was the worlds biggest ship builder, and as trade fell fewer ships were needed. This hit the working class areas where the ships were built. The formula whereby the elite paid no price for economic failure continued once again with the workers at the bottom paying the price. The welfare on offer was pitiful. The Jarrow Hunger March, which took place in October 1936, has become synonymous with the catastrophic economic situation in Britain. Once again it was the same story as in Edwardian times; capitalism's crisis was the workers problem.

Three out of five Jarrow workers were unemployed, where a family of two adults and two children were forced to survive on 30 shillings[21] *(Remember that Roundtree found 21 shilling to be the poverty line in 1900)*. This benefit was only available for 6 months before it ran out. The jobs had run out and the government stood idly by, their liberal politics making them believe there was nothing they could do. This was the catalyst that would create the Beveridge report and mass social reform following the 1945 General Election.

Labour was to play a pivotal role in the government of World War Two. Historian Andrew Marr credits Labour members being in the war cabinet for backing Churchill's position of non-surrender in June 1940, whilst the

20   (Note: http://www.legislation.gov.uk/ukpga/Geo5/21-22/41/contents)

21   Private interview

other Conservatives present wanted negotiations with Hitler.[22] Under the 'total war' economy, Labour ministers helped ensure that Britain was able to focus, providing just enough from meagre resources. During this period Labour managed some small reforms but the main aim was to win the war. As summed up by this letter between Winston Churchill and friend and future Labour Chairman Harold Laski. *"In my view we ought to win the war first and then in a free country the issues of socialism and free enterprise can be fought over in a constitutional manner."*[23]

But there was one large step forward during this period. The design of the welfare state. It was accepted by almost all that victory meant change for Britain. The country could not return to pre-war poverty produced by financial liberalism, the all-out war economy had proved that planned socialism could work in Britain. The vision that was sold to troops was the promise of a New Jerusalem. Where social and economic justice could be found, not just wealth for the few but equality of opportunity and a chance at prosperity for everyone.

That vision gave hope to millions where none had existed before the war. The Beveridge Report is important not only for the history of the United Kingdom, but for identifying the place of the Labour Party in the history of British politics. Beveridge was a Liberal, but his vision pushed Britain to the front of what a modern state should look like. The Beveridge report was part of the coalition agreement which saw Labour enter a war government with the Tories and the Liberals, Labour Minister Without Portfolio Arthur Henderson told the House of Commons in June 1941 that the coalition was setting up a committee to be chaired by economist William Beveridge, *"To undertake, with special reference to the inter-relation of the schemes, a survey of the existing national schemes of social insurance and allied services, including workmen's compensation, and to make recommendations."*[24]

The vision the report produced, one of welfare, the NHS, education and pensions was implemented with gusto by Labour upon their election to government in 1945. This was to be the single biggest point of change for the slow revolution. The war industries remained nationalised and the planned economy became a socialist economy delivering full employment.

22

23 DLA 18/147 A letter from Sir Winston Churchill to Laski dater 25 March 1942, a reply regarding socialist policies in war time government.

24   (Hansard June 10th 1941)

In 1933 unemployment had peaked at 3.4 million around 21% of the working population, and by 1939 it was still 2.1 million or 10%. The government, despite huge war debts (far higher than anything now) moved towards an economy planned with the needs of everyone in mind, complete with nationalisation, the founding of the NHS and the consolidation of a Welfare State which looked after a person from cradle to grave. This really was a country for those who won the war, not the empty promise of earlier politicians. Harry Keen was a doctor when the NHS was founded. He told Ken Loach in the 2013 film, *"The Spirit of 45", "There was a real feeling of ownership about the NHS when it started. People felt that they were doing it themselves, that it was their possession. And they've lost that. And it's getting that back will empower people I think to live much more fulfilled and happy lives".*[25]

The next big tranche of reform came in the 1960s, once again through a Labour government. This time through the abolition of hanging, the legalisation of homosexuality, the ending of censorship, the legalisation of abortion, the creation of the Open University and the ending of the 11+ in most areas. Labours efforts in government in the late 1970s were not to yield the same results; they were more about the pursuit of power than social and economic justice. It was not until the late 1990s and New Labour that the latest chapter of the slow revolution could be played out.

The election of Tony Blair and New Labour changed the debate both in the Labour Party and Britain. Blair had adopted some of the terms of neo-liberalism but was prepared to spend big on the welfare state. However, Blair's acceptance of neo-liberalism has left long-term problems for future generations, whether this is in private interests running the welfare state, an unregulated banking sector or a narrow economy that lacks diversity. However, for all of New Labours failings, its biggest achievement was to put the public services right at the heart of the policy debate. There is a great deal of justifiable criticism as to Blair's extension of John Major's Public Finance Initiatives to garner investment, but the values that led to huge increases in public spending were sound.

But just what were New Labour's values? Writing for the Independent in 1996, current standard-bearer for the New Labour legacy Yvette Cooper attempted to answer this question.

"Equality. Just whisper the word and watch the middle classes squirm. The

25 Harry Keen quoted http://www.thespiritof45.com/Interviews-Archives/Health

successful and the privileged start counting their blessings and contemplating which they will have to sacrifice on the journey towards a brave new world. What was once a rallying cry for the outraged and the underdog to join the socialist cause sits uneasily with new Labour's pitch for middle England".[26]

It is interesting to note that Cooper was very keen to emphasise that New Labour was abandoning the concept of redistribution of wealth to correct social injustice. This is a very neo liberal approach which basically says that the wealth generators can keep their gains and the Welfare State would be used to pick up the pieces for those left behind. But at no stage would the wealthy be asked or expected to contribute financially to improve the lot of those not included in prosperity.

This mass expansion of the welfare state was seen through record investments in education, employment programs and hospital building. There was also record cash for local government to redevelop deprived areas, as well as a new system of working tax credits to supplement benefits. However, it is interesting that the biggest achievement of the New Labour government was the adoption of the minimum wage. A holy grail for social justice, and a very socialist act for such an un-socialist government.

---

26 (Note: *New Labour: What does it stand for?* By Yvette Cooper. *Independent 25th April 1996* http://www.independent.co.uk/news/uk/new-labour-what-does-it-stand-for-left-behind-1306672.html)

Chapter 3 - Old Labour, from 1900 to 1960

Now we have charted the route of the "Slow Revolution" from 1870 to the turn of the 21st century. It is important to understand the role of the Labour Party in the changing the direction of Britain. This chapter will chart the course of the Labour Party from 1900 to 1960, from its beginnings as a fledgling party in Parliament, to becoming the party that offered more reform in a single government than any other. This chapter is divided into pre-war and post-war governments.

"By the strength of our common endeavour we achieve more than we achieve alone"

There have been many academic books written about where the Labour Party came from. Yet if you want to understand the thinking or emotion behind the Labour Party, you need only to read Robert Tressell's one and only novel, published posthumously, *The Ragged Trousered Philanthropists.*[27]It tells the story of a bunch of painters and decorators and their travails, with uncaring employers who are only interested in making the biggest profit for the smallest outlay. The characters often argue and Tressell is constantly showing that they in fact facilitate their miserable existence by doing that very British of things, insulting their bosses behind their backs but then ingratiating themselves with said employers to gain the upper hand over their colleagues. Tressell uses various characters to illustrate the ideas of Karl Marx regarding the idea that employers, by and large, are like puppet masters watching their employees do all the work whilst they cream off the money. This process is never questioned because the employers create a hierarchy by making a few workers feel superior, but at the same time these employees are worried about the loss of their own privileges if those beneath them do not deliver.

27 *The Ragged Trousered Philanthropists, Tressell R- , Re-published by Gutenberg ebook project in 2009*

It was not until the mid-1800s that trade unions became wide spread within the industrial towns and cities of the UK such as Manchester, Liverpool and Glasgow. As we have touched on, pre-1945 capitalism was savage by modern standards and the contemporary idea of the welfare state was the workhouse. It was on the Clyde where Keir Hardie watched his sibling perish due to starvation. Hardie's father, along with his fellow workers were shut out of their workplace for fully six months during an 1866 shipyard dispute known as the "Clyde Lockout", which caused great suffering at a time when state welfare was virtually non-existent. Hardie was scarred by the sheer injustice of how such workers were cruelly and often fatally exploited by the yard owners who were determined enough to shut their business down for six long months just to teach their employees to know their place. In the 1890's Hardie, having worked as a miner, along with other trade unionists came to the conclusion that Parliament held the key to raising the lot of the working classes. Legislation could be passed to force employers to provide improved pay, working conditions and holidays, and if they failed to do so the law would make them comply. Progress would be across the board for the workers rather than piecemeal, and potluck dictating whether you had a decent boss. They made links with the religious, philanthropic wing of Gladstone's Liberal Party who in some cases endorsed union men such as Hardie to stand for Westminster. But fairly quickly Hardie realised that the Liberals were more than pleased to garner votes from the workers, whilst doing little to actually help them.

Thus as the 19th century came to a close, a variety of organisations such as the Independent Labour Party and the Labour Representation Committee evolved into what we now call the Labour Party. The breakthrough came in the 1906 General Election when 29 Labour MPs were returned, and by 1910 the Labour Party held 42 seats after that year's national poll. The formation of the LRC and its evolution into the Labour Party moved matters away from the Liberal tradition of benign regulation of work and poverty, and sought to take a more radical way of improving the lot of the working classes.

By the mid 1920's Labour had replaced the Liberal Party as the main opposition to the Conservatives in the House of Commons. Despite radical social measures such as the introduction of National Insurance, pensions and the bare bones of a welfare state, David Lloyd George's Liberal government had been swept from power in the 1922 General Election and the Labour Party was now 'his majesty's loyal official opposition'. The Tories fell into turmoil as the international situation in Europe caused an economic crisis at home, as cheap imports were driving down demand and production, resulting in rising unemployment. The death of Prime Minister Andrew Bonar Law after just 211 days in Office saw Stanley Baldwin replace him. Although he could have stayed in Number Ten for another four years the new Tory leader felt he needed a mandate from the people in order to stamp his authority on a Conservative Party hopelessly divided over our free trade relationship with Europe. Baldwin's gamble backfired in spectacular style as the Tories lost 86 seats, and although still the largest party with 258 MPs, Baldwin was defeated in a motion of No Confidence. He had fought the election on a platform of re-introduction of tariffs and so felt that the electorate had clearly rejected this proposal, and he was not prepared to lead a government with no mandate to charge import duty.

Despite being 67 seats behind the Tories, James Ramsay McDonald found himself as the first Labour Prime Minister. The maths clearly did not add up and his government fell after just nine months, but crucially his Housing Minister John Wheatley drove through a truly epoch making piece of legislation. The 1924 Housing Act allowed local councils to embark on a massive expansion of well-built, affordable homes due to a 30% boost in subsidies from central government for every house built, allied to a 50% increase in the time councils were allowed to pay back central government on loans taken out for social house building. This led to the building of 500,000 homes, another political issue from this period that remains today. Gradually we can see the patchwork of reforms coming together to create what we term "The Slow Revolution".

Ramsay McDonald's values were driven by his belief that socialists will find in the Gospels "*a marvellous support for his economic and political proposals.*"[28] Based on his actions in government McDonald appears to place "fairness" at the heart of his vision for the future. But the Labour government was short lived and it was alleged links to the USSR, and the now familiar antipathy of the Tory-dominated press, which destroyed McDonald's government and subsequent chances in the General Election of 1924.

The Boss Class looked at Labour's progressive policies for the promotion of workers interests and immediately took fright. They were given their opportunity to damage the electoral prospects when the Labour government decided not to prosecute the editor of the Communist Daily Worker, John Ross Campbell after an editorial called for soldiers and the military to mu-

28 *Socialism, Macdonald R, London 1907 P99*

tiny in the case of a workers' revolutionary uprising.[29] The vested interests made a great play on this political misjudgement and McDonald lost a vote of confidence in the Commons and went to the country. Further electoral damage was caused by the Daily Mail which published a letter purporting to have been written by a certain Grigory Zinoviev, a senior Soviet official to the Central Committee of Communist Party of Great Britain, calling for them to use McDonald's 1924 Trade Treaty with the USSR to encourage revolutionary activity and destabilise parliamentary democracy.[30] The letter was denied by the Soviets and later it was claimed to be the work of Russian monarchists residing in Berlin, but it wasn't until 1999 when Labour Foreign Secretary Robin Cook ordered a review of the case that the Zionviev letter was proved beyond doubt to be a forgery.[31] The subsequent 1924 election saw the Liberals obliterated, Labour lose 40 seats and left Stanley Baldwin and the Tories with a healthy majority but the upside was that the Labour Party was now the undoubted main party of opposition.

The 1929 General Election returned MacDonald to Downing Street but again with no overall majority. However for the first time the Labour Party became the biggest Party in the Commons, and enjoying the benign support of Lloyd George's 59 MPs the government was able to restore rights lost by workers in the wake of the General Strike, embark on a programme of slum clearance and appoint the first ever female cabinet minister when Margaret Bondfield became Minister of Labour. Note that little reform had taken place in this period in fact, some years very little legislation was passed. Despite Ramsay's McDonald ignominious exit from the Labour Party, after forming a national government it fair to say that a number of radical measures were attempted to improve the conditions for workers. As previously mentioned, the 1930 Coal Mines Act could have had a tremendous effect on the lives of miners but was not enforced by the pit owners, and Labour did not have the clout to ensure compliance due to being a minority administration. The idea was that no man was expected to work more than a 7 ½ hour day, and the government wanted to intervene directly to regulate production as a means to stop owners flogging their men beyond endurance to see off competition from other pits. It was not until

29 *Daily Worker 25th July 1924 quoted by Spartacus Education http://www.spartacus.schoolnet.co.uk/TUcampbellJ.ht*

30 *Actual edition was Saturday 25th October 1924. Quoted by University Of Warwick "Stalinism in Europe." September 2013 http://www2.warwick.ac.uk/services/library/mrc/studying/modules/docs/stalinism*

31 *Official: Zinoviev letter was forged Jury L, The Independent – 4/2/1999*

the war years and subsequent nationalisation in 1945 that life underground became centre stage in the coal industry.

Homes fit for a civilised society once again took centre stage with the government embarking on a slum clearance via the 1930 Housing Act. Step by step the Labour Party was changing the Victorian acceptance that workers lived in abject poverty, and that was just the way things were. As seen before, as a result of the Act nearly ¼ million slums were cleared and by the outbreak of war in 1939 700,000 new homes had been constructed.[32] The message was that government had a key role to play in the conditions that people were forced to live in, and that Labour politicians would actively lead the way in ending poverty. They would not leave it to the market or use charities to take the edge off the worst circumstances for families in trouble. The second Ramsay MacDonald Labour government was determined to improve everyday life for all, not just the industrial working class. It succeeded in passing the Agricultural Marketing Act in 1931. This was important because it guaranteed minimum market prices for hard pressed farmers and their workers. This industry was and still is notoriously volatile and the act gave much needed protection to the agricultural sector. The Agriculture Wages Board, founded by Lloyd George as part of his 1909 People's Budget was strengthened by MacDonald and lasted right until 2013 when they it was abolished by Lib Dem Farming Minister David Heath.[33]

Predictably that Labour government fell and the 'Hungry Thirties' was a disastrous decade for the UK working class. The Jarrow March, which took place in October 1936, has become synonymous with the catastrophic economic situation in Britain. Situated in the North East and reliant on the ship building industry, Jarrow had become, according to one of the 207 marchers who completed a walk from their town to Parliament, '...a filthy, dirty, falling down, consumptive area." with unemployment standing at 70%.[34]

This was a grim period in British history and was documented by George Orwell in "*The Road to Wigan Pier*". The book is split into two sections with the first part seeing Orwell living in digs and observing the day to day grind of life as the woman of the house desperately tries to make the

32(Note: http://www.parliament.uk/about/living-heritage/transformingsociety/towncountry/towns/ overview/councilhousing/)

33(Note: *This withering assault on farm workers' wages is a race to the bottom, by Polly Toynbee Guardian 25th Oct 2012* http://www.theguardian.com/commentisfree/2012/oct/25/withering-assault-wages-race-bottom)

34 (Note: http://www.bbc.co.uk/history/british/britain_wwone/jarrow_01.shtml)

money last so she could feed the family, *"Rent and clothes and school-bills are an unending nightmare, and every luxury, even a glass of beer, is an unwarrantable extravagance"[35]* Meanwhile the unemployed man of the house suffers the ritual humiliation of applying for Public Assistance. In chapter two this is brilliantly summed up, *"This business of petty inconvenience and indignity, of being kept waiting about, of having to do everything at other people's convenience, is inherent in working-class life."[36]* In a chilling passage Orwell talks about the level of debate by politicians about the amount of money that people should, or should not be able to live on. *"When the dispute over the Means Test was in progress there was a disgusting public wrangle about the minimum weekly sum on which a human being could keep alive."[37]*

The Thirties have many parallels with today's economic crises, and the crushing of aspiration for young people is a recurring tragedy in our era. Walter Greenwood wrote *"Love on the Dole"* in 1933. Set in a Lancashire mill town the Manchester Guardian told its readers at the time, *"We passionately desire this novel to be read; it is the real thing."[38]* What comes across when re reading Greenwood's tome is that the aspirations of young people then and now tally up. The wish for independence, a steady income and the respect that comes from it, to better oneself so that you have a more enriched life than your parents. The degradation that comes from an empty and poverty stricken daily existence is clear, and today's young people will empathise with the plight of Harry Hardcastle. Dispensed with at 18 years old by factory owners who would rather pay virtual slave wages to under 15's, he is desperate for the respect of his girlfriend and the hours of grinding boredom and self-loathing, rowing with his parents and assorted issues with his peers leads him to make poor decisions borne of zero control over his life.

Then there is Larry. An eloquent and self-educated Marxist he is regarded as a bit of an odd ball, "up on himself" by the slum inhabitants he grew up with, he struggles with his health and the infuriating inertia of his peers who just don't seem to get it until it is too late about the motives of the factory owners. Getting drunk and other things seem to be their priority

---

35 (Note: "The Road to Wigan Pier" 1937 George Orwell \penguin Modern Classics page 114

36 (Note: "The Road to Wigan Pier" 1937 George Orwell \penguin Modern Classics page 114

37 (Note: "The Road to Wigan Pier" 1937 George Orwell \penguin Modern Classics page 114

38 (Note: Guardian 7th August 2010 quoted by John Harris http://www.theguardian.com/books/2010/aug/07/rereading-love-dole-walter-greenwood

as they sleepwalk on to the dole heap. The character of the pawnbroker resonates, is also in clear evidence in modern Britain, this time through legal loan sharks. It's when we examine texts like these we see Britain and the harshness of financial liberalism and we see things haven't changed.[39]

The Wall Street Crash and the subsequent Great Depression destroyed the Labour government and caused a terrible split in the Party as, despite advice to the contrary from economists such as John Maynard Keynes, Prime Minister MacDonald and his fiscally-orthodox Chancellor Phillip Snowden refused categorically to run a deficit budget and increase public spending to stimulate the economy and protect jobs. As a result unemployment soared to 20% and the export market for UK goods suffered a cataclysmic fall of 50% by the end of 1930. The Labour government, to the total fury of many within the Party who just could not understand why MacDonald and Snowden were prepared to stand idly by whilst the workers bore the brunt of the greatest economic crisis in history, dissolved itself and formed a National Coalition government with the Tories and Liberals. This contrasts hugely with the New Deal in America which saw unemployed put to work building state infrastructure works, many of which remain as the backbone of America today, demonstrating that it's great for governments to invest in times of need.

The Labour Party turned in on itself in the wake of a crushing defeat in 1931 when it polled only 30.7% of the popular vote, lost 225 seats and ended up with just 52 MPs. This included new leader Arthur Henderson losing his Burnley seat. George Lansbury, who was leader of the Labour Party between 1932 and 1935, was stunningly out of touch with the needs of 1930s UK voters. The problem, compounded by age, could be summed up by his total naivety of the intentions of Adolf Hitler, saying if he were Prime Minister he, "would close every recruiting station, disband the Army and disarm the Air Force and say to the world: Do your worst."[40] This provided the backdrop to Clement Attlee being asked to lead the Labour Party in an interim capacity for the 1935 General Election. This election produced a surprisingly strong showing for Labour: the vote was trebled, there was a swing of 7.2% to the Party and 102 seats were gained. This is despite Lansbury's inept leadership, which culminated in his resignation just as the election was called. The result secured Attlee's leadership of the party and his subsequent place in British history.

39 Note: "Love on the Dole (1933) by Walter Greenwood Vintage Classics *ISBN-13: 978-0099224815*

40 *Speech by George Lansbury, June 1933.*

1940- 1960

The outbreak of war was an advert for Labour. Total war would shake the old guard of European politics, propelling the continent into the cold war and onto the path of modernity we know today. But the war itself was almost lost before Labour had chance to serve in government. It was only the ineptitude of Neville Chamberlain and his government that allowed for the creation of the national (coalition) government. Labour was to play a pivotal role in the national government, led by Churchill, with Attlee serving as his Deputy Prime Minister.

In opposition the Labour Party had reservations about entering a national government with the Conservatives in the face of war. They did so, but they reserved two rights: firstly the right to criticise the government and the secondly they did not enter into any government under the premiership of Neville Chamberlain. When entering the War coalition in 1940 the Labour Party did well in terms of the number of positions it gained in the government in comparison to its size in Parliament and the 1935 general election showing. There were two reasons: to recognise the Labour's popularity in Britain and because of the unpopularity of the appeasement policy of former Conservative Prime Minister Neville Chamberlain. Clement Attlee joined Prime Minister Winston Churchill's five-man war cabinet and by 1945, 17 Labour MPs had become ministers. The work of Aneurin Bevan and Herbert Morrison in the war effort was noted by the general public and did much to bolster the image of the Labour Party. After the 1942 cabinet reshuffle Clement Attlee was appointed Deputy Prime Minister.

Labour ministers were able to make social reforms such as the Catering Wages Act (1943), The Education Act (1944) and the creation of the 1942 Beveridge Report, which although not implemented during the war, was to be the blueprint of the welfare state and the backbone of Labour's policy agenda post 1945. Small steps forward in the slow revolution. But it was clear there was no doubt in the mind of Labour MPs that the war would be won and there would be a post war election victory for Labour. Finally, the slow revolution would yield the social reform in Britain that campaigners had worked for over 50 years to achieve.

Given the evils of Nazism, support amongst the British people for the war was generally strong. Perhaps more surprising was the willingness to support and get involved in the war effort amongst Labour Party members.

Many constituency Labour parties got involved with entertaining and catering for injured soldiers paid for by donations from members and supporters. This shows a deep patriotic love for Britain that is often dismissed by many on the right in Britain, who often claim that they are the most patriotic.

The war turned the UK from a country in steep decline at home, and with rumblings of discontent with Empire abroad, into a more coherent society, as central government stepped in to ensure that the country was run as efficiently as possible. The first task was to hold up the Axis tide that saw the Nazis sweep through all before them in Europe, and Japan conquer vast swathes of the European-controlled parts of the Far East. Britain's next aims were the total defeat of Hitler and to join with the USA in vanquishing Japan. The socialist style demand economy in the UK had unintended consequences for the British working class, most of them positive in the long run. According to economist Mark Harrison, Gross Domestic Product (GDP), which economists use to measure output, rose three fold in the UK during the war years following steep decline during the 1930's.[41] The dramatic upturn in output was not only attributed to military production, but also reflected an increase in mining, and farming activities as the UK looked to be as self-sufficient as possible. This required two things to make this happen. Firstly there was a planned economy and secondly there had to be an effective and enthusiastic workforce. The former was achieved by central government taking direct control of industrial output and production. The mines and shipyards came under Whitehall control, as well as the land. Every aspect of working life was dictated by the government. In response to this Churchill took the unprecedented step of bringing the head of the Transport and General Workers Union, Ernest Bevin into the cabinet to take charge of the Ministry of Labour. Bevin ensured that to win government contracts meant that employers must recognise trade unions, and as a result union membership increased by three million during the war.[42]

Workplaces were turned upside down by the hemorrhaging of men into the services and the burgeoning of the unions and a planned economy led many workers, especially women to see that maybe Socialism wasn't the nightmare that it had been made out to be by the press and Tories during

41 (note: "The economics of World War II: an overview" (1998) by Mark Harrison Cambridge University Press ISBN978-0-521-62046-8.)

42 (Note:The Labour Movement and World War Two by Professor Mary Davis, Centre for Trade Union Studies, London Metropolitan University http://www.unionhistory.info/timeline/1939_1945.php)

the inter war period. This coupled with the realisation that the war effort could not be for a return to pre-war poverty and financial liberalism ensured that the Tories accepted the Beveridge Report and its findings.

The Beveridge Report is important not only for the history of the United Kingdom, but for identifying the place of the Labour Party in the history of British politics. At the time of its conception Britain was the last man standing in the fight against the evils of Nazism. The Soviet Union was still allied with Hitler and the very survival of Britain was on a knife-edge. Yet the Labour Party was still prepared to argue the case for social reform, and still had the fire, energy and vitality to envisage the world as it should be, and to strive to make it happen. Labour's values of Socialism were, despite the country being at a low ebb, overwhelmingly optimistic. Not even the bombing of civilians in the Blitz and the relentless arrival of telegrams informing families of the death of loved ones could quell Labour's thirst to create Utopia in England's Green and Pleasant Land. Maybe some of the dull, faceless and visionless politicians today should take note.

The 1945-50 Labour government

The war government came with an electoral truce between the three main parties, which allowed a number of independents to gain entry to Parliament and by 1944 the Labour Party was gearing up for the first general election in Britain since 1935. With the surrender of Nazi Germany in May 1945 the Labour Party NEC voted that Labour should leave the War coalition in accordance with the wishes of Herbert Morrison. This was against the requests of Clement Attlee, who along with Winston Churchill wanted to keep the War coalition together until peace in the Far East had been achieved. Labour left the coalition leaving the Conservatives in government alone. The popularity of Churchill with the British people was unquestioned, but the public had fallen out of love with the Conservative Party as a whole.

The General Election of 1945 was a seismic national event even though this was in an era of open-air political discussions where politicians spoke in front of small local crowds. Many servicemen were still abroad and the war against Japan was still being fought. As a result it took over three weeks for the result of the election to become clear. The parliamentary majority of 146 seats for the Labour Party represented a landslide, and the fact that Labour took 11.9 million votes or 49.7% in comparison to 36.2% by the Conservatives was perhaps the biggest political shift ever in modern electoral history. Many people were still keen to blame the Conservatives for the mistakes made in the run up to the war such as the Munich agreement. Memories of pre-war unemployment and poverty were still raw. Much had been made during the war years of the Britain the soldiers would come home to, academics wrote short books for soldiers in which they were promised a Britain where class barriers were broken down, the unregulated pre-war capitalism and resulting poverty were done away with, to be replaced by a mixed economy, full employment and welfare state. Why not? Class barriers had been broken down as everyone mixed in the services or in munitions factories; the war had been fought by the people and the victory belonged to the people. Victory should not be claimed only by the capitalists and the upper classes. Labour argued that the outcome should be different from other conflicts. The British people gave this idea a massive endorsement at the ballot box.

The 1945 Parliamentary Labour Party (PLP) was different from its predecessors. Now only one third of MPs had union sponsorship, the new intake was made up of men (and some women) of all ages, including middle class professionals as well as workers from the shop floor. Many of the newly elected Labour MPs had returned from the front line and had proudly campaigned in uniform, including future heavyweights Denis Healey and Roy Jenkins. The new party had an unusual togetherness, discipline and sense of direction. Attlee as leader of the party quickly accepted the invitation from the King to form a government, despite calls by some for a leadership election. Much has been made of the quiet demeanour of Clement Attlee; Sir Winston Churchill famously made the quip Attlee was *a modest man, with much to be modest about.* Historian Lord Hennessy notes the contrast of the shyness of Clement Attlee with the pomp and circumstance of his predecessor Winston Churchill. However despite this quietness Attlee soon gained a reputation as the master of the surroundings in Downing Street and the inner workings of government. He surrounded himself with political heavyweights such as Aneurin Bevan, Stafford Cripps, Herbert Morrison and later Hugh Gaitskell and Harold Wilson.

The post-war Labour government was notable for many achievements and some failures. The fledgling Labour government had to ensure that Britain had a strong place in the new international order whilst also funding the new and promised domestic social reforms that they wanted to implement. There was the major challenge of dismantling a war economy that had mobilised almost every adult person in Britain. This government was associated with nationalisation of industry as part of the transition from a war economy. The programme of nationalisation started with the Bank of England and was met with little opposition from the Tories. Next came the coal industry, canals and the railways. The nationalisation of the road haulage industry was more contentious and met with opposition, but the public ownership of the utilities such as gas, electricity and water proved popular. Finally, and with most opposition, came the nationalisation of the efficient and profitable steel and iron industries. The return of these industries to the private sector under Thatcher proved to be highly contentious.

Part of Nye Bevan's remit was to do something about the desperate state of housing in the UK following the damage inflicted by the Luftwaffe (20% of pre-war housing stock was rendered useless), added to the fact that virtually no houses were built in Britain for the duration of the war. We were very much a nation of renters in the 1940's. 57% of houses were privately leased, with only 10% being rented from local authorities. This sector saw the biggest post-war boom with nearly 750,000 council built homes springing up around Britain in the five years of the Labour government. These brick houses were augmented by the surprising popularity of prefabricated dwellings, which could be assembled within three days. 168,000 such homes were put up by 1948. Given the circumstances Bevan's building programme was a triumph of willpower over reality as Nye's passionate belief in creating a Socialist paradise, a New Jerusalem was put into practice.

Labour also began the process of implementing the Beveridge Report, starting by bringing together private, charity and insurance based hospitals to create the National Health Service. The school leaving age was raised to 15, university scholarships increased and the National Insurance Act was also implemented. The government gave local authorities the power to build over 200,000 new homes, thus rebuilding a country damaged by the blitz and many of these houses remain standing to this day.

If you asked a Labour Party member what they thought was the party's greatest ever achievement then we suspect that the vast majority would plump for the foundation of the National Health Service, which opened its doors to serve the medical needs of the nation on 5th July 1948. The NHS encapsulates all that is great about the UK because it is based on those most British of traits: fairness and equality. "Free to all at the point of use". The evidence over the decades is crystal clear. The UK public hold the NHS to be sacrosanct and even during the years that Thatcher totally dominated the political scene, Labour always led in opinion polls when it came to the question of which party had the best policies on healthcare. The story of how the NHS came to be results from a consensus amongst 1930s mainstream politicians that something had to be done about the gross inequalities of access to healthcare across the nation. Depending on where you lived, free access to doctors and hospitals was either provided by the local authority or by charities, and it was hit and miss as to how effective free healthcare was in reaching those in chronic need.

The Beveridge Report of 1942 had its opponents over the way social reform was to be implemented after the war, and Labour cabinet minister Ernie Bevin went as far as to call the report a Social Ambulance Scheme, but the ethos was clearly accepted across the political spectrum as Beveridge called for an end to, "*squalor, ignorance, want, idleness and disease.*"[43] Churchill gave his blessing to the report in 1943 accepting the aim of full employment as a governmental responsibility, and welcoming the expansion of free health care provided by the State. How this was to be done proved to be a more difficult proposition. Nye Bevan was appointed by Attlee as Health Minister following Labour's landslide victory in the 1945 General Election, with the responsibility of setting up the NHS. The Welshman faced almost implacable opposition to his plans from the powerful doctors' professional body, the British Medical Association (BMA) who feared their medical decision making would end up being directed by politicians and they would become civil servants with no independence. Bevan was forced to compromise over the issue of private work and NHS contracts for doctors. He bitterly regretted having to do so in order to get the BMA onside with literally a handful of weeks to spare before the NHS opened for business. *"I stuffed their mouths with gold,"*[44] he said with some bitterness. There was also the tiny matter of how on earth a country shattered by war and crippled by associated debt was ever going to pay for a programme delivering free healthcare for all, from cradle to grave. The anti-American strain that has always existed in the Labour Party would do well to remember that President Truman's largesse in agreeing to a loan of some $68 billion at today's prices, with interest of only 2%, was the key to the UK not only being able to get back on its feet, but have some hope for a bright future. Economist John Maynard Keynes negotiated the loan whose last repayment of £45 million was lodged with the US in December 2006. Without the loan the Great Britain would

43 *The Beveridge Report uploaded by The BBC* http://news.bbc.co.uk/1/shared/bsp/hi/pdfs/19_07_05_beveridge.pdf

44 *The birth of the NHS, Published in the Independent,* http://www.independent.co.uk/life-style/health-and-families/features/the-birth-of-the-nhs-856091.html 2008

have faced a very bleak future and been in perpetual crisis, similar to that of Weimar Germany following World War One.

Despite a deficit five times that found in the immediate aftermath of the 2008 banking crisis, Labour invested in health and housing thereby creating jobs, putting money into the pockets of the population who spent it, thus creating demand for manufactured goods. Allied to tax increases on the rich, the money borrowed from the US saw Britain have a chance to move forward. Without these gambles we would have been finished as a world power and struggling to provide even the basics for our people. From the struggles and sacrifice of war there was great demand for social reform and Labour was once again the party that delivered social justice. This was the slow revolution delivering action. None of this *"we can't do anything because of the national debt"*, like we have today. These were strong politicians, who had had enough of being ruled by international economics and bankers. These were men (and women) who implemented change, this was the reform that Britain needed to deliver social and economic reform and from the most precarious of situations.

The Labour government also faced some expensive foreign policy challenges. It was important that Labour made policy decisions that protected Britain in the face of the threat of the USSR and the atomic age as well as securing a sound footing for Britain in the new international order, especially with the policies of decolonisation and the divide between communism and the capitalist west. Labour had to take a strong foreign policy line and many within the party accused the government of adopting an 'un-socialist policy.' The Labour government chose the nuclear option and aligned itself with the United States, if for no other reason than to stave off the threat from the now aggressive USSR. The natural Labour policy would have been to remain independent of both the Communist USSR and the capitalist USA, acting as a bridge between the pair with closer ties to post war torn Europe. Whilst many of the world's top scientists took part in the Manhattan Project a decision was taken by Congress in the United States in 1946 to keep any further arms development inside the USA, forcing Britain to develop its own weapons. Attlee's decision to pursue the nuclear option was not the catalyst for the later arms race: it would have happened anyway, and it also helped preserve Britain place in the new international order. At a time when decolonisation and the resulting loss of economic might could well have relegated us down the international pecking order. Further expensive cold war expensive policies included the expansion of the intelligence services, dealing with the threat of espionage as well as updating the war plan to ensure policies were in place in the event of nuclear holocaust.

Whilst Labour had pursued an aggressive and expensive programme in government, perhaps the most radical of the 20thCentury it faced the same problem it would be accused of time and time again in future governments, balancing the books. Post war, the economic issues facing the new government were huge. Hugh Dalton as Chancellor had to deal with the end of the lend-lease agreements with America. This armed the UK and kept us supplied with food, but it had left Britain running a balance of payments deficit. The government had to arrange a high interest large dollar loan, which gave Britain the cash it needed to both recover from the war and implement the social reforms that the government had been elected to introduce. Fortunately unemployment remained low and food subsidies helped to keep inflation under control. However the Cold War began to undermine Britain's economic performance and a recession in the USA impacted here as the UK was in effect a dollar economy. The decision was taken to devalue from $4.03 to $2.90, which in modern political economic theory seems a rational act and which allowed Britain to export and improve the balance of payments. But devaluation proved politically unpopular, and following the 1950 general election, economic performance was one of the key reasons given as to why Labour underperformed. Although the government's popularity had waned somewhat since the 1945 landslide, the parties found themselves neck and neck by polling day; in fact Labour polled 46.1% to the Tories 43.5%, leaving the Labour government with an overall majority of just 6.

For the people this was a time of austerity; they felt there was little or no reward resulting from the sacrifices of total war. Austerity meant a lack of improvement of the quality of life for the British people. The stubborn deficit in the balance of payments led to continued food rationing right into the 1950s. The British people looked to their American counterparts where young middle-class families had the latest mod cons, and it left them craving a higher quality of life. Parallel to UK's food rationing, America's middle class expanded; they had TV sets, rock and roll music and big modern refrigerators.

Post 1950

The 1951 budget by Labour's chancellor Hugh Gaitskell proved to be unpopular with the public and split the government in two. It proposed tax increases, spending cuts and payment for NHS items that remain charged for today such as dentures and spectacles. Many constituency Labour Parties were against the proposals, seeing it as attacking one of Labour's greatest achievements, and the row provoked the resignations of ministers Nye Bevan, Harold Wilson and John Freeman from the government. In a climate of division in Labour ranks Winston Churchill's Conservatives won the 1951 General Election despite Labour polling their highest ever number of votes (13.9 million) 1.3 million more votes than the Tories. The Conservatives had a 16 seat majority when their National Liberal and Ulster Unionist allies were counted. The 1951 election was remarkable for a turnout of 84% something modern day politicians should take note of. For the Conservatives, it was a fortunate victory at a fortunate time, as the beginning of the 1950s saw an end to the war time austerity, and the beginning of prosperity and American style consumerism which coincided with the end of rationing.

Although the Conservatives had electioneered on moving away from socialism, the Tory ministers of the 1950s actually continued to commit themselves to full employment and the mixed economy. This was compounded by the need to retain the new, highly popular welfare state reforms. Labour had been a government of social justice, despite horrendous economic conditions. Voters were satisfied with reforms in education, insurance and health provision, and as such the post war consensus was born. This consensus was more than a commitment to state welfare: it was the commitment to a mixed economy and the commitment to full employment. A commitment to social justice that both the main parties would maintain. There was also cross party agreement on policies such as nuclear armament that kept Britain at the table of super powers with a permanent seat on the UN Security Council. This unwritten consensus on the big issues between the main parties remained in place until the late 1970s and the election of Mrs Thatcher.

The Labour government lost power in 1951. There were a variety of reasons including the Korean War and the continuation of rationing of sugar and clothes. The Tories Manifesto promised a swift end to rationing. [45] As in

45 (Note: David Knastor Austerity Britain, 1945–1951,Bloomsbury Publishing, ISBN 978-0-7475-7985-4)

the Hungry 'Thirties the Conservative ideology was the antithesis of social-ist collectivism. The 1945 Labour government believed that society should be organised so that in bad times those at the sharp end should be helped by redistribution of wealth, and by including everyone in shaping the fu-ture of the country. This principle of universality saw a multi-millionaire receive free healthcare, and also sharing the burden of rationing with the poorest in society. The other reason that Labour lost power was down to good, old-fashioned political infighting. The splits in the Attlee govern-ment arose over the decision to introduce prescription charges in 1951, as previously explained.

The 1950's were difficult for the Labour Party, mainly due to the rising af-fluence in society and a feeling amongst the electorate that the Party's rai-son d'être was to fight poverty and unemployment. It was almost as though certain sections of the growing middle class felt that they didn't need the Labour Party anymore and wanted to embrace the consumer society. Writ-ing in the Journal of Modern History in 2005, social historian Peter Gurney asserted that, *"As austerity receded after 1950 and consumer demand kept growing, the Labour Party hurt itself by shunning consumerism as the antith-esis of the socialism it demanded".*[46]

Maybe this attitude of no longer needing the state to better oneself once you have reached a desired standard is a recurring phenomenon amongst voters that was witnessed during the Thatcher era. A decision taken in self-interest, regardless of the plight of one's fellow citizens. But by modern standards the 1951-55 Conservative government was far to the left of any government we might see today. But ultimately an increase in aspiration and infighting within Labour ranks caused a pause in the slow revolution. Hire purchase gave the average family access to household aids such as vacuum cleaners and washing machines. Women particularly found this a major boon and responded by voting Tory in their droves. Labour had vot-ed against extending household credit in 1954 and were seen by some ele-ments of the working class as being kill joys, taking money in taxes which could be spent on pleasure. Alan Silitoe's seminal 1950's novel "Saturday Night and Sunday Morning" sees the antihero Arthur Seaton reflecting these feelings on a regular basis: *"If you don't stop that bastard government from grinding your face in the muck, though there ain't much you can do about it"*[47]

46 (Note: Peter Gurney, "The Battle of the Consumer in Postwar Britain," Journal of Modern History (2005)

47 (Note: "Saturday Night and Sunday Morning" (1958) by Alan Silitoe. ISBN: 0007205023)

Throughout the 1951-55 government the Tories continued with the programme of rebuilding Britain, and they also managed to bring more people into the direct tax bracket, but at the same time reduced income tax rates. Inflation was kept under control through these taxation policies via good relationships with the trade unions. Prime Minister Winston Churchill was once again active on the world stage. However the 1955 election was conspicuous for his absence. Churchill had retired just a few weeks earlier, and in his place was Anthony Eden. If the Tories polled over 1 million fewer votes in 1951, they certainly had a democratic mandate in 1955 taking 900,000 more votes than Labour, which translated into a majority of 60 seats.

The Labour Party continued to be divided between Bevan, who was seen as the beacon on the Left and Gaitskell who was perceived as more pragmatic and less ideologically driven than his Welsh colleague. Following the 1955 defeat and at the age of 72, Clement Attlee stood down as leader of the Labour Party that November. Even with the exit of Churchill from the political stage, the 1950s remained a Conservative decade. Labour was unable to capitalise on the Suez Crisis, which divided Britain, undermined democracy and almost bankrupted Britain. The next general election, which took place in 1959, should have been Labour's for the taking. They had devised a programme for government; however Gaitskell became unstuck on economic policy detail after proposing no direct tax increases. Conservative Prime Minister Harold MacMillan was able to challenge the Labour position on paying for proposals such as the abolition of the eleven plus and increased pension payments through indirect taxation. Labour fell 1.5 million votes behind and the Tories recorded a thumping 100 seat majority. The lesson for the slow revolution, if you want social and economic reform, you had best make sure your sums add up.

Chapter 4 - Old Labour, Politics of the 1960s: The Labour Government, Accompanying the Social Revolution

Much has been written regarding the social revolution that took place in the 1960s. The baby boomers that lived it and revelled in it have recollected their youth and experiences time and time again. No generation before or since has managed to experience such freedom: freedom of music, freedom of speech, freedom of fashion, freedom of expression. They lived in the first consumer society, they revolutionised popular culture, brought celebrity into the mainstream, and initiated the first throwaway society. However this chapter will not re live the 1960s. This chapter will look at how the political events combined with the social revolution created a radical 6 years of Labour government lead by a brash opportunist, with the popular touch in Harold Wilson.

As 13 years of Conservative government dragged on there were a number of crises and events which gave signs of the change that was to come. The Tory government was very much the old order and the Labour government that was to follow was very much the new. The Conservative government of 1951-64 was led by four Prime Ministers: Winston Churchill, who retired at the top; Anthony Eden, pushed from office following the Suez Crisis; Harold Macmillan, who failed to oversee the modernising of his party or the economy and left office amid fears of ill health following one of the biggest sex scandals ever to hit politics; and finally Alec Douglas-Home, who renounced his peerage to serve one year as premier before narrowly losing the election of 1964 to Labour.

Eden was elected as a popular Prime Minister in 1955, but the 1956 Suez Crisis left Britain isolated and out of favour with the United States who were bank rolling Britain in times of need. The conflict forced one of Britain's most embarrassing moments and forced Anthony Eden from office. But still the British people put faith in his successor Harold Macmillan and the Conservatives over a divided Labour Party. Despite this biggest of re-prieves, the Tories failed to realise that they needed to modernise and widen their inner circle of government. Macmillan's government was stuffed full of the upper class elites from yester year, a fair number of whom were related by marriage. This really was the elite ruling over Britain. By not observing the warnings, Macmillan had made a grave mistake. Many of the Ministers he appointed were to underperform and eventually he sacked most in one reshuffle that became known as the *night of the long knives*. There would be three incidents that led up to this. These three events would leave a mark on the nation. They were the Notting Hill riots, the Polaris missile protests and the Profumo affair. All of which rocked the psyche of the nation.

The Notting Hill riots related to an ongoing political theme through this period and to in some guise to this day, that politically poisoned word, immigration. During this period Commonwealth citizens were allowed to enter Britain as they pleased with their British citizenship. At the time this wasn't seen as an issue. Britain needed workers after the war and anyway, why would Commonwealth citizens leave their nice warm climates for our soggy shores? Notting Hill is now one of the most sought after parts of London so it's somewhat ironic that this would be the area where racial disharmony broke into riots. These tensions were a clash of the new vibrant immigrants of Caribbean origin and the white working class Teddy Boys of the 1950s. This was the start of the debate regarding multiculturalism and immigration and many of the debates still continue to this day. The basic problem seemed to have been the contrast in life style between some of the young Caribbean men and some of the young British men of the time. The young men arriving in Britain were often alone, without family, community or religious guidance. They did what many young men would do in this situation: worked hard, listened to music, drank, chased girls and had a great time. The British attitude didn't help. If one house in a street had a black household, the white residents often took fright and moved on to other rented housing, thus the vacancies created were filled by other Commonwealth immigrants.

Disrespectful attitudes and words regarding race were used and it became a lethal cocktail. The young working class white men of the 1950s, constrained by the socially conservative nature of the time as well as the class system, grew frustrated by the changing world and this intimidated them. This is a similar and recurring theme, which blew up with the 2001 race riots in

56

the North of England. Tensions are stirred between white working class men and ethnic communities which for one reason or another are seen as detached and advantaged, when often nothing is further from the truth. The riots themselves are a matter of history. Something small triggered them, they lasted for a number of days and heavy punishments were handed out. In the aftermath of the riots, the Notting Hill carnival was set up, a two day event each August Bank Holiday which celebrates the multiculturalism of London and has a major place in London's annual calendar.

The Campaign for Nuclear Disarmament (CND) symbolised a divisive issue that came to the forefront of UK politics in the 1960's and again in the eighties. Nuclear weapons split the nation in the balance between our moral standing and our foreign policy need to protect the nation. The essential picture is that Britain, financed by the United States, had a foreign policy need to protect its position in the world order, especially in the face of the growing conflict between the USA and the USSR. No matter how much Britain may have wished to act as a neutral player and a bridge between Europe, the USA the USSR, it was unable to because of its financial commitments to the Americans. However, the UK's potential use of weapons of mass destruction, which could eliminate humanity worried many and what resulted was a social movement, CND, which was similar to the peace protests in the USA and captured the culture of the times. To people of a certain age the Campaign for Nuclear Disarmament holds a special place in the heart. CND had two halcyon eras of mass membership and influence within the higher echelons of the Labour Party. But what CND really exemplifies was the difference between idealism and practicality, that many on the left of British politics have spent generations grappling with. The geo-political state of the world meant that the press saw CND at least as do-gooders and at worst in league with communists.

Ironically CND was formed in response to Nye Bevan's 1957 decision to renounce his opposition to the UK holding an independent nuclear deterrent. The New Statesman received so many letters in response to writer J.B. Priestley's demolition of Bevan's position in the magazine, that editor Kingsley Martin decided to set up a pressure group with philosopher Bertrand Russell, Michael Foot and renowned peace activist Peggy Duff. It launched in London in February 1958 and attracted a plethora of high profile supporters including leading clerics, cricket legend John Arlott, actor Charlie Chaplin, sculptor Henry Moore and author Doris Lessing. CND's stated aims were, "the unconditional renunciation of the use, production of or dependence upon nuclear weapons by Britain and the bringing about of a general disarmament convention".[48] The campaign caught the popular mood for many on the left sick to the back teeth of yet another long era of Tory rule, and CND provided a rallying point for, in particular, the so called intellectual Left.

The Atomic Research Establishment based at Aldermaston in Berkshire formed a focal point for the fledgling CND to organise around. A tradition of marches from the nuclear facility was begun in 1958, and by 1962 15,000 people were taking part. The aim of CND was to persuade the Labour Party to adopt unilateral disarmament as party policy. Labour conference voted for this stance in 1960, but Labour Leader Hugh Gaitskell vowed to, *"fight, fight and fight"*[49] the decision. And the 1961 Conference obliged by overturning the previous year's vote. This did serious damage to CND's credibility. They had based their campaign amongst the political classes with the aim of persuading the Labour Party to act when it returned to government. Because it wasn't a movement that sought to build pressure by recruiting ordinary people, once it had lost the argument within the Labour Party its influence soon waned.

As the 1970's ended, Cold War tensions rose considerably. The Soviet invasion of Afghanistan and the election Ronald Regan, an avowed and enthusiastic communist hater meant that the spectre of all out nuclear war once again stalked the planet. The deployment of short range nuclear weapons by both powers in the European theatre ratcheted up tensions even further. The 1983 downing of a Korean civilian airliner by the Soviets, plus NATO exercises in Europe which spooked the USSR placed the very survival of humanity on a knife edge.

This fear was reflected in popular culture by the BBC screening the truly horrific docudrama *"Threads"*[50] in 1984, following the US production, *"The Day After"*[51] (November 1983). Both films depicted the aftermath of nuclear war and produced an unprecedented response from the public and politicians alike. Reagan's response to *"The Day After"* was especially interesting. He wrote in his diary that the film was *"very effective and left me greatly depressed,"*[52] and that it changed his mind on the prevailing policy

48 http://en.wikipedia.org/wiki/Campaign_for_Nuclear_Disarmament

49 Labour Party conference, 5 October 1960

50 Threads, directed by Jackson M- distrusted by BBC- 1984

51 The Day After, directed by Meyer N, distributed by ABC- 1983

52

on a "*nuclear war*". This was a dramatic change of tack from his infamous speech delivered in March 1983 when he described Soviet foreign policy as "*the aggressive impulses of an evil empire*".[53]

The hotting-up of the Cold War proved to be a spur for the renaissance of CND. As NATO prepared to deployed cruise missiles in Europe in 1983, 300,000 marched in London to protest. In addition more civil disobedience occurred, as camps such as that at the Greenham Common US air base in Berkshire sprung up. But CND's greatest success was the adoption of unilateral nuclear disarmament as a central policy objective by the Labour Party for the 1983 election.

The nuclear issue neatly split the Labour Front bench along left/right lines with Healey (a former Defence Secretary who believed that "*Nuclear weapons are preventing wars*"[54]), Hattersley and the Gang of Four (who went on to form the SDP) all in favour of retaining the bomb. Benn, Kinnock and Foot, however, supported the CND position. The truth about CND and the anti-nuclear movement is that they failed to make the argument with Thatcher's core "white van man" constituency who was not ashamed to be a patriot. They allowed the perception to fester that it was somehow anti British to support de-weaponisation. In the 1980's the public were scared of the USSR.

We cannot underestimate the impact of the Profumo affair and how it fatally undermined the perception that the ruling class were born to inherit and exercise power. The scandal itself was rotten and sordid from start to finish, and symbolised how Prime Minister Macmillan had failed to modernise the government. From the Labour perspective it showed that the moral superiority of the upper classes was nothing more than smoke and mirrors. The story begins with Christine Keeler, a young and beautiful girl from a working class background, who found herself working in a bar in Soho where she met Stephen Ward. Ward, in his later 40s by the time he met Keeler, was trained as an osteopath, although it's not quite clear how genuine his qualifications were. After acting as a medic in the war he treated patients such as Gandhi and Winston Churchill. He even drank with and painted portraits of royalty, and it was patients in these kinds of circles who allowed Ward to begin to mix business and pleasure. One of Ward's

---

53 *Speech by Ronal Reagan, accessed from http://voicesofdemocracy.umd.edu/reagan-evil-empire-speech-text/ 1983*

54 *A complete Fantasy R Hattersley Published in The Guardian http://www.theguardian.com/commentisfree/2006/dec/04/comment.military 2006*

patients was Lord Astor, who allowed Ward the use of his vast Cliveden estate. Ward had a string of fashionable girlfriends and a group of girls who surrounded him; he claimed to be *"sensitive to their needs and stresses of modern living."* These girls were introduced to the high flyers Ward associated himself with - the Profumo affair came about as the result of one of these meetings.

In July 1961 Ward held a party at the estate of Cliveden, at which Stephen Ward introduced Christine Keeler to the Secretary of State for War, John Profumo. Profumo and Keeler began an affair that continued for some time. This in itself was not unusual at the time; married politician befriends and begins an affair with a younger mistress. However what was not known was that Keeler was also having an affair with a known Russian spy named Yevegny Ivanov. Whether Ivanov was using Keeler to extricate secretive information from Profumo over pillow talk is another matter, but the affairs remained a secret to all but the intelligence communities. This was until the trial of one of Keeler's former lovers, a drug dealer who was accused of using a firearm in the flat that Keeler and Ward shared. During the trial, rumours of a love triangle between a call girl, a government minister and Russian spy began to circulate. Profumo was dragged into Parliament in the dead of night by his party Whips and interrogated. He denied the affair and then crucially lied about it at the dispatch box. When the scandal hit the public domain, Profumo had no choice but to resign both as the cabinet minister for war, and as an MP. Profumo left public life and dedicated himself to carrying out good deeds but the scandal continued and in doing so caused damage to the government. Ward was arrested and found guilty at trial of living of immoral earnings. However, the night before the last day of his trial he took an overdose of sleeping pills and entered a coma. A guilty verdict was found in his absence but no sentence was passed due to his death three days after the verdict was passed. The scandal shocked the nation and contributed to the downfall of Macmillan as Prime Minister, given that issues of espionage were deemed to be the responsibility of the Prime Minister. Whilst the Notting Hill riots and the Cuban Missile crisis encapsulated the times, it was the Profumo affair that gave us the strongest signal that there was about to be a tidal wave of change in politics. This was the political elite, ruling over the British, playing with people's lives at its worse.

Did the government learn? Lord Alec Douglas-Home was appointed by the Tory inner circle as the Prime Minister following Super Mac's resignation in October 1963, another symbol of how the elite were running the country with little accountability. There were two main problems the United Kingdom was facing. British industry had fallen into decline and behind our major competitors, and a huge budget deficit was appearing on the government accounting books which ultimately was a burden Labour was to inherit in 1964. This was masked from the public view because unemployment began to fall in 1964 and the economic situation seemed to be superficially improving. Nevertheless, with the parliament reaching the end of its five-year limit, late 1964 saw a general election and Labour finally returned to power after thirteen years with a majority of just four seats. This was increased to a majority of 96 in the subsequent March 1966 election. The new Labour Prime Minister was a cocky Yorkshireman by the name of Harold Wilson; Wilson was a departure from the Tory elite and was sharp on economics and witty in debate. However, privately Wilson was seen as an opportunist and a player who was not to be trusted, but he rode the wave of 1960s cultural revolution to grab power.

The Labour government was the parliamentary embodiment of the 1960s cultural revolution with liberal attitudes and the wish for a fairer society. Once again a Labour government was to put social justice as the heart of the agenda. The slow revolution on this occasion was to reflect the change in social attitudes above all else. Many of these reforms were given life by Roy Jenkins. Jenkins, as Wilson's Home Secretary, was a one-man social revolutionary, who made wide scale reform possible. This was not by the conventional means of using the Labour Party to adopt policies such as getting rid of capital punishment, or allowing women the right to choose abortion as it would have proved very difficult, especially as there is a parliamentary convention that "moral" issues should not be whipped and MPs be allowed to vote with their conscience. The sixties was a decade of immense social and ethical change in the UK. At the start of the 1960s the theatre was subject to government appointed censors, divorce was a middle class only option then widely frowned upon, back street abortions were killing women (it was thought 15% of maternal deaths were a result of unsafe terminations, or women being forced to use the crudest and cruellest methods), suicide and attempted suicide were criminal offences, hanging of criminals and birching of offenders was practised, and homosexuality was against the law. There was, and maybe still is a very strong streak of social conservatism in the UK. Persuading the Labour Party to adopt social and moral reform as a serious campaigning platform would have proved impossibly divisive. Jenkins instead threw the weight of the government behind Private Members Bills, and worked with the Leader of the House to ensure that there was enough parliamentary time available for debate.

Capital punishment was one of the most controversial issues facing mid-20th century Britain. Between 1900 and 1949 621 UK citizens had been executed, but the 1950s and early 1960s had seen a succession of hotly contested hangings. In 1950 Timothy Evans, a Welsh lorry driver, had been hanged for the murder of his wife and child in the Notting Hill multi occupancy house where a man called John Christie resided in the basement. Evans was a drunken working class man and had form for domestic violence. In addition he had fled the scene on discovering the bodies. An open and shut case if ever there was one. But in 1953 Christie moved out of 10 Rillington Place and the new tenant discovered three bodies behind a false wall. It turned out that Christie had butchered six women over ten years, and it was he and not Evans that had murdered the victims Evans had been hung for.

Public disquiet was further roused with the execution of teenager Derek Bentley, whose mental age at the time of his hanging was that of an 11 year old. He and 16-year-old Christopher Craig had set out to burgle a sweet warehouse in Croydon; Craig was in possession of one of the many guns in circulation at the time in the wake of World War Two. The burglars were cornered on the roof of the building and Bentley was arrested. Craig approached the police waving the gun and Bentley exhorted his friend to, "Let him have it Chris!" Craig fired and PC Sidney Miles was fatally shot. The prosecution successfully persuaded the jury that Bentley had encouraged Craig to fire, whilst Craig argued years later that his friend's intention was for him to hand over the weapon. As Craig was too young to hang, Bentley was executed in January 1953 on the grounds of joint enterprise and amongst a furore of public condemnation. In 1998 the Appeal Court quashed Bentley's conviction, confirming the Royal Pardon granted in 1993.

1955 saw the execution of Ruth Ellis, again under controversial circumstances as Ellis was sent to the gallows for the murder of her abusive and unfaithful lover David Blakely. Women's rights campaigners pointed to Ellis suffering a miscarriage as a result of being punched repeatedly in the stomach by Blakely, an event that contributed to Ellis becoming disturbed and exhibiting bizarre behaviour. The Judge Cecil Havers, father of future Attorney general Sir Michael Havers, wrote to Conservative Home Secretary Gwilym Lloyd George recommending clemency on the grounds that this was a crime of passion but on 13th July 1955 Ruth Ellis was executed, to a cacophony of public outrage.

The issue of Capital Punishment would not go away. When Roy Jenkins became Home Secretary he was horrified to find outside his office a board containing the names of those due for execution which moved along day by day until the date of their hanging. He replaced it with a drinks cabinet. Long-term abolitionist and Labour MP Sydney Silverman introduced a Private Members Bill in 1965, which called for the suspension of execution for a five-year trial period. The aim was to investigate whether or not ex- ecution acted as a deterrent. The murder rate remained largely the same, so vindicating the argument that there was in fact no deterrent value to hang- ing and in 1970 the three of the four UK countries abolished the Death Penalty with Northern Ireland joining the ban in 1973.

Divorce in the UK had generally been the preserve of the middle classes, and the need to prove "fault", especially for women in abusive relationships threw up barriers, especially to working class women. The upper hand was definitely with men. Mortgages, bank accounts and household incomes were largely the preserve of men due to their traditional role as the bread- winner, and the concept of a married woman going out to work and having a separate bank account was anathema to many in the UK. In 1969 back- bench Labour MP Bill Wilson introduced a Private Members Bill that pro- posed a "no fault" divorce after a two-year separation, and where one party would not consent, divorce would be granted after a five-year period. This was a seminal piece of legislation as it sent the message to women and men that the law was being shifted away from men controlling their spouses. This work was built on by the second Wilson government when in 1976 it passed the Domestic Violence and Matrimonial Proceedings Act which gave added protection to women who were trapped in violent relationships, particularly when their partner was the sole name on the mortgage or rent agreement and refused to leave the family home.

Abortion is a subject, which is guaranteed to up the temperature in any debate because for many it represents a life and death issue. But by the 1960s the protection of working class women from back street abortionists was becoming an imperative. Although the advent of the pill had given women far more reproductive control, and undoubtedly the number of women seeking and being injured or killed by botched abortions was in decline, there was still a distressing undercurrent in UK society that placed women, especially those who could not afford to bribe an unscrupulous doctor, in considerable danger. The figures are difficult to pin down. The *"Hospital Inpatient Enquiry"*[55] of 1967 extrapolated mortality reports from Aberdeen and concluded there were up to 100,000 illegal abortions performed every year in the UK, whilst a *National Opinion Poll s*urvey gave a figure of 30,000.[56] Either way these figures demanded that action be taken. David Steel's backbench private members bill became the government backed Abortion Act and allowed women to have the right to an abortion on the NHS providing two doctors agreed and certain loose criteria were met. It came into force in April 1967.

The treatment of gay, lesbian, bisexual and transgender (GLBT) UK citizens under the law has provoked controversy throughout the post war period, but when it seemed that the police were actively targeting the GLBT community with a policy of entrapment, the Tory government of the 1950s decided to commission a review of antiquated laws that made it a criminal offence to follow a GLBT lifestyle. Alan Turing is considered by those in the know to be the father of modern computers and he was a renowned code breaker during the Second World War, credited with smashing the Nazi code system, which seriously damaged the German war effort. Turing was gay, and in that era this was an "offence" punishable with prison. In 1952 after being robbed by a former partner, Turing told police they had been in a sexual relationship. He was prosecuted for gross indecency, and sentenced to prison but instead was "allowed" to accept injections of female hormones coupled with chemical castration in an effort to "cure" his urges. He was stripped of his clearance and kicked out of the security services. Alan Turing committed suicide in 1954. The public outcry encouraged Tory Home Secretary David Maxwell-Fyfe to set up a review around LGBT issues. The Wolfendon Report of 1957 concluded:

"Homosexual behaviour between consenting adults in private should no longer be a criminal offence [finding that] homosexuality cannot legitimately be regarded as a disease, because in many cases it is the only symptom and is compatible with full mental health in other respects."[57]

But Maxwell-Fyfe, who subsequently had been made Lord Chancellor, stated in a Lords debate that he felt the public had little interest in the issue, and the matter was quietly dropped. The sixties saw a number of attempts by Labour backbenchers to have decriminalisation put on the statute book

55 http://www.nhshistory.net/chapter_2.htm

56 http://www.historyandpolicy.org/docs/abortion_act_1967.pdf

57 The Wolfenden Report, 1957

and the large majority achieved by Wilson in the 1966 general election made it easier to have the necessary legislation passed. Although these votes were not whipped, most Tory MPs, despite a grand tradition of enthusiasm for non-marital sexual antics, were still pro the status quo. Leo Abse was the Labour backbencher charged with piloting the legislation to drop the ban on GLBT lifestyles. Although lesbianism was not a criminal offence as it was thought that the Victorian legislators believed that it didn't exist. Far from the ideal solution the Sexual Offences Act of 1967 provided a starting point for the acceptance of GLBT as equal citizens. It set the consent age at 21, but in 2001 the Labour government equalised the age with heterosexual citizens at 16, and in 2005 civil partnerships were introduced. This was the latest chapter in the fight for equality as part of the slow revolution. One that took direction from the Suffragettes - but it wasn't all smooth sailing.

1988 saw the Tories attempt to reverse the trend of acceptance for the GLBT community. Clause 28 of the Local government Act was deliberately provocative, divisive and stunk of prejudice. It clearly and unequivocally stated that it was against the law for local authorities, including teachers, to accept *"the intentional promotion of homosexuality"*.[58] Teachers were banned from inferring *"the acceptability of homosexuality as a pretended family relationship"*. Later David Cameron was forced to apologise for this grotesque piece of legislation, and as part of his drive to detoxify the Nasty Party brand he said in 2009 that Section 28, *" was a mistake and had been offensive to gay people"*.[59] The work done by successive Labour governments has altered public feeling on this issue, and whilst no one should be complacent and there is still work to be done, the acceptance of the GLBT lifestyle is a proud legacy dating back to Roy Jenkins' creation of the means to liberate UK law from its most out-dated attitudes on moral issues.

Whilst Roy Jenkins had assisted with the implementation of crucial and progressive legislation, Harold Wilson managed to create a Labour government that was not as left leaning as before whilst at the same time modernising British government. Once again the Labour Party had been at the centre of the social reform and social justice. Wilson as Prime Minister was at the centre of everything modern occurring in Britain in the 1960s, whether it was being seen with the Beatles or being at the forefront of new communications technologies. Britain in the 1960s was a changing place as the old bombed out working class cities of pre-war Britain were

58 *Local government Act (1988) accessed from http://www.legislation.gov.uk/ukpga/1988/9/contents*

59 *David Cameron apologises to gay people for section 28 Watt N, The Guardian, 2/7/2009*

being torn down and replaced by clean concrete metropolises. This was the promised modern age bought directly to the masses. In addition to the Jenkins policies the Labour government introduced the Open University which subscribed to the emerging Labour policy that education was the key to social mobility and as such quality education should be available to all. The Open University has allowed thousands of people to transform their lives through education. The Open University was mirrored by the reforms in secondary education whereby the grammar school system was done away with.

Tony Crosland is a revered and iconic figure not only within the Labour Party but also across politics as a whole.[60] Crosland felt that the grammar school system that had evolved in the wake of the 1944 Education Act meant that far too many mainly working class students were written off as failures if they did not pass the 11+ exam, which was the basis of selection for Grammar Schools. Pupils who flunked the exam were then crammed into ailing and underfunded Secondary Modern schools, and then expected to find a job at the age of just 15. Only between 15 and 25% of pupils in any given area gained access to the grammar school system, and whilst there are plenty of working class kids who "made good" under the system, middle class parents who feared that their children might fail the exam relentlessly drilled their offspring with past papers and a market in private tutoring just for the one off test sprung up across the nation.

Susan Crosland quotes her husband as saying, *"I'm going to destroy every fucking Grammar School in England",*[61] and with typical passion Crosland embarked on creating a comprehensive school system for England where Local Education Authorities (LEAs) encouraged the schools they funded to abolish selection. Most complied and by 1970 the vast majority of LEAs were so far down the road to switching to the comprehensive model that new Tory Education Secretary Margaret Thatcher could not reverse the trend. On her watch more comprehensive schools were created than under the previous Labour government and there was nothing she could do about it.

No legislation was required for LEAs to scrap Grammar Schools, but Crosland nevertheless secured a parliamentary vote on the principle in January 1965. He then moved forward by issuing a government Circular (10/65) which used the word "request" regarding abolition of the 11+ and

60 *The Future of Socialism A Crosland, Constable republushed in 2006*

61 *Tony Crosland by S Crossland Published by Jonathan Cape 1982 p. 148*

an end to selection. In effect Crosland had the LEAs just where he wanted them, as new money for school building would not be granted to any LEA who held on to the existing system. Most went for abolition, although a few LEAs held out including Kent and Buckinghamshire, and of 3127 secondary schools in England only 164 are still Grammar Schools as of 2014. Despite 18 years in power between 1979/97, the Tories lacked the stomach for the intellectual fight that would be required to reinstate the Grammar school system. Crosland had made the argument that comprehensive schools were a major tool in breaking down the barriers for working class children to excel, and to develop at their own pace rather than having to get involved in a break neck paced race to overtake their middle class peers who came from homes where learning was passed on by osmosis, where books were readily available and part of the routine in the home, where children had their own room and one parent could afford to stay at home as the main care giver. If taken in the round, it could be argued that Crosland's passion and commitment to reforming education was the biggest single legacy of the Wilson years, as it liberated millions of ordinary children to aspire to carry on in education for as long as they wanted, to be given access to the best teachers and facilities, and to smash through the class ceiling that grammar schools put in place and that restricted life chances for the majority of our nation's children. This was further evidence of social justice and the slow revolution. Brought about by Labour and not Conservatives. Later we will discuss how the long term effects of Thatcherism has led to a decline in social mobility, at this point we should note that social justice and socialist style equality from the Open University and the Comprehensive system had encouraged social mobility. That has become a clear aim of the slow revolution. Social mobility is something conservatives claim to have a monopoly on, this is a falsehood and should be exposed, with evidence for what it really is.

However, not everything was ethically right with the Labour government; they faced several hard decisions and made some poor choices. The vilest decision made by the Labour government surrounded immigration and may go some way to explaining why this topic is such a sensitive subject for the Labour Party today. The 1968 Commonwealth Immigrants Act banned persecuted refugee Asian Kenyans from entering Britain. The legislation was seen as a knee jerk reaction to quell anti-immigration murmurs amongst the Labour voting electorate, and the bill was pushed through Parliament with unreasonable haste not allowing time and consideration of the proposed legislation. Asian Kenyans had been marginalised in their own country and they were arriving in the UK at the rate of about 1,000 a month under the aforementioned legislation that allowed Commonwealth citizens to come to the UK. The influx of arrivals was picked up on by the media and talk spread like wildfire amongst working Labour voters. If the fuel for the fire was laid bare then Enoch Powell's *Rivers of Blood speech*[62] ignited the anti-immigration feeling throughout Britain. As a result Powell needed round the clock protection and re-stoked the anti-immigration arguments that resulted from the 1958 Notting Hill riots.

The second tricky decision taken by Wilson was not to speak out against the war in Vietnam. Despite intense pressure from the USA to join the American invasion, Wilson resisted the call to arms, a minor miracle that without doubts saved tens of thousands of young British men from being slaughtered in the face of an unwinnable battle. However Wilson refused to speak out against the war. How could he when the USA could have stopped the supply of cash keeping the UK in business? However peace protesters in Britain were highly sceptical of this move, unfairly so. Although it was a tough decision, on this occasion Wilson made the correct one, to keep British men from being slaughtered and keeping our economy and welfare state going.

It is hard to explain just how vital the financial support from the United States was and what a precarious financial situation the Labour government had been left in by the Tory elite previously in charge. The Labour government had no illusions about the scale of the deficit problem facing them, although it had been almost hidden through the 1964 election. Labour's new Chancellor of the Exchequer James Callaghan identified an undisclosed economic deficit of around £800million, (6.7% of a £12.7 billion budget – in today money an unidentified black hole of £48 billion). In fact the seeds of the 1967 crisis were sown by Tory Chancellor Reginald Mauldling's mishandling of the economy which resulted in him apologising to incoming Labour Chancellor Jim Callaghan for leaving the £800 million deficit.

"*Sorry about the mess, old cock*"[63], said Maulding as Callaghan arrived for his first day in the Treasury following Labour's narrow victory in the 1964 General Election. The fact of the deficit had been kept quiet and immediately put Callaghan on the back foot. With a minuscule Commons majority survival was the name of the game as Wilson's first period in Number Ten began.

62 *Speech by Enoch Powell, Birmingham 1968*

63 *Quoted in the Guardian 17th May 2010 http://www.theguardian.com/politics/2010/may/17/liam-byrne-note-successorsaid*

The most obvious political solution would have been to devalue the pound on day one. Callaghan could have blamed the Tories and put the issue to bed, but this was too risky. It would have made imports more expensive for the consumer mad society, and could have damaged the government credibility with its wafer-thin majority of just 4. Wilson as a sharp economist and man in touch with popular feeling realised this would be political suicide. His way of attempting to bring the crisis under control was the technique of central economic planning. He created a Department of Economic Affairs, not as a rival but as a complement to the Treasury. A radical initiative, the idea was that the new department would produce a strong active modern economy and the Treasury would write the cheques and keep the accounts up to date. However the reality was anything but this. The Wilson government wanted to end "stop-go" economics, or what we describe today as "boom and bust" but inflation and interest rates remained high and strikes were adding pressure to the pound. The dreaded devaluation was discussed and avoided with further stopgap measures such as increasing tobacco duty, a wages freeze and control of monetary flow into foreign cash. Despite an increase in unemployment the measures seemed to be working, the pound was slowly recovering and Britain was once again exporting. Slowly the government could bring interest rates back down to get people borrowing again.

In early 1966 Wilson took a massive gamble by deciding on a snap election. He figured that as Ted Heath had barely got his feet under the table as Tory leader, and was awkward with the media, Wilson could present himself as a strong and responsible leader for the nation. His easy charm and better understanding of popular culture contrasted with Heath's wooden demeanour and stiff presentation. But the deficit continued to be an issue, and poor trade figures meant there was an (unfounded) fear that Labour could get the blame for the Tory hangover. However in the March 1966 general election Labour romped home and increased its majority to 96.

Wilson's golden touch saved the Labour government as his administration was buffeted from every angle. The seaman's strike in May 1966 damaged export figures and drove foreign investment overseas meaning the pound came under pressure. The Bank of England stepped in but Wilson baulked at the idea of devaluation as he felt that such a move would see the UK lose face and attract even more pressure from the markets. The economic news continued to be gloomy throughout 1967. Then from nowhere conflicts between Arab states and Israel, and a civil war in Nigeria knocked the UK's oil supply and altered the import/export balance. By September the monthly trade deficit was £52 million. The next set of figures however forced Wilson's hand. October 1967 saw the UK record its worst trade figures since the War and that month's deficit was £107 million.

Wilson's chancellor and other senior ministers such as George Brown and Tony Crosland were persuaded that devaluation was the only way to defend the pound from damaging speculation and to reboot the economy based on exports. But Wilson decided to try and pressure US President Lyndon Johnson into giving him a cheap long-term loan instead, to no avail. LBJ's lack of support made devaluation a certainty. To cap it all as far as Wilson was concerned, his "tired and emotional"[64] Deputy Prime Minister George Brown, still smarting from the failure of his pet project the Department of Economic Affairs was informing the Commons bars that he would challenge for the leadership unless Wilson acquiesced on devaluation. This spooked the markets even further and by the third weekend in November Wilson caved in and agreed to the devaluation of sterling to the tune of 14% from $2.80 to $2.40.[65]

The value of the pound these days is no longer fixed and is free to move in value as the market dictates, so this issue would not arise in the same guise today. At the time devaluation made British exports more competitive, but the added expense made it harder for the government to maintain military bases aboard. The government had vacillated for three years before being forced to take this step, which arguably should have been taken on day one after the 1964 election. Devaluation damaged the reputation of the Prime Minister. Wilson only made matters worse when he blurted out on TV *"the pound in your pocket will still be worth the same."* [66] This added insult to injury in the eyes of the British electorate and Wilson had lost his shine as Prime Minister, and was never really to regain it.

Callaghan had tactically denied devaluation was on the cards during a Commons debate in order not to attract more pressure from the markets but felt that he had to do the decent thing and resigned. The short-term result of sterling's devaluation was a boost to exports and the economy recovered to such a degree that Wilson decided to go the country in June 1970 with a comfortable poll lead. But a rogue set of balance of payments which

64 *Tired and Emotional: Life of Lord George Brown by Peter Patterson (1993)*

65 *The Great Devaluation Myth Published in The Economist* https://www.thesaturdayeconomist.com/the-great-devaluation-myth--uk-and-sterling.html July2011.

66 *Speech by Harold Wilson 1967, can be viewed at http://www.youtube.com/watch?v=-IHVQU9BSks*

showed a deficit, provided an open goal for Heath. Reminding the country of how Wilson had attempted to spin and trim his way out of devaluation struck a chord with a public who just wanted a quiet period of economic stability. They decided that the man with the boat, rather than the man with the pipe was the best way to achieve such stability.

Chapter 5 - Old Labour- The 1970s

In many ways the 1970s proved to be a real tipping point for the socialist experiment in the UK. As we will see, the decade started with the social consensus between the Conservatives and Labour and ended with a return to financial liberalism, albeit it's modern and larger, American cousin neo-liberalism.

The big question remains, why did the UK ditch the political way of thinking that through collective aspiration had seen the lives of millions of Britons improved? Why did this decade leave a scar in the minds of British people? The people moved on from this way of thinking; putting personal greed ahead of the bettering of the whole society. It would take Labour the whole of the 1980s to understand this shift, eventually accepting many of Mrs Thatcher's reforms with New Labour.

We should briefly examine the culture of the time. The decade began with the breakup of the cultural phenomenon that was the Beatles, the fall of the Labour government and UK sport in uproar over the Apartheid Regime in South Africa. It ended with the election of Thatcher, the Labour Party in meltdown and the rise of electronic music and sexually ambiguous pop stars. And in the middle came the whirlwind that was punk rock.

1970 saw the UK cultural scene in rude health. Two influential films, "Get Carter" and "A Clockwork Orange" were in production. The Rolling Stones and the Who carried the Union Jack high over the US following the success of the Beatles in breaking America and Francis Bacon was leading a cohort of brilliantly original British artists that included David Hockney and Lucien Freud. It was the culmination of the swinging 'Sixties and definitely was the original "Cool Britannia". The UK was confident at home and at ease on the world stage.

The city of Leon in Mexico may seem an odd place to chart the decline of Britain but on June 14th 1970 the football World Champions were England. Sitting on a 2-0 quarter final lead against rivals West Germany and wanting to keep his best player fresh for the inevitable semi, Alf Ramsay substituted Bobby Charlton. The iconic survivor of the Munich air crash that decimated his Manchester United team in 1958, Charlton seemed to epitomise the optimism of 1960's Britain as he overcame tragedy to lift the European Cup in 1968. England went on to lose 3-2 in extra time. Ramsay took the blame. Four days later the optimism of the Wilson Labour government went up in smoke and the Tories returned to power unexpectedly.

What followed was a decade blighted by poor industrial relations and an economy that went into a tailspin following the oil shock of 1973. Anger took over from optimism as Johnny Rotten snarled about with the hit record, "Anarchy in the UK", and soccer fans went on a seemingly weekly rampage in crumbling stadia and then were escorted home by British Rail on the notorious "Football Specials" which used virtually derelict rolling stock to ferry about drunken men looking for trouble.[67]

"Viva Espana" and Brotherhood of Man's success at Eurovision dominated mid 'seventies mainstream music seen on TV. But in London clubs, and then into the provinces, a much harder-edged and darker genre was enticing young people. Whilst Val Doonican crooned on Saturday night TV, and the Black and White Minstrels entertained the nation young men and girls sporting shocking hair styles and clothes, pogoed and spat on each other for fun.

Punk rock, which hit the mainstream in the UK during the Silver Jubilee summer of 1977, seemed to somehow encapsulate a sense of hopelessness and nihilism that had wrapped itself around Britain. The Ripper murders paralysed the police in the North, and the kicking to death of a teacher, Blair Peach at an anti-Nazi Rally in London during 1978 summed up such sentiments. The proto-Nazi imagery used by bands such as the Sex Pistols, allied to ambiguous statements on race by established stars such as Eric Clapton[68] were a reminder that if channelled by right wing extremists such as the National Front, such anger could have lead the UK down a very dark path. The Clash provided the youth with a left-wing version of punk, and the rise of Rock Against Racism (RAR) provided a multi-cultural antidote. Bands such as The Specials and UB40 took their cue from RAR with their multi-ethnic makeup and reggae influence, which morphed into the ska movement. Of course we could touch on the troubles in Northern Ireland, which escalated during this period. A struggle where politicians, elites and

67 (Note: "City Psychos" (2002) by Shaun Tordoff, Milo Book Ltd. SBN-10: 190385413X

68 (Note: The South Bank Show 2007, ITV Productions)

religion turned working people on each other.

The 1970s was a transition period, a transition between the white heat of the 1960s, a decade where economics would be modernising Britain. An era of motorway networks, large comprehensive schools and the birth of the consumerist Thatcherite Britain. This was the decade where Britain would enter the European Economic Community. The European issue is one that has ebbed and flowed through out UK politics since the war. Rejected by Paris on two occasions Edward Heath was the prime minister that took the UK into the Common Market in January 1973.

By nature socialists, and the left in general tend to favour being outward looking, and working in cooperation to achieve progress. Yet it was the Tories, ironically given their travails with it in the last twenty years or so, who embraced the concept of a common European economic approach. This is because capitalism seems to have very few problems presenting a unified front if money is at stake. Europe had the potential to become a capitalist club where with tariffs abolished money could flow easily. And with fewer restrictions on labour movement it would be possible to drive down wages and encourage a race to the bottom as workers could be brought in if local wages were seen as too high. This was brought into popular culture by the hit TV show "*Auf Weidersen, Pet*", where workers from all over the UK congregate in the West German city of Dusseldorf to work on building sites, much to the chagrin of the locals whose wages have been undercut.

These ideals are what attracted business to the European project. The UK right started to spurn Europe in greater numbers when the Maastricht Treaty of 1992 tried to bring enhanced workers' rights to the UK, and it became seen as socialism through the back door. Labour has always been split over Europe, indeed Wilson was forced to accept Benn's plea to make the issue one of personal choice rather than cabinet policy when the in/out referendum offered by Labour took place in 1975. The difference with the Tories is that Labour has done a better job of ignoring the issue as much as is possible.

There is little doubt that the Labour government between 1976 and 1979 was the least radical of the century, and the slow revolution ground to a halt. Tony Benn summed up, saying, "Labour believes in nothing anymore other than staying in power."[69] This is evidence that when Labour loses sight of social justice and focuses on power at any cost it loses its way. There

69

is little doubt that the 1970s were a failure for socialism and Labour politics in the UK.

Andy Beckett's 2009 book, "When the Lights Went Out", postulates that Edward Heath and the Tories deliberately over reacted to the autumn 1973 miners work to rule, which morphed into an all-out strike in January 1974, in the hope of recreating a Blitz like siege mentality amongst the British people which would blame the unions for disruption to everyday life. Beckett argues that coal stocks remained manageable and that Heath was too hasty in implementing his emergency plans.

The Three Day Week has passed into British folklore. Mention this era and many families have a story to tell. Lib Dem Energy Secretary Ed Davey reminisced, *"My early memories of childhood in the 1970s include being allowed to light the household candles during one of the power cuts that were much more common then".*[70] Patrick Jenkin was the young Energy Minister forced into the limelight by Heath, and he exhorted the UK public to enjoy the challenge of brushing their teeth in the dark, and John Noakes encouraged people to make the best use of bath water.

Ask Britons of a certain vintage about the 1970's and alongside Jack "we're the Sweeney and we haven't had our dinner" Regan, "Viva Espana", Bernie Inns, and prawn cocktails served with Blue Nun wine, will come British Leyland. The state owned motor company seemed to epitomise all that ailed UK industrial relations in that decade, and the press used the antics that went on at the plant to smear the trade union movement for years to come.

Tony Benn nationalised the carmaker in 1975 with the idea that worker participation in management would usher in a new era of cooperation.Jonathan Coe in his 2001 novel, "The Rotters Club"[71] shows how class issues and the inherent social tensions meant that Tony Benn's dream was pie in the sky. Professional industrial managers and working class union men felt ill at ease with each other and had radically different stakes in what they were doing. Relationships at British Leyland broke down on a regular basis and the Longbridge plant near Birmingham became notorious for snap walkouts over issues such as soap dispensers and matters relating to the canteen. BBC journalist Peter Taylor said that notorious Communist Party

70 (Note: Energy Networks Association Tony Glover July 2013   http://www.energynetworks.org/blog/2013/07/01/it%E2%80%99s-energy-security-stupid-and-the-answer-smarter-networks-and-a-strong-role-for-gas!/)

71 (Note: (ISBN: 9780141033266)

shop steward Derek "Red Robbo" Robinson, *was credited with causing 523 walk-outs at Longbridge, costing an estimated £200m in lost production between 1978 and 1979".*[72]

Nationalisation and government directed industrial planning policy seemed in the minds of UK voters to be dead in the water because of perceived union militancy, which often resulted from poorly trained managers. The Labour Party seemed inexorably linked to this due to their failure to obtain a formalised way for the government and the unions to work together.

What we today refer to as "sleaze" has soured Wilson's legacy and sealed a perhaps undeserved reputation as a trimmer and fixer, rather than a man with a political vision. His second stint as Prime Minister was tainted by growing paranoia regarding cabinet plots and a theory, (later vindicated in former MI5 secret agents Peter Wright's book *'Spycatcher"*), that he was being bugged by the security services, as they feared he was a Soviet mole.[73] In addition his Political Secretary Marcia Williams came to dominate him, a theory vindicated when Wilson's Resignation Honours List was published in April 1976. Williams became Lady Falkender.

Relationships within the Labour Party were at best strained, and at worst broke into open warfare. Benn and Foot were the conference darlings and both were superb orators, capable of rousing the comrades. Foot was Deputy Prime Minister when he made this extraordinary speech to the Commons in January 1976 in the run up to the infamous IMF incident later that year, *"The crisis afflicting this country, along with other countries of the Western world, is a crisis of capitalism. It is a crisis of the dominant economic system that prevails in all those countries."*[74] Meanwhile Healey, the Chancellor was roundly booed at that September's Party Conference as he tried to explain what had led him to seek help from the IMF. Foot's analysis may have been correct, but in the context of collegiate government it was a poor thing to say given the volatility of the markets and the pressure his cabinet colleagues were under at the time to balance the books.

The fall of the Callaghan government was somehow typical of the times for the Left. Machinations and wheeler-dealing were the order of the day

72 (Note: Transcript of 2002 BBC documentary "True Spies "by Peter Taylor http://news.bbc.co.uk/nol/shared/spl/hi/programmes/true_spies/transcripts/truespies_prog2.txt)

73 (Note: published July 1987 ISBN: 9780440201328)

74 (Note: Hansard, 20 January 1976, Col. 1126)

as the government limped into the spring of 1979. It was severely damaged by the prime minister's vacillation over calling a snap election in the autumn of 1978 (echoed by Gordon Brown 29 years later) and the Winter of Discontent. Wilson's wafer thin majority of three achieved in October 1974 was soon wiped out by the usual cycle of deaths within a parliamentary term. The government stumbled on but in March 1979 opposition Leader Margaret Thatcher felt confident enough to force a no confidence motion which would lead to the fall of a government being decided in the Commons for the first time since 1924. What followed was pure political melodrama as every single vote was tallied by the Whips' Office. Sir Alfred Broughton, a terminally ill Labour MP offered to travel as if he died in the ambulance within the Palace of Westminster then his vote would count. Common sense prevailed but "Doc" Broughton's absence cost Callaghan the vote, which was lost by one. Broughton died a week later.

In Place of Strife? Cracks in the Consensus: The unions and the government 1968-79

The story of Britain between 1968 and Margaret Thatcher's entry into Ten Downing Street in 1979 and the subsequent move as a country towards neo-liberalism largely revolves around the relationship between the trade union movement and the government, both Labour and Conservative. Nationalisation of many sectors of industry after 1945 meant that trade unions would now be negotiating with managers who represented the government of the day and whose priorities were not necessarily those of the old fashioned 'Boss Class'. Unlike the pre-war privately owned industrial sector the managers were not the owners therefore the pure profit motive, although not totally removed from the equation, was not the overriding be all and end all of how and why state owned industries were run. But by the 1960s some right wing elements, especially in the press felt that the unions now had too much power. Wildcat strikes called by militant shop stewards became a major headache for the Wilson government, which had taken office in 1964. A strike by the National Union of Seamen (NUS) in the summer of 1966 encapsulated the Labour government's union-related problems. The NUS was desperate to raise the plight of their workers who were notoriously badly paid and worked long hours in a dangerous industry. They expected a Labour government to help them after 13 years of Tory domination which had seen seamen's wage packets driven down in relation to other workers. The ship owners rejected demands to cut the working week from 56 to 40 hours, and government supported them because they feared the subsequent overtime payments would stir up inflation. A strike ensued and the dispute saw ports come to a standstill, a bad month for the balance of payments figures and a run on the pound. Eventually a compromise was reached but Wilson was determined that the unions would never cause him such problems in the future. Relations between the union leaders and the Labour government that held office between 1964 and 1970 were usually cordial. This was the era of beer and sandwiches provided by a Labour Prime Minister for visiting union dignitaries. But the problems lay on the front line where shop stewards leading a handful of workers had the ability to paralyse workplaces with snap walkouts, and strikes called on the hoof with little reference to democracy. Due to conventions about not crossing any union picket lines this meant that wild cat strikes could cause immense disruption in and around an affected workplace.

Wilson moved darling of the Left Transport Minister Barbara Castle to the post of Employment Secretary. He also made Castle First Secretary of State, which saw the MP for Blackburn become at the time the most powerful female politician in UK history. Castle took up her post in April 1968 with the remit to reform industrial democracy and to bring the trade union movement into step with what was required if Britain were to achieve better economic growth to rival the economic expansion seen in France and Germany. Whilst standards of living rose on the Continent there was a feeling of stagnation in Britain. Strikes increased relentlessly and Castle wanted to arrest the perception that the unions and their thirst for stoppages were to blame. She failed and the number of days lost to strikes peaked just as Labour left office in 1979 at nearly 20 million from a base of around 1 million in 1950. Castle's White Paper proposing a way forward in industrial relations was called *"In Place of Strife"*, a play on words referencing a book by left wing hero and founder of the NHS Nye Bevan entitled *"In Place of Fear"*.[75] The proposals seem quite reasonable when looking back forty odd years further on, but at the time what Castle was lining up for the unions, to them, presaged emasculation of their movement and their ability to meet speedily their members' needs. This was a time when unions were popular with the public at large, a time before the mention of British Leyland caused the sight of mass meetings followed by mass walkouts to spring to mind in the public's imagination. *"In Place of Strife"* suggested mandatory

75 *In Place of Fear, A Bevan Kessinger Publishing (2010 Edition) In Place of Strife, Published 1968 by The Secretary for Employment and Productivity accessed from http://www.nationalarchives.gov.uk/ cabinetpapers/themes/industrial-unrest.htm*

ballots before strike action, and a cooling off period of 28 days before labour was withdrawn. Crucially the White Paper gave the government the power to settle wildcat strikes on their own binding terms, and if rules were broken unions faced the prospect of being fined. The issue of secondary picketing was, however not addressed.

The Labour cabinet - and the party as a whole - were split, and "*In Place of Strife*" had quite the opposite effect to that alluded to in the title. Many Labour MPs were union-sponsored and felt that Castle had put them into a no win position with their backers. There was a feeling from some that Castle and Wilson were seeking to pick a fight for the sake of it, and their aim seemed to be about stamping their authority on the Party. In Place of Strife was dropped. Instead of the unions having some say and control in their reform, the rejection of Castle's White Paper inadvertently led to the unions falling victim to union-busting legislation in the last quarter of the century. Whilst it is easy to look back, if the Party and the unions had made the necessary leap of faith and imagination to adopt Castle's Bill the whole history of the Labour Party and our nation as a whole would have been different. Just think. No Winter of Discontent, no victory for Thatcher and all that that entailed for the Left. The Bill was rejected because Jim Callaghan, Tony Benn and others placed their own standing above that of the Party, and similarly Roy Jenkins and Tony Crosland who stood in a more centrist position were seduced by the prospect of Wilson resigning and their own elevation.

Labour suffered a shock defeat in the June 1970 General Election. Despite Wilson's monumental loss of face regarding "*In Place of Strife*", a 1968 humiliation involving devaluation of sterling and the Party being split over entry into the Common Market, the polls in the early part of 1970 encouraged Wilson to go to the country a year before he had to. Yet against all the odds Heath pulled of a stunning victory and secured a majority of 31. But how would Heath deal with the unions? Having spent time with leader of the Transport and General Workers Union Jack Jones in 1930s Spain as part of a fact-finding mission about the Civil War, Heath did not have the knee jerk anti-union bias of many of the younger Tories such as Keith Joseph or Norman Tebbit. Heath had served as Minister of Labour in the previous Tory government and his reputation from his time in post did nothing to unnerve trade union leaders. There seemed to be no underlying antagonism and the TUC didn't foresee any major problems going forward. The consensus approach seemed fit for purpose. But behind the scenes radical Tories were lining up to take the unions on. The 1971 Industrial Relations Act saw the Tory right in the ascendancy for the first time. Although Sir Keith Joseph was officially kept out of the loop by being assigned the Social Security portfolio, and Thatcher was put in charge of Education, the fingerprints of both are all over this Bill. The trade unions and the Labour left were now paying the price for kyboshing "In Place of Strife" as the Act legislated to severely limit strikes by the imposition of a binding Industrial Relations Court which was granted swingeing powers to fine unions who backed wildcat strikes and failed to heed Court rulings, no matter how unjust they seemed.

Festering resentment and a sense of guilt over *"In Place of Strife"* saw the trade union movement enter the summer of 1971 in a militant mood. The miners had always been the romantic heroes of the working classes and it was the Nation Union of Mineworkers that took centre stage by demanding an eye watering 25% pay rise to recognise the danger of their work and the long term health damage that could result from years spent underground. Heath was determined to hold pay increases below 8% to dampen down the risk of inflation so the miners were offered 7.5%. As pay, unlike the 1980's pit closure programme, was a national issue affecting each and every member of the NUM, a national ballot was called and in the autumn of 1971 the miners voted for their first national coordinated action since the General Strike commencing with an overtime ban in November to speed up the depletion of coal stocks. The strike began on 9th January 1972 and by mid-February the Heath government was in full retreat and forced to settle by a brilliantly plotted and executed NUM campaign which involved the blockading of ports unloading coal, encouraging other unions to refuse to move coal stocks and most famously Arthur Scargill made his name by organising a total blockade of the Saltley coking depot in Birmingham. Saltley was vital to gas and energy supplies to keep the lights on across the Midlands and by shutting it the NUM had the government exactly where they wanted them, on the run and desperate for a way out. Heath was forced to accept the recommendations of an independently appointed judge who was tasked with looking into miners' pay and who called for an increase of 20% for mineworkers, thus totally busting Heath's incomes policy in one fell swoop. The Tory Right was incandescent that the government had been forced into such a humiliating climb down, and despite the 1971 Act it was the unions who had dictated the response to the Tories' incomes policy and therefore Heath's ability to control inflation.

Further pressure was piled on the Heath government with the relentless rise in unemployment, which had stood at 582,000 in June 1970 when Labour left power, but by early 1972 the psychologically damaging 1 million mark was passed. Evidence is clear that Heath himself placed protecting job right at the forefront of his agenda. We have seen how his government was not afraid to nationalise ailing industries such as the Clyde Shipbuilders, but any plans Edward Heath had to revive the UK economy and improve the job market were wrecked by another dispute with the National Union of Mineworkers. The pay award of 1972 had seen the miners rise to the top of industrial pay "league tables", but inflation soon eroded their position and by late 1973 they had slid to 18th by this way of calculating salaries. Then out of left field came events that would strengthen the miners' hand: war in the Middle East. The result was an Arab flexing of economic power via capping oil production which forced prices of an up till then cheap source of energy. Suddenly a commodity that had cost $1 a barrel shot up to $12 within a year leading to a crisis of supply on the petrol station forecourts and the lowering of the national speed limit in the UK to preserve petrol stocks. Thus domestic and industrial energy demands began to look once again towards coal. To say that there was ill feeling between the Heath government and the trade unions was an understatement. Heath simply could not understand why the unions failed to appreciate his largesse in nationalising to save their jobs nor their unwillingness to enter into pay restraint. For the unions' part they were furious over Heath's intent with the 1971 Act and the government's constant hectoring of workers, urging them that the only way to stabilise the UK economy was to strangle inflationary pressures via wage restraint. But as inflation rose sharply to 10% in 1973, and onwards to 16% by 1974, the unions wondered why their workers should bear the brunt, as Heath demanded an 8% upper limit for wage increases. The oil crisis gave the NUM the leverage they required. The story of the Three Day Week, which caused power rationing across the UK, is well documented. Then as the dispute unfolded, and after only three and a half years in office, the Prime Minister decided to go to the country asking the question "Who Governs?" Andrew Marr summed it up in his book *A History of Modern Britain*, with the quip, *"not you mate"*[76] and with that Harold Wilson was back in Downing Street albeit as the biggest party in a hung Parliament, despite polling 200,000 less votes than the Tories.

The failure of *"In Place of Strife"* now became the spectre at the feast during the Wilson/ Callaghan government that was in power for the next five

76 A History of Modern Britain" A Marr, Published by Pan 2009

years. The Labour Party has traditionally been heavily reliant on funding from the trade union movement and the unions were determined to take their pound of flesh as Wilson struggled in opposition. Emboldened by the success of the miners in 1972, Wilson had been forced into accepting a document called The Social Contract which ostensibly was meant to deal with the perennial 'inflation versus wage claims' dilemma but really put the unions in the driving seat as Labour were committed to repealing the hated 1971 Industrial Relations Act. In addition workers were to be protected from inflationary pressures via a system of food subsidies and price controls. On the industrial front the Contract tied Labour to promises of government investment for companies in trouble. The Trade unions refused to sign up to compulsory wage restraint and the inevitability of a serious breach between the unions and the Labour government became reality with the Winter Of Discontent in 1978/9. First of all Wilson called NUM Leader Joe Gormley into Number Ten and settled the pay dispute at double what Heath was prepared to pay, which placed the miners back at the top of the industrial pay scale. The public were relieved more than anything to see the lights come back on. Wilson sensed the mood and called a fresh election for October 1974, which delivered a thin but workable majority of three in the House of Commons. Wilson, who allied a fearsome intellect with an uncanny ability to read his colleagues and the public, came to realise virtually right away that he was struggling to grasp details of government that he had soaked up with aplomb during his previous six years in Number Ten. In addition he was quickly fatigued. Thus in late 1974 he took the very private decision to go on his own terms within two years, and later Harold Wilson was diagnosed with Alzheimer's disease.

Inflation was the theme that dominated the late 1970s UK economy, spurred on by price controls and the oil crises. Jumping to 16% in 1974 inflation spiked at 24.2% in 1975, which was a disaster for low paid workers and wealthy savers alike. But the perception that the TUC were calling the shots around economic policy of the Labour government seemed to be on the mark when Chancellor Denis Healey upped tax on unearned income to an incredible 98% and the upper rate of income tax peaked at 83%. Despite crippling tax rises, and due to his commitment to helping the low paid ride out the inflationary wave, Healey was unable to balance the books. Printing money was not an option as it would simply encourage inflationary pressures and weaken the pound.

It was the same old story for Labour: economic woes. So in 1976 Healey and the Prime Minister James Callaghan were forced into accepting a loan from the International Monetary Fund who demanded public spending cuts as a condition of the loan. Whichever way you look at this, it was a humiliation for the UK and fatally damaged Labour's credibility for a generation regarding economic management. Despite further industrial turmoil, Healey had made an astonishing discovery. The Treasury had made a monumental mistake in calculating the UK's borrowing requirement meaning that much of the IMF credit access remained unused. The economy began to recover due to the Black Gold pumping ashore in the guise of North Sea Oil. We were now self-sufficient in gas and inflation in the summer of 1978 dipped below double figures, in part due to dabbling in monetarist theory, which was used by Margaret Thatcher in her first term as Prime Minister. The polls gave Labour a slight lead and going into the autumn of 1978 election fever gripped the nation. However Callaghan decided to wait until spring 1979 as the signs for economic growth were good but the curse of pay and the unions blew up in spectacular style. Failure to control wage increases due to the unions' refusal to enter into an incomes policy with the Labour government made the events of the winter of 1978/79 depressingly predictable.

Callaghan and Healey were determined to hold pay rises to 5% to build on the success in reducing and finally getting control of inflation once and for all. The unions flexed their muscles to achieve rises way above 5% and private companies failed to toe the line with Ford awarding 20% and Vauxhall awarding 8.5% pay rises. Low paid public sector workers looked on. In January 1979 the Transport and General Workers Union supported their members who worked in the haulage industry in their strike which saw a 20% wage increase awarded. The public sector started to react. The Royal College of Nurses demanded a 25% settlement, ambulance drivers followed suit and a domino effect rippled across the NHS. The sight of picket lines around hospitals filled the nation's TV screens. Gravediggers in Liverpool struck and were awarded 14% with the prospect of burials at sea being considered. The strikes were a public relations disaster for Callaghan who was caught on camera taking a dip in the Caribbean during a G8 Summit, which seemed to encapsulate that Sunny Jim was fatally out of touch and too much in hock to union power. His opportunistic rejection of 'In Place Of Strife' had resulted in the worst industrial relations problems since the General Strike of 1926. Other matters relating to devolution for the Celtic nations finally saw Callaghan's government lose a vote of confidence in the Commons in March. The election was called for 3rd May and the biggest swing since 1945 saw the Tories march into Downing Street with a 43-seat Commons majority.

Chapter 6 - The 1980s, the Decade that Changes Everything

Like her or loathe her, Mrs Thatcher and her policies changed Britain. Whether this was for better or for worse depends on your political outlook. It is easy for us to look back now and mock the 1980s. But for us it was the decade that changed everything.

The decades that followed the 1980s have merely been copies, change the music, change the fashion, and change the faces. We are just copying that 1980s blueprint. The technology has been updated but neo liberalism and the policies that Thatcher introduced changed the way the UK is run and the values system that underpinned it. It could be argued the 1980s were the first generation to be bought off by the appearance of wealth, the idea that we could all be stakeholders in a home and share owning country. This is not a new theory; however one of the key themes to this book is that the party of Thatcherism, or neo-liberalism, is the root cause of chronic problems that we face today.

But before we explore these issues we must begin to understand life in the 1980s. Although it doesn't seem so long ago, in reality it really is ancient history. The Labour Party during this period was nowhere to be seen, as this decade belonged to Thatcher whilst Labour was fiercely divided, on the verge of breaking up and at a policy crossroads. The 1980s were a decade punctuated by savagery of war in Northern Ireland and its overspill into the rest of Britain, the Miners' strike, civil disorder, football hooliganism, innovations in fashion (the mullet) and music, financial liberalism and the rise of the consumer society. This was the generation when the nationalised industries were sold to private interests that make huge profits today and exemplify the huge inequalities that exist in our generation.

On the face of it, the 1980s was the decade when we, the British people, become extremely selfish. To the casual observer, the "loadsa' money" boom years and Thatcher stating "there's no such thing as society"[77] symbolised a change away from finding a collective solution for the problems of the UK towards a selfish me, myself and I approach. However this does not explain phenomena such as Live Aid. The huge one off 1985 concert at Wembley seemed to signal something very different about the British people.

The story of that summer's massive pop concerts in aid of those caught up in the horrors of African famine is well documented. Rock star Bob Geldof, having witnessed BBC reporter Michael Buerk's truly shocking testimony of the dire situation facing millions in Ethiopia and surrounding nations, mobilised the UK pop industry to release the biggest selling British single of all time. "Do They Know It's Christmas?"[78] raised millions for the stricken famine areas and despite enormous logistical difficulties 13th July 1985 saw a packed Wembley Stadium put on the biggest pop show in history. But more importantly people across the UK felt as if they had an active stake in the event, and were doing something positive to help those less well off than themselves. For a generation brought up on conflict, this event had a profound impact. It showed that there was a collectivist way to confront problems. But despite Thatcher's non-involvement with Live Aid and her refusal to waive VAT on the Band Aid record, she was re-elected just two years later. What was wrong with the voters?

The Smiths, Billy Bragg, the Style Council and U2 amongst others provided the soundtrack for these troubled times.

"*I was looking for a job, then I found a job but heaven knows I'm miserable now*",[79] intoned Morrissey, singing lyrics of alienation over Johnny Marr's disconcertingly optimistic jangling guitar lines. This quintessential Northern band chimed a chord with young people who were facing a bleak future of unemployment or mind numbing toil for low pay.

Take for example lyrics by *The Clash* in 1982, which sum up the decline of feeling of youth culture in Britain. "*If you can play on the fiddle, How's about a British jig and reel? Speaking King's English in quotation. As railhead towns feel the steel mills rust water, froze, In the generation Clear as winter ice, This is your paradise, There ain't no need for ya, Go straight to hell boys.*" These tangled lyrics talk of deindustrialisation, that working class Britain had had

77 *Interview in Woman's Own by Douglas Keay Published in 1987 published by The Margaret Thatcher Foundation Accessed from http://www.margaretthatcher.org/document/106689*

78 *Do they know it's Christmas? By bob Geldof and Midge Ure distributed on Columbia and Phonogram*

79 *Heaven Knows I'm miserable now By Marr and Morrissey, distributed by Rough Trade 1988*

its meaning and culture taken from it by a British elite.

The 1980s were the real beginning of the everyday Americanisation of UK culture with shows such as "Dallas"[80] and "Dynasty"[81] portraying a glamorous wealthy life we could all aspire to. But this was also the last politically rebellious generation. The rebellious streak didn't just show through in music, but in strikes, civil unrest and in TV. The Tube ran on Channel 4 between 1982 and 1987.[82] It was produced by Malcolm Gerrie and filmed live from Newcastle, and it summed up the cultural tastes from the north of the UK for that generation. It was outspoken, rebellious and commercialised. Nothing is present on the airwaves today on the same scale reflecting those values.

Unless you came from the comfortable middle classes with their connections to interesting, well paid work, or you were one of the very few working class kids who made it to university, there was very little on offer for ordinary teenagers once they left school in 80s Britain. Liverpool band the Christians made an interesting comparison with the 1930s in their 1987 top ten single, "*Hooverville*"[83]. Referencing the shanty slums that built up around Great Depression era US cities, and as a riposte to Norman Tebbit's exhortation for the unemployed to "*get on your bike*" the band sang, "*The doubt of work sends the out of work man, to city a hope and a home. One door shuts here another two slam, yes he's homeless he's hopeless alone.*" It was the sense of despair and hopelessness in working class communities that was the worst aspect of this terrible era. And we see this being repeated in our own times.

Musician Billy Bragg articulated the situation the UK found itself in, but crucially he toured up and down the country urging young people to fight back. In 1987, along with the Style Council's Paul Weller, Bragg organised Red Wedge, which put on concerts by the Smiths, Elvis Costello, the Blow Monkeys and a variety of musicians with the sole aim of recruiting young people to join the Labour Party. Comedians such as Lenny Henry, Harry Enfield and Phil Jupitus took up the call to arms when Thatcher announced the date for the election (June 9th) with the sole aim of ejecting her from Downing Street. Whether or not Red Wedge and Bragg's pop formula were successful in the short term is debatable. But what it did do was imbibe

---

80 Dallas Created by Jacobs, D 1978-1991 distributed by Warner Bros and Lorimar

81 Dynasty Created by R & E Shapiro between 1981-89 distributed by CBS from 2006

82 The Tube Produced by Teen Tees Television between 1982-87

83 Hooverville By The Christians distributed by Island Records 1987

those young people with a sense of hope, solidarity and above all the feeling that they could change things if they fought back. The defeat of 1987 was a crushing blow, but the template for how to campaign was set, and culminated in the mass movement that ejected Thatcher from Number Ten via the Poll Tax rebellion.

The 1980's forced the UK to take sides, to make choices. It was in your face day after day via the TV and radio news and by mass readership of newspapers. In addition the tribalism was still there: loyalty to your class, profession, location, and even football team. This division has left a huge hangover for the UK. If after the war we had a consensus about how we could rebuild the UK and move forward, Thatcherism certainly ended it. How could the slow revolution have faltered in such a way? Could any of us have envisaged just what neo-liberalism would have been like? How did we return to such a pre-war way of running our country? What would the long-term effects be?

Thatcher moved the whole agenda to neo-liberalism. Late in 2002 Margaret Thatcher spoke at a dinner in Hampshire. At the reception one of the guests asked her what was her greatest achievement. She replied, "*Tony Blair and New Labour. We forced our opponents to change their minds.*"[84] This argument holds some truth as it is often argued that there is little to choose between the main parties. Nevertheless, whilst Blair was tolerant to neo-liberalism, he did use the state to its full capacity to lessen some of its evils with polices such as the minimum wage, doubling NHS spending, cutting class sizes, and by modernising schooling and radically committing the UK to reducing child poverty. There are lots of perceived reasons why New Labour failed to deliver in the long term. Many of them are due to a failure to reject Thatcherism outright. The result has led to many of the issues we face today such as, the chronic lack of affordable housing, suppression of wages, a debt culture, an aggressive and predatory system of banking and city finance to name but a few. This is why we would be foolish to simply close our ears to the influence that Margaret Thatcher had over the UK, not only during her time in power, but subsequently.

When Tony Blair was Labour's Shadow Energy Secretary, and Thatcher's government announced that the electricity grid and its supply would be broken up and sold off, he told the Commons on 31st October 1989 that the Tories should scrap such plans. But, crucially, at no point did he commit the Labour Party to reversing the sell off if it took office. In many ways, this

84 *Speech by M Thatcher, Hampshire 2002*

was the harbinger to Blair's notorious abolition of Clause Four in the Labour Party constitution, which stated that *"common ownership of the means of production"* was a core aim for any Labour government as a way to redistribute wealth in society. Indeed, when in power Labour did nothing to reverse the privatisations that were Thatcher's trademark. In fact New Labour privatised the Air Traffic control system, and Peter Mandleson made serious efforts for the break up and privatisation of the Royal Mail during his second coming as Business Secretary.

New Labour's preferred method of using the private sector in public services was via the notorious outsourcing process. The idea was that business would bid for contracts, such as building a hospital or providing IT, and then take all the risks such as raising the cash and organising staffing. This would leave public sector workers unencumbered, allowing them to deliver so called front line services such as caring for patients and teaching children. Thatcher had started this process of outsourcing when in 1983 she authorised that hospital cleaning be offered to the private sector. In 2002 an international report quoted by UNISON showed that there was a clear link between outsourcing and increasing rates of hospital infection.[85]

Thatcher's worst legacy is the chronic state of our housing market. Labour under Jim Callaghan had considered allowing council house tenants to buy their rented properties, but with the proviso that for every sell off, a new home must be built. Thatcher's ideas were very different. She believed that social housing tenancy encouraged a slothful attitude to life. She had the idea that the discipline of having to pay a mortgage would somehow galvanise working class people. The policy of not replacing social housing absolved the state and politicians of providing housing for those that needed it. By 1989 new homeowners were contending with soaring interest rates, suppressed wages, inflation and the spectre of yet another recession. In the long term, housing, both social and private, was one of the biggest problems facing the future of the UK.

Nigel Lawson's 1988 budget created a housing bubble that burst with catastrophic consequences, but the idea of home ownership was now ingrained into the British psyche. It was all part of Thatcher's "aspiration" plan which would see ordinary people become shareholders and mini capitalists. They would stand on their own two feet and the state could be pared right back. Living in social housing being a stigma, poor houses for poor people. But

85 *Lethbridge, Jane University of Greenwich (2012)Empty promises: the impact of outsourcing on NHS services. http://gala.gre.ac.uk/8084/*

perhaps the most surprising statistic came in March 2013 when a Daily Mirror investigation found that a third of ex-council homes sold in the 1980s under Margaret Thatcher were now owned by private landlords. This tells us that the right to buy scheme has actually choked off the chance for people to become home-owners because of the chronic lack of new build in the private sector, which allied to the virtual cessation of councils building homes has simply driven prices up and made the market the preserve of a new generation of landlords who took their cue from the post war slum rental exploitation.

Perhaps the most iconic, and well-observed analysis of Thatcher's Britain was provided by comic Harry Enfield. In 1988 the star of Channel Four's "Saturday Night Live" came up with a cockney plasterer character who was cashing in on the late 80s housing boom and obsession with property make overs. *Loadsamoney* was crass, loud and obnoxious, constantly waving a wad of money, no doubt earned "cash in hand". He was ostentatious in his tastes but only gave 10p to help free Nelson Mandela. His alter ego was an unemployed Geordie, *Buggerallmoney,* which served to reinforce the shocking north/ south divide that existed in the UK under Thatcher's rule. This was particularly the case after the 1987 general election when the Tories were virtually eliminated from urban seats north of Watford, and fared especially badly in Scotland. But the truth was that the Tories had established a firm grip on the south by peddling the myth of aspiration, and by portraying the north as reliant on state hand-outs whether through the benefits system, or via state subsidised industry.

Tony Blair realised that the only way for Labour to return to office was to end the perception of tax and spend, and also convince so called Middle England that their aspirations would be catered for by not raising income tax and using dog whistle Tory issues such as crime and fiscal responsibility to woo the voters. Ultimately this meant Thatcher's privatisations were not reversed; indeed New Labour had gained an appetite for private sector involvement. In addition central planning of the economy was off the agenda and a light touch attitude to the vagaries of an unfettered financial system, as begun under Thatcher with the Big Bang in the City which got rid of much regulation, sowed the seeds for the banking disaster of 2008.

So how would we describe the hangover from Thatcher's Party? She did change the way we did things. Restructuring of the economy led to 3million unemployed and an unemployment and benefits culture which we still suffer from today. Thatcher's legacy was not that New Labour aped the Tories, but that they were handcuffed by her rebooting of the political agenda. We can certainly see privatisation, increased fuel costs and high unemployment as a real hangover. Added to this the houses crisis we see today has come directly from Thatcher. But did Thatcher make us more selfish as a society?

The Thatcher government

The previous chapter concluded with social unrest prior to the 1979 election. But the post war consensus was alive and well up until around 1977, for example Ted Heath's government had nationalised Rolls Royce and the Upper Clyde Ship Builders, both heavyweights of industry and under severe financial pressures. It was only when Labour Prime Minister James Callaghan spoke of the need to end Keynesian economic practice in favour of monetarism in 1977 that the beginning of the end was apparent. Mrs Thatcher had become leader of the Conservative Party in 1975 and she used the period between then and the election in 1979 to build a bank of policies. Whilst Prime Ministers of the post war consensus believed that unemployment was the greatest threat to economic progress, Thatcher along with Sir Keith Joseph who was inspired by economist Milton Friedman began to take a more liberal or Laissez- faire approach to politics.

In Mrs Thatcher's memoirs *The Downing Street Years,*[86] Mrs Thatcher outlined her vision of decline in Britain identifying it along the lines of social, economic and foreign policy. Similar theories have been outlined by both Tony Blair and David Cameron. Whilst her theory of British decline was in dispute, taking the time to undertake an intellectual journey allowed the Conservatives to map out an agenda for government with policies that remain the blue print for the Conservatives today.

Thatcher argued that social decline had been brought about by the large welfare state and that the unrest caused by the trade unions, that economic decline had come about due to large nationalised industries and that foreign decline was symbolised by Britain along with the west was losing the Cold War *"Three challenges of long term economic decline, debilitating effects of socialism and the growing Soviet threat".* [87] Once Thatcher had identified the British decline she set about defining a number of policies inside

86 *The Downing Street Years, M Thatcher Harper Collins, 1993*

87 *The Downing Street Years, M Thatcher Harper Collins, 1993 p9*

the new right philosophy to identify decline. The Centre for Policy Studies published several key documents in the late 1970s which were to be the foundation of Tory policy under Thatcher, including *Second Thoughts On Full Employment*[88] which lobbied for an end to the commitment for full employment and *The Right Approach To The Economy,*[89] which preached the values of monetarism and supply side economics. Andrew Gamble recognised Thatcher's election victory *"brought into office a government that was determined to end British decline and the crisis of state authority by making an ideological and political break with social democracy."*[90]

Prior to Tony Blair's election to government in 1997 he, like Thatcher, had identified a British decline. Even more startling, Blair's identification of decline mirrored that of Thatcher's. By 1996 Blair had published *New Britain: My Vision of a Young Country.*[91] In this critique of the British political economy, foreign policy and British society, he identified that under John Major the areas of British decline that Thatcherism had sought to reverse had returned. Blair argued that Thatcherism did not liberate people but neglected them. Blair noted *"Across Britain I see enormous untapped potential, children in classes too big, people in their 20s who have never had a job, trains vandalised, city centres clogged up.*[92]*" "My ambitions for Britain are defined by this gap between potential and performance.*[93]*"* But whilst Thatcher had set about dropping the post-war consensus commitments to full employment turning to market-driven supply-side dogma, Tony Blair's answers were to modernise the Labour Party by dropping clause 4, by moving Labour to the centre ground, and by accepting both the role of the markets and their limitations. Blair's policies would see the adoption of neo-liberalism in an uneasy co-existence with the state, whose role it was to prepare people for the neo liberal economy as well as protecting them from the dangers of it, through welfare.

Thatcher needed solutions to what she identified as sluggish economic performance, which she identified as low productivity, over manning and

88 *Second Thoughts On Full Employment published by Centre for Policy Studies accssed from http:// www.cps.org.uk/publications*

89 *The Right Approach to the Economy published by Centre for Policy Studies accssed from http://www. cps.org.uk/publications*

90 *Privatization, Thatcherism, and the British StateAuthor(s): Andrew Gamble P2*

91 *New Britain T Blair Published by First Estate 1996*

92 *New Britain T Blair Published by First Estate 1996 Pix*

93 *New Britain T Blair Published by First Estate 1996 Px*

restrictive economic practice. Monetarism demanded that the government control and reduce the supply of money into the economy in order to bring inflation under control. But restricting the supply of money proved stubbornly hard to do as a spasm of serious civil disorder in July 1981 was blamed in the eyes of many on poverty caused by the collapse of inner city employment prospects. Unemployment doubled from 1.5 to 3 million but the government continued on its path. Mrs Thatcher was saved by two key factors: Michael Foot was portrayed by the right wing press as out of touch, and the sudden flare up of war in the Falklands. By 1981 UK industrial output had fallen by 20% and up to £8 billion a year in North Sea oil was spent propping up the economy. Thatcher's government ended the policy of a redistributive tax system, favouring indirect taxation, pushing VAT from 8% to 17.5% during her premiership and extending fuel duty. By 1982 the monetarist experiment was effectively at an end, public spending grew in the wake of Geoffrey Howe's March Budget and by the mid 1980's the concept had died. The battle to curb inflation was not won, although it was brought under control temporarily. By 1989 inflation burst through the 10% barrier, interest rates were pushed to 15% and housing repossessions began to increase, peaking in 1991 when over 75,000 homes were taken back by building societies, and which equated to 0.77% of mortgages ending in default.

In the previous chapter we touched on the programme of nationalisation versus privatisation as a debate regarding ends and means. The end goal for a Labour politician is to see a fairer more equal society. In 1984 privatisation began, firstly with British Telecom and then British Gas, and the argument of the government would be that the people were able to buy shares and directly own these utilities, Harold Macmillan simply called it "selling off the family silver."[94] The people were able to buy shares in a company they already owned, but in reality many of the shares were purchased by hedge funds taking the opportunity to take profits. Arguably this has bought the telecommunications market into the modern age of the Internet; however, commodities such as fuel or heating for the home are now being squeezed for mass profits. By 1992 42 major companies employing nearly one million workers had been sold off. Wages were driven down, unions side-lined and workers terms and conditions eroded. Crucially any democratic control over how companies providing vital services were run became virtually non-existent, whilst many of the national sell offs had been undervalued.

94 Speech by Harold Mcmillan, 1985 which can be viewed at http://www.youtube.com/watch?v=G1ssGrq5S3w

Labour in the 1980s

But where was Labour through this period? Michael Foot will always be unfairly associated, for people of a certain age: with two things; the donkey jacket and Labour's manifesto for the 1983 Election, *"A New Hope for Britain"*[95], which earned the memorable sobriquet, "The Longest Suicide Note in History" from Gerald Kaufman.[96] Both of these memories are grossly unfair to a man of considerable intellect, oratorical flair, and journalistic integrity but above everything an almost all consuming passion for the Labour Party and social justice. Let no one forget that Foot was a deeply patriotic man, which explains why he felt it so personally as he witnessed the industrial carnage wrought upon the UK and his Ebbw Vale constituency.

Nothing can disguise the disaster of the 1983 Election when Labour totally misjudged the mood and needs of the nation. However it could be argued that the Manifesto was, with two notable exceptions of Europe and disarmament, in some ways the right document, just at the wrong time due to its misjudgement of the psyche of the contemporary electorate. The Manifesto makes for an interesting read. It proposes the reduction of class sizes to 30 at Primary level plus the introduction of an Education Maintenance Allowance, both radical policies which the Blair government introduced, and goes on to call for much greater regulation of the financial sector, including pensions, and the formation of a government-controlled Investment Bank to encourage lending for small business and industry, something which was on the table in the wake of the 2008 economic crash brought on by a lack of active regulation.

The UK was on its knees; well and truly the sick man of Europe. Margaret Thatcher's poll ratings were amongst the worst in history. A Gallup opinion poll in September 1981 gave the Tories just 23% support which would have seen the Party wiped out in any forthcoming General Election. Then a series of monumental blunders by the Tories delivered them every desperate politician's dream: a just war. *"I will never hand over our people to a bunch of fucking Fascists"*.[97] Not Thatcher, but her predecessor Jim Callaghan speaking in 1978 when noises were emanating from Buenos Aires regarding Ar-

95 *A New Hope for Britain Manifesto published by The Labour Party, a copy can be accessed from http://www.labour-party.org.uk/manifestos/1983/1983-labour-manifesto.shtml originally released in 1983*

96 *Gerald Kaufman Labour MP for Manchester Gorton*

97 *Hugo bicheno- "I will never hand over our people to a bunch of fucking Fascists" "Razors Edge: The War in the Falklands", byHugo Bicheno ISBN-10: 0753821869*

gentina's claim of sovereignty over the Falkland Islands. He sent a nuclear submarine to this remote part of the Southern Atlantic where a number of rocky outposts were home to over 1,000 UK Citizens. The Military Dictatorship (Junta) realised he meant business and backed off.

When on 19th March 1982 a party of Argentine "scrap metal merchants" landed on South Georgia and raised their national flag, there was a panicked reaction from London and HMS Endurance was dispatched with a handful of Marines from the tiny garrison based at the Falkland's capital Port Stanley. The Argentinian group was sent packing. The irony was that the Tories'1981 defence review, which saw the sacking of Tory Defence Minister Keith Speed for speaking out against naval cuts, had actually recommended that Endurance be withdrawn leaving the Islands in the South Atlantic with no full time naval cover. In the wake of the South Georgia diversion, Argentina's Junta leader General Galtieri decided to launch a full-scale invasion in the first week of April. All of a sudden the whole of the UK knew where the Falkland Islands were and Thatcher had her salvation. The Falklands War is used as an excuse by many on the left as to why Labour crashed so badly when Thatcher called an election in June 1983, citing her terrible pre-war poll ratings as evidence. However, the voters looked at the Thatcher government and reasoned that they were doing, despite the gloomy global economic prospects, a bad job of fixing things. Who, apart from the most dyed in the wool one-eyed Tory ultra-loyalist could have thought any different? A large section of her cabinet, if not in revolt, were seriously concerned by her utter determination, in the face of much evidence, to soldier on with monetarism and its inevitable fall out. Therefore surely all Labour had to do was sit back and watch as poll after poll battered the Thatcher government, and her own competence ratings?

But political life doesn't work like that. Despite the electorate clearly endorsing our entry into the EEC in 1975, just eight years later Labour arrogantly told the voters they had got it wrong and a Labour government would take us out. Despite the popular mood against overt meddling by government in industry, Labour failed to take note and called for even more regulation and interference. In spite of the fear of Soviet expansion into Western Europe Labour decided on a purely unilateral approach to weapons control when they could have easily called for more international debate and discussion on the issue. The Labour Party was right, the voters wrong and misguided. Ignoring fears over trade union power in the wake of the Winter of Discontent the manifesto simply proposed a blanket repealing of all anti-trade union laws, and even suggested that firms would be forced to have workers representatives in the boardroom: laudable, but given the circumstances pie in the sky.

Foot was also beset by internal Labour Party issues that became public and made it look as though the Party was more interested in themselves than the nation as a whole. These were truly desperate times for the Labour Party. In June 1983 they suffered humiliation at the ballot box, polling just 27.6% of the popular vote and losing 80 MPs with a swing against of 9.3%. Despite polling 700,000 fewer votes compared with 1979, the vagaries of the electoral system saw Mrs. Thatcher's majority increase to 144 and her political confidence became emboldened as she moved into her second term. The Labour Party was in disarray and Michael Foot resigned the leadership.

Despite being far more comprehensively turfed out of Number Ten by Margaret Thatcher, Jim Callaghan continued unchallenged as leader of the Labour Party for a further 17 months. However the rise of the left, led by Tony Benn saw the formation of the *"Campaign for Labour Party Democracy"* whose aim was to shift power from the Parliamentary Labour Party (PLP) to the membership. This would be achieved by the leader being elected via an Electoral College system of which the PLP would form a part along with the trade unions and CLP delegates.

The ultimate irony of this reform cannot be overstated. The left saw the college as a conduit to having their darling, Tony Benn elevated to the leadership and the so called right feared a takeover by the Bennites in selection meetings. They fought the democratisation of the Party tooth and nail.

To this end Callaghan quit the leadership before the college process could come in to force. The idea was to stop the left and ensure the PLP elected his protégé and bête noir of the left, Denis Healey as Labour Party leader. Roy Hattersley (Healey's campaign manager*)* summed up Foot thus, *"a good man in the wrong job, a baffling combination of the admirable and the absurd"*.[98] Now Benn decided the time was right to strike. With a hated Tory government in power, a left wing leader of the Labour Party, and the members now empowered it was his moment in the sun. What could go wrong? The answer was simple. The democratisation of the Party did not deliver the hard left victory as many centre/right Labour figures feared. Instead Healey was re-elected as Deputy Leader and subsequent elections

98 *Oxford Dictionary of Political Biography edited by Dennis Kavanagh, published by Oxford University Presshttp://www.answers.com/topic/roy-hattersley*

delivered Neil Kinnock, John Smith, that renowned hard left disciple Tony Blair, and Ed Miliband to the summit of the Party. Not a head banging lefty amongst them.

But four leading members of the PLP had seen enough. The wrangling and posturing over who should have the most influence in the electoral college, plus their existence in the Westminster bubble inert from the opinions of the rank and file membership saw Dr. David Owen, Shirley Williams, Bill Rodgers and Roy Jenkins take the momentous decision to split from the Labour Party in March 1981.

Rodgers and Owen were sitting MPs, the latter having served as Jim Callaghan's Foreign Secretary, and Jenkins had been a political heavyweight in the 1960's Wilson governments, going on to lead the European Commission. Williams was Education Secretary when she lost her seat in the 1979 general election. This was no knee jerk reaction, and the "Gang of Four" had credibility within the Party and crucially free access to a Tory press for whom this "War of the Comrades" was manna from heaven. It was compounded by a bloody and ill tempered so-called "Special Conference" in January 1981. In full view of the media the Labour Party delivered the best fight at Wembley Arena since Alan Minter and Marvin Haggler had slugged it out for the middleweight crown the previous year. It was agreed that the unions should have a 40% block vote in the leadership college, that Labour would quit the EEC and ditch nuclear weapons if elected to power. The weekend was ill tempered and despite Foot and (surprisingly) Hattersley begging the Four to stay in the Party, the game was up.

Owen's home provided the backdrop and on 25th January 1981 the Four issued the *Limehouse Declaration*, which signalled their intent to quit the Labour Party. The Council for Social Democracy was formed which evolved in to the Social Democratic Party. The SDP was formally unveiled as new centre left UK political party on 26th March 1981, and in a leadership contest held in 1982 following Roy Jenkins' return to the Commons at the Glasgow Hillhead by election, the former Labour Deputy Leader defeated David Owen in a one member one vote run off. In the coming months 28 Labour MP's and one Tory, Christopher Brocklebank Fowler defected to the SDP. Outside the House future Tory Health Minister Anna Soubry found an ally in ex-Communist Party member Sue Slipman. Adair Turner and Andrew Adonis, future New Labour ministers became a part of a somewhat motley crew.

The SDP love in with the anti-Labour media ensured former Labour Education Secretary Shirley Williams was returned to the Commons as the first elected SDP MP at the Crosby by election, which took place in November 1981. The Tories and Labour were both badly damaged. As the main opposition the by election hurt Labour more as sitting government parties almost expect a ritual kicking midterm, and this was an especially turbulent year for the Tories as their poll rating crashed to just 23%. The Labour Party vote crumbled with a 15.9% swing shattering their chances. Jenkins secured an unlikely win in the Glasgow Hillhead by election of March 1982, barely weeks before the Falklands War. He inflicted a 14% swing against the Tories, but worryingly for Labour, in a solidly working class constituency, he damaged their candidate by an 8% swing. Labour would regain the seat in 1987 with the candidate being none other than George Galloway.

What did the SDP effect have on the Labour Party? The differences with this parliament are instructive. Due to the Lib Dems involvement in government, the Labour Party is the only mainstream, wholly UK opposition party. They do not have to compete for anti-government votes and as a result poll strongly even in the wake of the 2010 election debacle. Back in the day, the SDP provided a strong and credible alternative with heavyweight political figures and the draw to be able to mobilise activists at election time. This meant that with the election of Foot, and the casting of the SDP as the traitors to the Labour Party, intellectual and practical debate took a back seat. The retreat to the thumb sucking certainty of unrefined socialism threw the Party out of any meaningful contention for power.

The losers were the UK public as Thatcher stormed through the turmoil on the centre left. The vagaries of the first past the post system were brutally exposed at the 1983 UK general election. Despite polling 7.7 million votes (25.4% share) against Labour's 8.4 million (27.6%) the SDP and their partners the Liberals only managed 23 seats compared to Labours 209. Even more remarkably, the Tory vote fell by over ½ million votes, yet they gained 62 seats.

The SDP had decided in 1983 to stand in a pact with the Liberals who had been politically irrelevant since the fall of their strangely charismatic leader Jeremy Thorpe in a 1976 sex scandal. They had only managed a paltry 11 seats at the 1979 election. David Steel, the leader of this rump of MPs was so enthralled by the rise of the SDP and the opportunities that they afforded the Liberals, that he famously, and quite ludicrously exhorted his members in his 1981 conference speech to, *go back to your constituencies, and prepare for government"*. The SDP provided a strong and credible alternative with heavyweight political figures as well as a knack of being able to mobilise street activists for the party. Ultimately this split the anti Tory vote. The statistics suggest that Labour lost 3 million votes from 1979 that went straight to the SDP/Liberal alliance as their vote increased by around 3 million.

The damage in the long term for Labour was immense, the defeat scared many members of the Parliamentary Labour Party into thinking that they may never return to office. But the shift in politics wasn't to last, as by the 1987 general election, rancour in the SDP between the egos of Jenkins and Owen, who had succeeded as leader, saw the SDP go down to just five MP's. Steel, as Liberal Leader was portrayed as the junior partner in the Alliance and suffered at the hands of ITV's satirical hit show, "*Spitting Image*" where the Scottish MP was cast as David Owen's simpering stooge puppet, intoning, "*Oooo David!*" in sycophantic admiration. As their popularity waned, a media savvy Labour Party re-emerged, closer to the centre ground where the SDP has tried to be. The SDP was effectively finished as a force in UK politics (unless you live in the seaside town of Bridlington) and despite the protestations of David Owen it was wound up and merged with the Liberals to become the Lib Dems by 1990.

The Party was over, but the SDP dragged Labour back into the mainstream and after the 1992 defeat, the emergence of Tony Blair and New Labour can be credited to the influence of the SDP. In our era Progress (sic) with their virulent anti trade unionist stance can be seen as the political grandchildren of Dr. David Owen who loathed their place in the Labour Party and especially their usurping of the PLP as sole choosers of the leader. In the Labour Party Neil Kinnock became leader of the Labour Party in 1983 with an overwhelming 71% of the vote. Left wing candidates Eric Heffer and Peter Shore were beaten out of sight. Roy Hattersley, seen as being on the right of the party secured the deputy leadership forming what the press called the Dream Ticket.

Kinnock's working class Welsh background played well with the Labour membership, and his early parliamentary career saw him cast as a rebel. He famously remained in the Commons during a Queen's Speech due to a lack of enthusiasm for the concept of monarchy. Foot had initially brought him into the shadow cabinet as Education spokesman. Neil Kinnock faced a daunting challenge: to reform the Labour Party, tune it in the real world and the concerns of the Public, and become a credible alternative Prime

Minister to Margaret Thatcher. He succeeded by and large on the first two requirements, but fell well short in the Prime Ministerial stakes. Two huge issues, Militant and the miners' strike defined the first half of Kinnock's nine-year period as Labour Leader.

Militant Tendency was a sect whose ideology was based on the ideas of Russian Revolutionary Leon Trotsky. Whilst they decried Parliament as a tool of the bourgeoisie ruling class, and preached a programme of agitation, they saw the Labour Party as a host for them to recruit members to the cause and even managed to secure parliamentary seats for four of their members by taking over constituency Labour Parties. Hounding of sitting Labour MPs by Militant members was not unheard of and Robert Kilroy Silk resigned his parliamentary seat due to constant harassment by Militant activists, although judging by Kilroy Silk's subsequent political career, they may have had a point.

It was the militant control of Liverpool that proved to be the final straw, and June 1985 saw the Militant-led Liverpool City Council set a deficit budget and demanded that the Tory government make up the difference, as indeed Tory Local government Minister Patrick Jenkin had done the previous year. But 1985 was different. Thatcher was in no mood for compromise and Militant knew this. By September it was clear that Central government would not lend a hand. Militant's aim was to force the government's hand, cast them as the reason why wages would not be paid, encourage a local General Strike which they hoped would spread across the country and drive the Tories from power. So in September 1985 a fleet of taxis was hired by the Council to deliver redundancy notices to its staff. The public was disgusted and Neil Kinnock saw his chance to get rid of Militant forever, stamping his authority on the Labour Party at conference famously saying, *"I'm telling you, and you will listen, you can't play politics with people's jobs and with people's services."*[99] Eric Heffer stormed off the platform and Militant's poster boy Derek Hatton shouted, *"Liar, liar"*, but from then on Militant was effectively finished in the Labour Party. Kinnock had sent a clear message of unity to the Party as a whole, and a message to the country that the Labour Party was on the road back to mainstream Democratic Socialism, which addressed the needs of those not present in the hall.

It was now Kinnock's time; he had weathered the storm and come out fighting at conference finding his voice in that amazing Bournemouth speech.

99 Speech by Neil Kinnock, 1991 you can view a report on this at http://www.youtube.com/watch?v=bWLN7rIby9s

How would he take advantage of his unchallenged status as Party leader with an election barely eighteen months away? Kinnock's chance to stamp his authority on the Commons, and prove himself to be a viable alternative Prime Minister to Thatcher came on 27th January 1986 when Labour tabled an adjournment motion condemning the government's handling of the takeover of the Westland Helicopter plant which was on the point of collapse. The cabinet was split over the solution. Defence Secretary Michael Heseltine favoured the Yeovil-based company being bought by a European consortium involving British Aerospace whereas Thatcher and her Industry Secretary Leon Brittan preferred a takeover by a US company, Sikorsky. A complicated set of events culminated in Heseltine storming out of cabinet and resigning in front of the assembled press in Downing Street, followed by the revelation that Brittan had leaked letters to the press with the aim of damaging Heseltine. The government was in disarray and Thatcher's dictatorial style of running her cabinet was being openly questioned. Westland was a major crisis, which threatened to see the Prime Minister's authority eroded and could have even resulted in her resignation. But a poor Commons performance by Neil Kinnock in support of the motion, described by the Guardian as "inept",[100] let Thatcher off the hook and seriously damaged Kinnock's prospects of casting himself in the role of "Prime Minister in waiting".

Post 1987

For the 1987 general election Labour had a more moderate manifesto that reversed policy of withdrawal from the EEC, but the programme still called for more 1970s style government control of industrial policy. Significantly Labour said its vast programme for job creation would be paid for by taking back Tory income tax cuts. This laid the charge of taxing aspiration for high flyers, and restricting voters' freedom to spend their income as they pleased. At least this is how the Tories spun it, and despite Peter Mandleson winning all the plaudits for running the best and slickest campaign in Labour history, the policies, the spectre of Militant and a popular Tory programme that focused on Labour's weaknesses and their strengths allied to a hostile press meant the best result Labour could hope for was that they would remain ahead of the SDP/ Liberal Alliance and retain the role of the official opposition. This was achieved and Labour gained 20 seats. Total destruction had been averted and the groundwork laid for a comeback. The

100 Maggie - The First Lady By Brenda Maddox (2004) ISBN-10:0340825464

Alliance had been seen off as possible rivals.

Arguably the biggest policy that affects life in the UK from this period was the 'Big Bang'. In 1976 the government had decided to outlaw the cartel of the City and a long lasting legal case ensued, a battle the City was likely to lose, meaning there would be enforced reform. This was until Cecil Parkinson, Secretary for Trade and Industry, urged prominent members of the City to self-reform and self-regulate. There was a three-year gradual reform. This saw the banks and finance houses explode in size hence the sobriquet Big Bang even though it was more of a staged process than is remembered in the public imagination. These reforms were in line with other privatisation efforts of this period that saw chief executive pay rocket. It was these new, unregulated markets that have caused a number of the issues that caused the 2007-2014 financial crises. The banks of the pre regulation era were cautious whilst the new financial institutions indulged in high risk behaviour and self-regulation means they failed to set the safety measures in place to spot a problem.

The Tories' fortunes continued to rise and Lawson's 1988 Budget was rated the most popular in recent history. Taxes were slashed. The upper rate of income tax tumbled from 60 to 40% reflecting the aspirational mood of the country where people felt that get up and go should not be punished through high taxation. The basic rate was cut by 2p in the pound as £4 billion was pumped into the economy mostly, however, benefiting the richest third in society. Lawson's give-away gave the Tories a staggering poll rating in September 1988 of 50% whilst Labour languished in the doldrums. Nine years into her tenure Margaret Thatcher seemed unassailable and the Labour Party appeared as far away from power as ever.

But all of a sudden Lawson's give away blew up in his face. Due to a technicality in the Budget that involved mortgage tax relief, house buyers had until 1st August 1988 to set up their home loans and gain full relief. This meant that the spring and summer of that year saw an almighty scramble to beat the deadline. The sale of council homes (at a discount) and the virtual elimination of local authority house building meant a shortage of available houses to buy, thus burgeoning demand saw house prices rising unsustainably quickly. Mortgage companies fuelled the spike by offering for the first time 100% loans, an unheard of practice. Prices in London were rising at a rate of £1000 every month for a three-bedroom home in places such as Uxbridge and Hayes as homeowners began to feel wealthy and the tiresome subject of property values became the subject de jour in the pub and at work. The fallout from Lawson's largesse in his March Budget was starting to be felt at that year's conference, and when the Tories convened in Brighton that autumn there was thinly veiled criticism from Thatcher towards her chancellor in her keynote speech. The prime minister was faced with the truth that Lawson's stimulus package was the antithesis of her monetarist policy, which she and Geoffrey Howe had pursued in the early part of her time in power. For Thatcher the twin enemies were high inflation allied to high interest rates, both of which were back on the scene due to the pumping of money into the economy as a result of Lawson's instant tax cuts.

Thatcher's economic guru was an academic called Alan Walters, who was an enthusiastic supporter of monetarism and had played a large part in drafting the controversial 1981 budget, which controversially sought to squeeze the supply of money in the economy by squashing consumer demand in the midst of a recession. Walters had left for a university job in the US in 1983, but by 1989 Thatcher decided he was needed once again by her side, as she had lost confidence in Nigel Lawson's ability to deliver low inflation and interest rates. Lawson opposed the proposed poll tax: Walters supported it. Lawson wanted to fix our currency exchange rates with our European trading partners by joining the European Exchange Rate Mechanism (ERM): Walters preferred the pound to float on the exchanges as the market demanded. The differences between the two men were insurmountable and Lawson resigned. Thatcher was made to see by her colleagues in cabinet that an unelected advisor could never be seen to take precedence over a minister and Walters left his post almost right away.

Margaret Thatcher's legendary domination of her cabinet was severely damaged by Lawson's resignation. Her authority was for the first time coming under scrutiny. The Europhile and until then largely anonymous backbencher, Sir Anthony Meyer stood as a 'stalking horse' (he was dubbed the Stalking Donkey by sections of the media) against Thatcher. This act was intended to then provoke a more credible candidate to come forward. None did, but in total 60 Tory MPs failed to endorse their leader, and the damage done to Margaret Thatcher was terminal.

Without doubt the 1980s had changed the way of life for the British people through the way our economy was run, our prospects of employment, the way we borrowed money, home ownership, everything. At the start of the 1980s many of us went to work for nationalised industries, but by the end some of us owned shares in them. Some say that Thatcher set the middle classes free; others say she polarised and oppressed parts of society and her successor, John Major, would continue with her policies, as it could be argued has every Prime Minister since.

The final chapter of Mrs Thatcher's premiership was proof beyond doubt that her policies were not liberating her people but oppressing them and in doing so creating great inequality in society. In 1988 Thatcher's government passed legislation which introduced a 'community charge' to replace the local tax on homes which had previously been set at a percentage of the rental value. This system was called the Rates. The new community charge or poll tax meant that every person had to pay a set levy decided by the local authority regardless of income. This caused great unease in communities around Britain, for many of the middle classes who had let the injustice of the Thatcher government slip by because it did not affect them now found themselves being a victim of Thatcherite policy for the first time. The tax was due to be introduced on April 1 1990. The day before, thousands of people took to the streets of London and at around 11am the protests turned violent. But there was to be no U-turn by Thatcher. By the time John Major was re-elected in 1992 he had abolished the tax. However in the meantime hundreds of thousands had failed to pay their bills. Some moved and did not re-register in new homes; some shared rooms and local authorities could not keep up with student populations who moved regularly. This policy eroded much support for the government. By 1990 Thatcher's government majority had slipped below 100, she was beginning to lose her shine and the electorate was clearly wanting change. Labour's opinion poll leads were steadily, if not spectacularly increasing and to the backdrop of unpopularity, opposition and civil unrest her cabinet did what they had not had the courage to do before.

In November 1990, The Deputy Prime Minister, Geoffrey Howe resigned over Thatcher's refusal to take Britain closer to the single European currency. The following day political rival Michael Heseltine, who had resigned back in 1985 over the Westland affair, announced he would challenge Thatcher for the leadership. Only Tory MPs were entitled to vote. In order to win outright under Party rules, Thatcher needed 15 clear percent over her rival, but she secured an advantage of 13.9% and intended to carry on into the second round of voting. However this picture became clear: whilst many of her government would support her in a second round, she would not win. She stepped down and John Major was elected as the Conservative Party leader and new Prime Minister.

Labour should have been surging ahead in the polls as the decade ended. The Tories were in disarray over the poll tax, Europe and Margaret Thatcher's leadership, and having seen off a leadership challenge from Tony Benn, Kinnock sought to move the Party into a position where it had a genuine chance of winning a general election. Kinnock appointed Margaret Beckett to the post of Shadow Chief Secretary to the Treasury in 1989. Beckett, it seems, took the decision that one of Labour's biggest mistakes whilst in opposition was to come up with grandiose plans such as starting up an Educational Maintenance Allowance and promises to renationalise key companies such as British Telecom without giving evidence of how they would be funded. This allowed the Tories to wheel out the tax and spend argument which concluded that Labour plans, which were costed at £35 billion by the Tories during the 1987 General Election campaign, always involved hiking taxes, something that hit Middle England the hardest, precisely the voters they would need to court if Labour were to ever again regain the keys to Downing Street.

Between 1989 and the run up to the 1992 General Election many key policies, particularly around nationalisation, were dropped. In the forefront of this drive to bury state ownership as an issue in any coming election was one Anthony Lynton Blair who, as Shadow Energy Secretary, made no commitment to renationalise the electricity industry when it was broken up and sold off at the end of the decade. This was a new move. Previous Tory selloffs such as BT and British Gas had been met with a Labour promise to take them back into state ownership. Not anymore.

As radical policies waned, it could be argued that from 1985 onwards the Labour Party's emphasis moved more towards media management as a tool to make the Party electable and to tone down the image created by the 1983 Manifesto. Labour was indelibly linked to high taxes and meddling in the economy at a time when business was looking to free itself from the undoubted over regulation of the 1970s. Peter Mandelson walked into Labour's head office on Walworth Road, South London in October 1985 and along with Phillip Gould brought a much-needed professional attitude to dealing with the mass media. Despite the many naysayers, Mandelson and Gould were the main reason why the Labour Party swept to power twelve years later.

When Thatcher finally fell in 1990, it seemed only natural that her Party would fall with her in the next general election. But the old maxim that for an opposition to win they have to be seen as a credible alternative came back to bite Kinnock. Whilst the voters were happy to dish out an electoral kicking to the Tories in by-elections, Mid Staffordshire falling to Labour in a 1990 with a huge 24% swing against the government, the national picture showed the two parties neck and neck, with the Tories pulling slightly ahead. By January 1992 John Major's government was leading in the polls despite the Conservatives having been in power for 13 years, being hopelessly split over Europe, having to do a huge U-turn over the poll tax, and presiding over an economy in recession with unemployment on the rise. The voters perceived Kinnock as a loser, and the Labour Party had ditched so many policies, including disarmament and nationalisation without proposing an alternative vision that the electorate could only vote with confidence for Labour in a spirit of "well they aren't the Tories". This was never going to be enough to create a buzz around the Labour Party, to create the momentum that any opposition needs to defeat an incumbent government.

Chapter 7- John Major and the Birth of New Labour

In modern politics we mock senior politicians for being from privileged backgrounds, David Cameron and Nick Clegg being prime examples. However in 1992 we could not throw that accusation at the then Prime Minister John Major. By old fashioned standards John Major was at best working class, and today we may even label someone from his background as from the underclass brought up in a property shared with tax dodgers and down and outs. John Major embodies the social mobility that Conservatism promised: that with hard work and bit of luck, anyone can make it. At the 1992 general election the Conservatives ran posters with the slogan *"What does the Conservative Party want with a working class lad from Brixton? They made him Prime Minister."*[101]

We now know that John Major's 6 years and 6 months as Prime Minister would follow in a similar fashion to that of Mrs Thatcher, dominated by Europe, the economy and complicated with leadership challenges and sleaze.

In Europe, Major was confronted with The Maastricht Treaty which called for deeper integration of the European Union, specifically looking at a single European currency and a social chapter which entrenched the human rights of EU citizens- subjects which still divide the Tory party today. Major managed to jump his first hurdle as Prime Minister, having the social chapter removed and opt-outs on the single currency for the United Kingdom. These alterations gave him the status of political hero upon his return with his own Euro sceptic MPs; however this honeymoon did not last long. By 1993 when Major had to ratify the legislation through Parliament, he suffered numerous rebellions from his own back benchers and could only push through the legislation with a vote of confidence, which he won by 40.

As incumbent Prime Minister, John Major took an unusual step and fought the 1992 General Election on the streets. Instead of running a slick modern

101 Poster created for the 1992 General Election published by the Conservative Party

campaign, with highly managed speeches with select audience members, Major elected to stand on a turned over soap box and speak directly to the people. At times it got ugly but it worked. Major focussed the campaign on Labour's taxation policies and on their over slick campaign. Labour managed to make a couple of huge errors during the campaign. Major went on to overturn Labour's poll lead to return a majority of 18 seats with a record 14 million votes.

With a reduced majority and a declining economy Major had some serious challenges ahead. The boom of the late 80s had ended and economy was in recession. House values where depreciating, unemployment was over 2 million and interest rates at 10%. Under modern economic circumstances the government could have decreased interest rates; however in 1990, whilst John Major was the Chancellor of the Exchequer, Britain had entered into the Exchange Rate Mechanism (ERM) a policy which forbid sterling from fluctuating 6% either side of the then German currency, the Deutsche Mark. The pound entered the ERM near the bottom of this permitted range, and if it fell too far the government would be obliged to intervene. The UK had further problems including the deflation of the dollar in which many British exports were priced. On the 16th September 1992 there was a run on the pound, speculators acting on suspicions that the pound was valued too high. The run became known as Black Wednesday. The government at first increased interest rates to 12%, but this had no effect. British traders were selling sterling at an alarming rate whilst the government was burning £2 million an hour in an attempt to purchase the currency back.

Eventually Major and Lamont admitted defeat and removed Britain from the ERM. Although this saved the pound, it was also seen as a huge embarrassment on the international stage for Britain. The unexpected result was the start of a long road of over a decade of growth. Free exchange rates and the low interest rates that accompany them can be used to stimulate growth, borrowing and exports. The Major government ended the Thatcher policy of chronic under-investment in public services and began to spend, seeing it as the only way to stimulate economic growth in the UK. By 1994 the economy was back in growth, a boom which was to last until 2007. Subsequently unemployment fell from its 1993 high of 3 million to 2 million in 1997, facts that John Major was quick to point out on the day of his general election defeat.

The NHS under Thatcher and Major

Ideologically the Conservatives on the right of the party desire a health system in the UK that is run by private providers. During this period of Conservative government we saw this desire manifest itself in two ways. Firstly, the use of private firms in outsourcing, and secondly the creation of internal markets to create supposed financial discipline.

The 1980 Health Services Act repealed the previous Labour government's abolition of 'pay beds' in NHS Hospitals. The Thatcher government commissioned a report into the management of the NHS, which reported in 1983. It concluded, "*If Florence Nightingale were carrying her lamp through the NHS today she would be searching for the people in charge.*"[102] Commenting on the feeling that the NHS was different from everyday business due to lack of a profit motive, the report's author, Ray Griffiths said, "*These differences can be greatly overstated. The clear similarities between NHS management and business management are much more important.*"[103] It can be argued that the report, which has disappeared into history, is in fact a 'game changer', due to its mention of bringing business discipline in to a public service.

Manfred Davidmann, a leading scientist and consultant was asked by Thatcher for his analysis of what Griffiths said was "*a sixty year mistake*".[104] *(35 years in 83)* This is what he told the prime minister in January 1984, "*The impact of the proposed changes would be enormous. They would affect medical staff from top to bottom of the Health Service, they would fundamentally alter the relationship between administrators and other staff, they would affect the whole population.*"[105] Doctors, Davidmann said, should: "*be given rules, procedures and performance targets devised by what can be non-medical managers, that is executives.*"[106] This was the groundwork for the introduction of the so-called "internal market" by Thatcher and later built on by John Major. Labour abolished it in 1997 but later returned

---

102 "*The Griffiths Report 25 Years On.*" Health Service Journal 5th June 2009 by Peter Davies http://www.hsj.co.uk/resource-centre/best-practice/the-griffiths-report-25-years-on/5001481.article#.U0p-YmJdVcg

103 Report to Secretary of State for Health and Social Services 1983 quoted in NHS History http://www.nhshistory.net/griffiths.html

104 Reorganising the National Health Service: An Evaluation of the Griffiths Report by Manfred Davidmann 1985 http://www.solhaam.org/articles/nhs.html

105 Reorganising the National Health Service: An Evaluation of the Griffiths Report by Manfred Davidmann 1985 http://www.solhaam.org/articles/nhs.html

106 Reorganising the National Health Service: An Evaluation of the Griffiths Report by Manfred Davidmann 1985 http://www.solhaam.org/articles/nhs.html

to this policy. But it took fully five years from Davidmann's letter to Thatcher about Griffiths before she felt able to take her philosophy of the market into the NHS. The BBC summed up nine years later just what Thatcher's 1990 Health Act meant for the NHS, *"The aim was that GP fund holders and Health Authorities could use their purchasing powers to choose between competing providers and so obtain the best deal for patients. Contracts could be signed with hospitals and other health service organisations in either the public or private sector."[107]*

A study published in 2008 by Prof. Carol Propper for the Royal Economic Society made for interesting reading. Reflecting on evidence gathered as to the effect of the 1990 Act with its emphasis on targets she concluded, *"The study finds that the effect of competition on quality was to decrease hospitals 'performance in areas where it was not tracked – fatalities following emergency admission for heart attacks – but improved their relative performance on a well tracked aspect of performance – waiting times."[108]*

Damningly Propper went on to say this about competition in healthcare, *"Deaths from heart attack admissions have been argued in the US context to be the 'canary in the mine' – an overall indicator of poor clinical quality. This study finds that deaths were higher where competition was greater (in the implementation of the 1990 reforms)."[109]*

The number of managers employed in the NHS under Thatcher's reforms when they were actually implemented became a political hot potato. Speaking in the run up to the 1997 general election Lib Dem Leader Paddy Ashdown claimed that, *" Over the last 7 years, we have seen the number of administrators and managers in the NHS increase by 20,000, while the number of nurses has fallen by 50,000."[110]*

---

107 *The NHS: The Conservative Legacy, Produced by the BBC available from http://news.bbc.co.uk/1/hi/ health/background_briefings/your_nhs/85952.stm- September 1999*

108 *Competition Can Be Fatal: Evidence From The NHS Internal Market January 2008 Royal Economic Society Media Briefing http://www.res.org.uk/details/mediabrief/4377011/Competition-Can-Be-Fatal-Evidence-From-The-Nhs-Internal-Market.html*

109 *Competition Can Be Fatal: Evidence From The NHS Internal Market January 2008 Royal Economic Society Media Briefing http://www.res.org.uk/details/mediabrief/4377011/Competition-Can-Be-Fatal-Evidence-From-The-Nhs-Internal-Market.html*

110 *Speech Made by Liberal Democrat Leader Paddy Ashdown, Published by Swansea University - available from - http://www.britishpoliticalspeech.org/speech-archive.htm?speech=241 - March 1997*

Political sleaze

One of the key themes in this book (and its twin) is that political sleaze has undermined trust in politicians to the point that the voters have little or no confidence in the UK's political system. John Major's government became particularly associated with sleaze. In discussing New Labour, we should be clear that Labour has also failed in this area.

We shall start with an ailing Tory government that had lost credibility over economic management and was growing tired after nearly 14 years of government. Major decided to re-launch his ailing Administration, not by flagging up the boost to the economy from leaving the ERM which made our exports more competitive and pulled the UK out of recession, but by exhorting Britain to get "Back to Basics". He conjured up the image of, "*maids cycling their way to Church*" and "*warm beer*", as a template for the UK in the 1990s. But the real thrust of his speech to the 1993 Tory Conference revolved around longstanding Tory dog whistle issues such as traditional teaching, respect and family values. He declared: "*It is time to return to the old core values of neighbourliness, decency and courtesy along with self-discipline and respect for the law which are common-sense British values*".[111]

Given that the Prime Minister had recently had an undisclosed affair with former Health Minister Edwina Currie, it seems extraordinarily risky in retrospect for the leader of a Party with a rich tradition of sexual antics to invite such scrutiny, as inevitably the tabloid press now saw it as open season on exposing Tory MPs' personal peccadilloes and failings. Once the lid was lifted the press storm proved impossible to control and seven Tories were caught up in sex related scandals. Cabinet minister David Mellor's extra marital romps attired in a Chelsea strip[112] and MP Piers Merchant being pictured drooling over his teenage intern[113] were amusing fodder for the Red Tops, but the suicide of Transport Minister Malcolm Sinclair's wife after it was revealed that her husband had been unfaithful took the issue to

111 *Speech made by Prime Minister John Major, Published by Swansea University- available from http://www.britishpoliticalspeech.org/contact.htm- September 1993*

112 *Article published by The Independent, untitled but compiling ten political sex scandals-available from http://www.independent.co.uk/life-style/love-sex/top-10-sex-scandals-1709888.html?action=gallery&ino=6*

113 *Piers Merchant: Tory sleaze MP dies of cancer, leaving behind wife who stood by him after sex scandal Published by the Daily Mail- September 2009 Available from http://www.dailymail.co.uk/news/article-1215747/Piers-Merchant-Tory-sex-sleaze-MP-dies-cancer-aged-58.html#ixzz2xWtYv1jn*

a tragic new level.[114]

Next the press began to dig into the financial affairs of leading Tories, as the obvious charge of hypocrisy had been raised by Major's ill-judged speech. Chief Secretary to the Treasury Jonathan Aitken was found to have accepted undeclared favours from Arab businessmen and then compounded matters by forcing his daughter to lie on oath about a hotel bill from the Paris Ritz. Aitken was later jailed for perjury.[115] In 1994 Neil Hamilton was forced out as a junior minister along with fellow Tory MP Tim Smith for accepting cash from Mohammed Fayed in return for asking questions in Parliament.[116] Hamilton's determination to brazen the affair out did enormous damage to John Major as the Prime Minister chose to take his minister's word at face value and the matter dragged on and on until Hamilton finally resigned. 'Back to basics' had become synonymous with the phrase 'sleaze' as in 1993 and 1994 the press uncovered a number of political scandals. Further examples where numerous: Alan Clark was discovered to be having an affair with a South African judge's wife,[117] Stephen Milligan was found dead from auto erotic asphyxiation whilst five other prominent Tory MPs were having affairs.[118]

However, sleaze and scandal were not exclusive to the Conservatives. Labour came to power in 1997. Although in the early days of the Labour government the sleaze was not as wide spread it was still a shock and equally unpalatable. Tony Blair, as opposition leader, had said "the public will expect us to be purer than pure."[119] How right he was. Part of the reason Britain kicked out John Major, a popular Prime Minister, was the scandal in his

114 The Major Scandal Sheet- Published by the BBC available from http://news.bbc.co.uk/1/hi/uk_politics/202525.stm

115 Aitkin's Downfall Complete- published by the BBC- available from http://news.bbc.co.uk/1/hi/uk_politics/364174.stm- June 1999

116 Cash for Questions: The Scandal that should have changed British politics by Watt H Published in The Telegraph- available from - http://www.telegraph.co.uk/news/politics/conservative/10092681/Cash-for-questions-scandal-that-should-have-changed-face-of-British-politics.html May 2013

117 Clark scandal descends into tales of blackmail and lechery, by M Braid and R Williams - Published in the Independent- available from http://www.independent.co.uk/news/clark-scandal-descends-into-tales-of-blackmail-and-lechery-1419683.html - June 1994

118 A bolt from the Blue by N Cohen S Milligan Published in the Independent Available from http://www.independent.co.uk/news/uk/a-bolt-from-the-blue-stephen-castle-and-nick-cohen-on-the-events-surrounding-the-sudden-death-of-stephen-milligan-1393847.html February 1994

119 A Journey T Blair Published by Hutchinson 2010

government. Tony Blair was expected to eradicate foul play from British government.

The first major scandal, which rocked the government, came after just five months into the new administration. Before the 1997 general election, Formula 1 ring master and British billionaire Bernie Ecclestone had donated £1million to the Labour election campaign. Following the donation, a meeting was held in which Ecclestone and Blair discussed the phasing in of the tobacco ban in sport, a 1997 manifesto pledge. The argument being that tobacco funding backed 50,000 UK jobs through its sponsorship of Formula 1. Blair and Ecclestone were keen to note that the donation and the policy request were not linked; however the £1million donation was returned to avoid charges of buying influence over government policy. Blair was mortified that he could be thought of as anything other than, *"a regular sort of guy"*.[120] Soon after, in 1998, there was 'Lobbygate' when Labour advisor Derek Draper was caught on tape boasting that he could sell access to government ministers.[121] There were also sex scandals involving Ron Davies[122] and David Blunkett.[123] However up until the 2006 cash for peerages scandal and the 2009 MPs' expenses scandal, Labour was not seen as a party of sleaze but instead as a party of spin.

Spin at best is a byword for being romantic with the truth, manipulating the media with the facts of a story to create a favourable outcome. This works fine in practice, but creates great mistrust. Spin was associated with the Iraq war dossier, covered in the next chapter, when a journalist accused the Labour government of "sexing up" a government document regarding capabilities of the Iraqi army.[124] However the first real example of spin and a political scandal came in 1997 when revelations of an affair between

120 Account recalled in A Journey T Blair Published by Hutchinson 2010 Reported in the Independent 1997 http://www.independent.co.uk/news/blair-i-think-im-a-pretty-straight-sort-of-guy-1294593.html

121 Story reported by the Observer, reported here by the BBC http://news.bbc.co.uk/1/hi/uk_politics/128034.stm

122 Ron Davies resigns over gay-sex scandal Reported in the Yorkshire Post http://www.yorkshirepost. co.uk/news/main-topics/local-stories/ron-davies-resigns-over-gay-sex-scandal-1-2457949

123 I did something very wrong': David Blunkett's mistress Kimberly Quinn admits remorse over three-year affair Reported by the Daily Mail by I Gallagher http://www.dailymail.co.uk/news/article-1254365/I-did-wrong-David-Blunketts-mistress-Kimberly-Quinn-admits-remorse-year-affair.html

124 Alastair Campbell had Iraq dossier changed to fit US claims- by C Aims and R Norton- Toylor published in The Guardian available from http://www.theguardian.com/uk/2010/jan/10/alastair-campbell-iraq-dossier-inquiry January 2010

Foreign Secretary Robin Cook and his secretary were about to be made public.[125] On this occasion Cook was told by Downing Street to choose between his wife and his mistress and the story was spun as a divorce and not an affair. Whilst the Cook affair was insignificant in the face of the sleaze of the Major governments, the Ecclestone affair along with the resignation of Peter Mandelson didn't help Labour appear to be being straight with the public. Mandelson at the time was Secretary of State for Trade and Industry, a department he would later return to. He was good at his job and had been a leading figure in the Labour Party for over a decade. In late 1998 it was revealed that two years earlier whilst Labour was in opposition, Mandelson had taken a private loan to buy a house from fellow Labour MP and Treasury Minister Geoffrey Robinson and had failed to disclose it in the MP's register of interests.[126] The scandal cost both of them their ministerial jobs and the revelations shook the government to its core.

In July 2007 it emerged that the Labour Party had accepted £608,975 from a property developer named David Abrahams, and General Secretary Peter Watt was forced to fall on his sword, but the claims that Watt was the only person that knew about this very suspect donation, and that the money had been fenced via third parties, was seen as being risible and an insult to the intelligence of many in the Labour Party and the country as a whole.[127] However, whilst sleaze has damaged reputations and our trust of politicians many of these are insignificant in comparison with the more recent MP's expenses scandal.

New Labour

The death on 12th May 1994 of John Smith was clearly a tragedy. When the Labour leader died of a heart attack aged just 55, he had been Party leader less than two years. The night before his death he had addressed a dinner of more than 500 guests where he spoke the immortal words *"all we ask for is the chance to serve."* He was the leader of the opposition to Prime Minister John Major. Major lead a sleaze ridden Party deeply divided on Europe that had lost its poll lead on economic competence for the first time since 1964.

125 http://news.bbc.co.uk/1/hi/uk_politics/252341.stm

126 As reported by the Guardian http://www.theguardian.com/world/2000/oct/17/qanda.mandelson

127 Daily Telegraph 30/11/06 "David Abrahams, a generous giver" http://www.telegraph.co.uk/news/politics/labour/1570984/Profile-David-Abrahams-a-generous-giver.html

However despite the Tories being at civil war it was uncertain as to whether Labour would win a future general election, and if the Tories chose the time to go to the polls before the five year time limit for the 1992 parliament they still had a chance with Smith as leader of the opposition. Smith's Shadow Budget in the 1992 campaign had damaged Labour's chances by allowing the Tories to roll out the high tax, high spending argument. Mark Stewart wrote a wonderful chapter in the book *Prime Minister Portillo*[128] that balances both tributes to Smith and the doubt that still surrounded the Labour Party. There is no doubt Smith still had issues convincing the middle classes, especially on policies such as education and redistribution which were seen as out of date.

Smith's death bought with it a leadership election. The contenders for the leadership were Tony Blair, Margaret Beckett and John Prescott. Prescott and Becket both ran for the deputy leadership with Blair being elected leader and Prescott his deputy. It has been well publicised that a gentleman's agreement between Tony Blair and Gordon Brown was made following Smith's death, the so called Granita pact, after the curry house in Islington where it was made. In the deal Brown would step aside to allow Blair to run for the leadership in return for an enhanced role in the government and Blair would step aside around 2003.

This was the beginning of a powerful movement within the Labour Party, which came to be known as New Labour. A movement which consisted of some of the most talented politicians and advisers in British political history, such as Peter Mandelson, Alastair Campbell, Philip Gould, Gordon Brown and Tony Blair. They appointed young and talented political assistants who lead the Labour Party today including the Miliband brothers and Ed Balls. In addition there were heavyweights in the party from the union movement and local government such as David Blunkett, Jack Straw and John Prescott (as deputy leader and, in time, Deputy Prime Minister.) Prescott acted as a bridge between old Labour and New Labour and on many decisions of renewal Prescott was seen as the 'go to guy' for the green light. It was well known that in Tony Blair's 'Sofa Cabinet' most big decisions had to get the approval of Prescott, especially prior to 2003. Prescott as a person has been somewhat unfairly painted out of history by the media, who found it easier to ridicule him for his size and malapropisms when speaking. However 'Prezza' never gave the press what they wanted, and figures such as Alastair Campbell have gone to greater lengths to acknowl-

128 *Prime Minister Portillo M Stewart Published by Politico 2003*

edge the importance of Prescott in the government.

This new political project had talented people and would slowly win the blessing of the party, but there was one major problem: the party was still unelectable. They had been defeated in 1979, 1983, 1987 and 1992 and they could not muster a winning formula under the leadership of Callaghan, Foot, Kinnock or Smith. The brand had been damaged and was synonymous with economic incompetence. To add 'New' to Labour to create 'New Labour' was to rebrand and to symbolise a new era. This new era moved Labour politically to the centre ground, where it focused on economic competence. Many people now say that Labour is no longer a socialist party, and under the leadership of Tony Blair any lingering doubts were confirmed. Blair was inspired by the 42nd President of the United States, Bill Clinton. Both Blair and Brown had travelled to the USA in 1992 to take part in the Presidential Election; they witnessed first-hand how Clinton had overcome similar problems to that in the Labour Party in Britain in his own Democratic Party. The right in America had dominated presidential politics just as the right in Britain under Thatcher and Major had dominated Downing Street. The Democrats needed to modernise in the same way that Labour did. By the time Clinton stood as the Democratic Presidential candidate the Republicans had held the presidency for 20 of the previous 24 years. Bill Clinton, a young Arkansas Governor, came together with a number of progressive politicians to create what they called the New Democrat Philosophy. Their set of seven principles was the blueprint that New Labour was built on. In 1986 Clinton outlined these as:

Change is the only constant in the modern economy

Human capital is more important than financial capital

A constructive partnership between government and business is more important than the dominance of either

As a society we have to share the opportunities and responsibility

Government and private sector waste has to be punished

We cannot pursue our individual aims at the detriment of others in society

We must accept globalisation and interdependence.[129]

Bill Clinton practised a political policy known as triangulation, constructing

129 *My Life B Clinton Published by Arrow Books 2005 P 327*

a consensus became known as the political *Third Way*. Tony Blair would not call himself a socialist or a Conservative but a *Third Way* politician. He also practised triangulation, by attempting to build a political consensus by taking the values of the Labour Party regarding social justice but also accepting Tory policies such as the role of the free market, and rejecting unpopular Labour policies which he saw as making the party unelectable. The third way accepts that both the state and the market have limitations and advantages; this is not the view of either old Labour or the right wing Conservatives of the 1980s who had entrenched positions. Blair also noted the ideas of academic Anthony Giddens, who commented that under Blair Labour gave *"Particular attention to family life, crime and decay of community, a conscious attempt to relate the policies of the left to the concerns of the ordinary citizen."*[130] Blair attempted to turn Labour into a 'catch all' party. This aspired to appeal to all voters. It could even be called the depoliticising of politics. Policies such as fiscal discipline, health care reform, investment in education and training, regeneration and crime took centre stage as they affected the vast majority of voters irrespective of their voting history, or whether they had been engaged in the first place.[131] Blair, like Clinton, embraced globalisation and multiculturalism and sought to place Britain at the centre of Europe, a change from the Eurosceptic policies of Thatcher and Major.

The question was, could New Labour, triangulation and the 'third way' really contribute to the slow revolution? Could New Labour really push back the evils of financial liberalism? The aim of New Labour was to let neo liberalism get on and do its worse, the welfare state would come in pick up the pieces. This could work in theory, but really wasn't it just accepting financial liberalism that the founding socialist fathers of the Labour Party had fought to curb? On the back of this Tony Blair was accused of being an 'apolitical' leader of the Labour Party, only bothered by attracting votes. We would argue that this is the easy and somewhat lazy argument to make. If this is the case why did he put so much thought into the political position of the Labour Party in a similar vain to that taken by Margaret Thatcher and Sir Keith Joseph between 1975-79? The intellectual journey taken by the new right and Blair are remarkably similar. Like Mrs Thatcher prior to becoming Prime Minister, Blair had identified a British decline: even more startlingly Blair's identification of decline mirrored that of Thatcher's. By 1996 Blair had published *"New Britain, My Vision of a Young Country.*[132]*"* A

---

130 *The Third Way and its Critics A Seldon Published by Polity Press 2000   p4*

131 *The Third Way and its Critics A Seldon Published by Polity Press 2000   p3*

132 *New Britain T Blair Published by First Estate 1996*

critique of the British political economy, foreign policy and British society. He identified that under Thatcher and Major the policies they introduced to combat decline were now the cause of the decline. Blair was clear in his analysis that the Thatcherite policies of 1979-97 didn't liberate people; they neglected them:

"Across Britain I see enormous untapped potential, children in classes too big, people in their 20s who have never had a job, trains vandalised, city centres clogged up... My ambitions for Britain are defined by this gap between potential and performance.[133]"

Once Blair had identified the British decline he set about finding political solutions to reverse the situation. Whilst Thatcher moved the Conservatives to the right, Blair modernised the Labour Party by dropping clause 4[134] and shifting economic policy towards accepting the role of open markets. The Blair government's economic policy was a true display of the third way. By adopting a third way economic policy Blair allowed markets to act as agents of change whilst accepting the limitation of both markets and the state.[135] Blair mirrored Clinton by saying; "*We need to move beyond the old battles between the public and private sector.*"[136] Blair was keen to accept the role of markets but insisted on a system of regulatory authorities. However it's at the personal level where Blair realised that economic success could be unlocked. Blair recommitted the Labour Party to the 1945 Beveridge concept of full employment believing in "*unlocking human potential through education and training.*"[137] "*New Labour had offered an opportunity to counter some of the 'Thatcher-Major' sentiment through the implementation of centre left policies*" but "*New Labour endorsed markets and many aspects of the Thatcher-Major settlement*"[138] The 'third way' would balance economic, social and political interest whilst maintaining the UK's international competitiveness by embracing and tackling globalisation through contemporary opportunities such as the knowledge economy.[139]

---

133 *New Britain T Blair Published by First Estate 1996 Px*

134 *A Journey T Blair Published by Hutchinson 2010 P75*

135 *The Third Way and its Critics A Seldon Published by Polity Press 2000 P58*

136 *New Britain T Blair Published by First Estate 1996 P19*

137 *New Britain T Blair Published by First Estate 1996 P93/94*

138 *New Labour and the Politics of Dominance' by M Beech, Published by Basingstoke: Palgrave Macmillan – 2008 P2*

139 *The Third Way and its Critics A Seldon Published by Polity Press 2000 P72*

Chapter 8 - New Labour in Government

There has been much analysis of the Blair government in recent years. There is little doubt that Blair pushed Labour to the right, and had a great domestic reform agenda built on market dogma, but foreign policy issues overshadowed any achievements. We shall start this section by briefly examining the culture of the late 1990s and explore whether that aided Blair, and if he wasted the goodwill he was given. We will examine the positive changes of Blair and the negative decisions he made before asking if Blair blew his chance to truly change the UK for the better.

By the end of chapter seven we had identified that Tony Blair was developing a vision for the Labour Party and Britain. It is for this reason that Blair will go down as a key figure in the slow revolution. Not for his naivety in allowing the private sector in the public sector or his adoption of neo-liberalism, but for his investments into education, local government, overseas aid, and health.

Blair himself was also fortunate with timing. He was a charismatic man for a charismatic age. Blair was fortunate to be the leader of the Labour Party at the end of 18 years of a Tory government when the majority of the public could no longer be bought off with tax cuts. A time when people could see for themselves that the promises of financial liberalism were in fact little more than fantasy.

Blair offered what seemed like a genuine alternative to the voters in 1997 and the feel good factor of the UK at the time chimed with his charisma. In May 1997 Tony Blair swept into Downing Street surrounded by celebrities such as Oasis songwriter Noel Gallagher, who ten years later reflected on that era to the Scottish Mail on Sunday:

"I was brought up as a Labour voter. I come from a working class family and was on the dole for seven years. It was euphoric when the Labour Party got into power. It felt like it might be important after years of John Major and

Margaret Thatcher. He just MIGHT be one of us". [140]

The UK itself in the mid-1990s went into a period of soul searching. The 1991-2 recession had forced John Major into investment into the public sector to create economic growth. But society needed something philosophical, more than just economic changes. As well as the recession the endemic hopelessness in Britain seemed to be exemplified by the James Bulger murder in 1993. The details of this gruesome slaying of a toddler by other children are well documented. How could this happen? Further misery unfolded that autumn when the IRA killed two children in a botched attack on the northern town of Warrington. This at a time when life for those with low income was extremely rough, a time before a minimum wage and high unemployment. Had the country and the voters learned nothing?

Tony Blair with his bucket loads of charisma was just the tonic the UK needed, his positive "we can" attitude was a refreshing change from the "you should" message of the Conservatives. Whilst Gordon Brown would have made a thoroughly sound and logical Labour leader in 1994, can you honestly have seen him on the stage at the 1996 BRIT Awards being lauded by Oasis star Noel Gallagher as, *"the man!"* and imbibing young UK people with a sense that he was indeed their man?

Weighing up the options in 1994 many Labour activists saw Tony Blair as having stardust and wanted a piece of it. However this view wasn't universal. In a recent discussion a Labour Party member recalled *"Why would we want an arrogant posh boy who was distinctly pro market, lukewarm with the unions and dismissive of the views of others as our leader?"* However another said *"The sense of* wow, *this could be big suddenly slapped us in the face when in the 1995 local elections Labour took 50% of the vote."* People were flocking to Labour and by 1996 the deal was well and truly sealed between Blair and the British people. The sense of euphoria was palpable. The question was, was Blair just riding a temporary wave or was he the genuine man who could change the way the UK is run?

Cool Britannia: The Culture and Politics of the 1990's

But what was this wave? The wave was known as cool Britannia, a genuine feeling sweeping the nation that ordinary people once again had control of the

140 *Sun Mail November 12th 2006 quoted on http://stopcryingyourheartoutnews.blogspot.co.uk/2006/11/noel-on-tony-blair.html*

UK. This was to be the beginning of what was to become over a decade of the UK being at the front of the arts movement, a player on the world stage and there was a genuine increase in quality of life for people under Labour.

The Spice Girls blasted their way into our psyches in 1996 with Geri Halliwell at the forefront wearing her infamous Union Jack dress at the Brit awards. She became the face of cool Britannia. The Spice Girls seemed to represent the return of self-confidence to the working classes, five ordinary girls grabbing the pop world by storm. This was punk 90's style. Young people were doing it for themselves but with one crucial difference: this time the background was colourful, positive and can do. Geri Halliwell's Union Jack dress and Gallagher's similarly emblazoned guitar summed up the optimism surrounding the UK as the dog days of the Major government were finally coming to an end. D:Ream's "Things can Only Get Better"[141] was the election anthem for Labour in 1997, this in itself symbolising that Britain was changing direction with quality of life being put over stuffy out-dated politicians in grey suits.

The ultimate irony for Major and his chancellor Ken Clarke was that they had delivered a strong economy by running a socialist-style deficit budget, but would not be in power to garner the acclaim. Strong growth wiped out the overspend proving that targeted investment in public and private sector from the state worked. They had done it by increasing public spending and cutting stamp duty to stimulate borrowing on mortgages. Labour was inheriting a golden, socialist legacy.

The surge in optimism surrounding the UK was felt in many different areas. There was a cultural boom as the fashion and the arts were given a much needed lift from state investment. The UK was on the up, an exciting and vibrant place to be. But was it real, or just an illusion? A bit of both if the truth be told.

Noel Gallagher sums it up thus: "*I admit I got carried away by the whole Britpop-Cool Britannia thing. In hindsight, it turned out he (Blair) was just a politician like all the rest. Initially, we all thought something was going change... it didn't. (But) If you were to take the Iraq thing out of the equation, Labour do seem to have made a difference with things like the minimum wage. They also made education and health a priority.*"[142]

141 *Things Can only Get Better: Distributed by Magnet Records – 1993*

142 *Sun Mail November 12th 2006 quoted on http://stopcryingyourheartoutnews.blogspot.co.uk/2006/11/ noel-on-tony-blair.html*

The truth is Tony Blair helped Labour deliver the undeliverable; three General Election victories. To this day Tony Blair is the only Labour leader to win a general election since 1974. These victories showed that the UK had moved its thinking to become a more tolerant society that the public had moved towards a centre ground which politicians have now been reluctant to move away from. For 13 years Labour were no longer Downing Street Squatters, obliterating the myth that Labour was the party of opposition and the Conservatives where born to rule the country.

But ultimately the acceptance of the market as the panacea for what ailed the public services, plus a massive dose of hubris meant that Blair's career ended in failure. The rancour and ill feeling towards him now is precisely because he offered the ultimate hope for the left, that society can be changed and made more equal, forever.

Despite serving for ten years in Number Ten delivering wide ranging and positive changes for the UK, including economic growth the premiership of Tony Blair will only ever be associated with Iraq. To the point where all the positive changes he made, will be over shadowed by this one foreign policy disaster. It blighted his final years in power and meant that his resignation took place in the midst of a background hum of hostility, rather than in an atmosphere of reverential nostalgia which Blair seemed so desperately to crave.

Blair's presidential style of government meant that he experienced breathtaking personal highs, such as his victory stroll in Kosovo and the Belfast Peace Treaty of 1998. But being tethered in such a highly personal way to his government's actions also saw Blair endure some crushing lows during his ten years in power. If the petrol dispute had dragged on another few days, if he had lost the student tuition fees vote and if the Hutton Inquiry had pointed the finger regarding the Dodgy Dossier, he would have undoubtedly have been forced from power as he gambled his whole credibility each time.

Blair went through two distinct phases with the press and the public. Iraq is the dividing line. The pre-war Blair was desperate for approval and in hock to focus groups when it came to road testing policy ideas. Thus the first term seemed to be an exercise in remaining popular rather than using Labour's massive majority to push through radical reforms, particularly to the public services. Indeed Blair recognised this when he told biographer Anthony Seldon that he regretted not acting radically enough in his first parliament.

Seldon refers to the first term as, *"a learning experience"*, going on to opine, *"Only in the second and third terms did his personal ideas fructify into his "choice and diversity" agenda, extending Margaret Thatcher's liberal reforms into the welfare state."*[143]

Let's be clear here: Blair was no *"son of Thatcher"*. He joined the Labour Party and stood for Parliament at a time when Foot was the leader. The Social Democratic Party (SDP) was in its pomp but Tony Blair chose to remain with the Labour Party and was the candidate at the high profile Beaconsfield by-election in May 1982. Neil Kinnock saw something in Blair and quickly promoted him to the front bench. Blair was elected to the shadow cabinet by his fellow Labour MPs in 1988, and his closest political ally was Gordon Brown. During the 1980s Brown was touted as the next big thing in the Labour Party and served as a front bench treasury spokesman. Blair himself was no proto Thatcherite. In fact a letter surfaced in 2006 and was published by the Daily Telegraph in November of that year. It made for fascinating reading. Blair had told Michael Foot in July 1982 that he had *"come to Socialism through Marxism"*.[144] Whilst this could be dismissed as Blair buttering up his leader, it nevertheless roots Blair's values as far away from Thatcher as you could imagine.

The 1992 defeat had bruised Labour MPs and activists alike. In the wake of John Smith's untimely demise, they were looking for a sense of optimism. Blair managed to articulate a vision for Britain that was optimistic and charismatic, and that vision chimed with Labour's core ambition in 1994: power at all costs. This saw the ascendency of Peter Mandelson, Philip Gould and later on Alastair Campbell as spin and the rolling news agenda created by Sky in 1990 came to the forefront of tactics and policymaking.

Spin, as a tactic has been criticised as leading to the corrosion of trust in British politics. It was formulated in the USA, where the Bush Snr White House had spent around $200,000 over a four-year presidency, in the first two years Clinton's White House had spent over $1.2M.[145] But ultimately it had to be done, as the British press were distinctly anti-Labour. Deploying highly-trained press officers to out the parties 'spin' on any news topic often

143 BBC News Online "How will history judge Blair? http://news.bbc.co.uk/1/hi/uk_politics/6636091. stm Thursday 10th May 2007

144 Letter from tony Blair to Michael Foot in 1982, published here by The Telegraph in 2006 accessed here=http://www.telegraph.co.uk/news/uknews/1521418/The-full-text-of-Tony- B l a i r s - l e t t e r - t o - Michael-Foot-written-in-July-1982.ht

145 For the Love of Politics by S Beddell Smith Published by Random House 2007

allowed Labour to seize the agenda. This practice became essential when the Tories were in near collapse in 2002/3 it was the media and not the Tories that were the de facto opposition to the government.

There were still rumblings in the Party that John Smith's perceived tax and spend shadow budget during the 1992 election convinced voters that Labour had not fundamentally changed. Blair looked across the Atlantic and observed Bill Clinton moving the Democratic Party towards a way of delivering his own values, but in a different way.

The Third Way was Blair's plan to convince the voters that Labour had actually taken notice of a reframed world that had resulted from the Reagan/Thatcher era. This resulted in the rewriting of Clause Four of the Labour Party Constitution, a commitment to use the nationalisation of key industries to make society fairer. This was a watershed in Blair's leadership and had two main strands to it. Firstly it would stamp Blair's authority as leader, and secondly it would send a message to the voters that Labour had moved into the 1990s. Dropping the aspiration to public ownership of the means of production was a bold move. Whilst Kinnock had decided the idea in practice was unmanageable, for many Labour Party members Clause Four symbolised the Party's values from which practical policies flowed. We might not be able to take back the public utilities at the moment, but if it became possible we should do it. This was, and still is, the attitude of many Party members. By ruling it out completely, Blair seemed to be reframing the aims of the Party, moving in a more market orientated way and accepting capitalism had the answers.

The announcement of a Special Conference in 1995 which did indeed endorse the new Clause Four praising, *"the enterprise of the market and the rigour of competition* "stamped Blair's mark forever on the Labour Party. It could be argued, however, that Blair's core democratic socialist values remained intact. It was all about changing the means rather than the end. For example the UK desperately needed new schools and hospitals. Rather than tax the people, and then spend the money to deliver world-class public services, what Blair was doing was still delivering for the public, but getting the markets to put up the money, with all the attendant risk. What Tony Blair failed to grasp however, was that private companies such as Skanska who built the new Royal London Hospital,[146] were out to make as much money for their shareholders as they possibly could. This, in fact,

146 (Narrative) Context is *"Five Surgeons Quit "Appalling Hospital" Daily Mail 2nd Dec 2011http://* *www.dailymail.co.uk/news/article-2068939/Five-surgeons-quit-appalling-London-hospital-shortage-* *kit-nurses-beds-norm.html*

is their legal obligation. Blair may have deluded himself into thinking they were, *"regular guys"*, but the reality is that they are not motivated by altruism but by profit.

What really rankles with many activists is Blair's total lack of understanding of why the utilities and vital services were nationalised by the 1945 Labour government: keeping them out of the hands of private interests, and to make them to serve the many, rather than line the pockets of the few. It is as if none of the New Labour politicians had taken note of the Victorian, Edwardian or pre-war era. Did they think that nationalisation was just about power, something that Attlee did to make himself powerful? The long-term legacy from Thatcher's butchering and selling off is a utilities and fuel sector with sky high prices, making huge profits and hurting those of us who are already struggling with the basics of life. It is interesting that just twenty years later many Labour candidates, (if not MPs) are now in favour of public ownership of many of the companies Clause 4 turned its back on. It has certainly been a backward step for our slow revolution and a huge step towards economic injustice.

Blair's triumph over Clause Four won many plaudits and is credited with delivering the endorsement of The Sun newspaper whose owner, Rupert Murdoch, was especially impressed with the new sentiments of wanting a *"dynamic economy, serving the public interest with a thriving private sector"*. In 1997 the paper whose readership was ten million said of Labour Party Leader Tony Blair, *"The people need a leader with vision, purpose and courage who can inspire them and fire their imaginations. The Sun believes that man is Tony Blair."*[147]Note they were endorsing Blair himself, and not the Labour Party.

Tony Blair the great and the good

On 1st May 1997 in a blaze of glory the Labour Party won a huge electoral majority. They polled nearly 4 million votes more than the Conservatives and took a working majority of 179, in short, Labour had been told by the people "get on with it, do what you need to." This victory was a huge turning point, sending to the history books 18 years of Conservative government that for better or worse had fundamentally changed life in Britain. Labour

147 *It's the Sun wot's switched sides to back Blair Published in The Guardian By R Greenslade http://www. theguardian.com/politics/1997/mar/18/past.roygreenslade May 1997*

didn't just win the election: they took a landslide. Election night itself was alive with an energy that swept the United Kingdom rejecting the dogma of Thatcherism. Blair himself said, *"New Labour, New Britain did not seem like hubris, on the contrary, it chimed with the mood of the country."*[148] The Conservatives had lost 4.5 million voters.

Labour had the mandate to be radical, and they certainly started with a bang. There were a number of raised eyebrows on the Labour benches when new Chancellor Gordon Brown announced operational independence for the Bank of England right after the election. The plan, described as *"the most radical shake-up in the bank's 300-year history"*[149] was not in the 1997 election manifesto, and Bank of England Governor Eddie George was only informed at the last minute. Handing the power of the setting of interest rates to the monetary policy committee as well as responsibility for keeping inflation under control could disturb both the markets and could have spooked Labour's election campaign if it was in the manifesto. Only Deputy Prime Minister John Prescott and Foreign Secretary Robin Cook were consulted by Tony Blair and Gordon Brown prior to the announcement of independence.

Tony Blair used the political cycle as his reasoning for independence. To depoliticise the setting of rates helped both the economy and the British people. In his memoirs he notes that the British people paid less on their loans and mortgages closer to the election as the government looked to buy votes by lowering interest rates; however this would more than be made up for after the election as interest rates went up to slow down the inflation that had been caused by the low interest rates. This means one of key tools to help the UK economy was not being used to control inflation but to win votes by the party in government.

Labour promised to keep to the Tory spending levels of 1996 through to 1999. In addition to this they pledged to keep the top rate of tax the same. This was a big policy change for Labour, exemplifying the new direction the party had taken. Capital gains tax was reduced to 15%, showing that Labour was comfortable with people "getting filthy rich."[150] With a reduction in taxation Labour had to find other sources of income. Tony Blair

148 *A Journey T Blair   Published by Hutchinson 2010 p131*

149 *Quote by Ed Balls re-produced by BBC from http://news.bbc.co.uk/onthisday/hi/dates/stories/may/6/newsid_3806000/3806313.stm*

150 *Peter Mandelson gets nervous about people getting 'filthy rich' in The Guardian by Malik S, from http://www.theguardian.com/politics/2012/jan/26/mandelson-people-getting-filthy-rich January 2012*

was synonymous with the phenomenon of the stealth tax, increasing duty on tobacco, alcohol and automobile fuel as ways of increasing government revenue. Further sources of income were found through the privatisation of the air traffic control and a one off windfall tax on the utility companies.

In March 1998 the government released the Welfare Reform Green Paper which outlined manifesto pledges such as the minimum wage, tax credits and SureStart. The minimum wage was a manifesto commitment that guaranteed people a basic wage for an hour's work, and to increase it when there was growth in the economy. It seems strange to think that in 1996 a cleaner could receive less than £1 an hour, but that was life under the Conservatives. Labour's welfare to work policies recommitted the British government to full employment for the first time since 1979 and getting British people back to work was packaged as part of what became known as the 'new deal.' To get the economically inactive back to work incentives other than the minimum wage - such as tax credits - were introduced. Job centres were opened and the government invested in retraining the unemployed. In a similar vein to the government of Attlee, Labour had undertaken what seemed like a massive increase in spending but in reality between 1997 and 2005 spending only increased from 41% of GDP to 44%, with big increases in NHS spending from £58bn to £84bn.

For the first time since the Labour administration of 1974/79 the UK government now accepted that it played an active role and had responsibility in creating economic growth. The Thatcherite policy, which seems to have been adopted by Cameron and Clegg, dictates that markets and individuals will make an economic success of Britain. What Labour was saying was is that the government does have a role in stimulating economic growth through investment in infrastructure and reduction unemployment.

As previously mentioned, Labour had committed to keeping Conservative spending plans for its first two years in government, which was funded partly through a windfall tax of the utilities- raising £2.2 billion and privatisation of the air traffic control. After the two year spending freeze Labour undertook a spending review, which promised investment in education and the NHS.

In 1997 Labour had promised to "think the unthinkable" on NHS reform. The Tories had become synonymous with starving the NHS of funding and part of Labour's mandate was to restore funding to the health service. This investment began in 1999 and during the first Sunday of the new millennium, Tony Blair announced on television that Labour would increase NHS spending to the levels of our European counterparts. Blair replaced old Labour favourite Frank Dobson who had taken the reigns of the NHS in 1997 with New Labour true believer Alan Milburn and between them they devised a 10 year plan which renegotiated contracts, aimed to push up standards, introduced the choice agenda, and reintroduced the internal market. They also made large changes to structures through trusts, business management, procurement and funding of building to increase quality of outcomes. Blair's long-term aim was to reduce waiting lists from 18 months to 6 months, and by the 2005 general election to 18 weeks.

This increase in NHS spending was mirrored by increased investment in education, as education Secretary David Blunkett, supported by assistant Andrew Adonis, had an agenda of pushing up standards and this was to be the beginning of a small education revolution under Labour. Many within the Labour movement have accused Blair of the total abandonment of socialism in education policy; however Blair cannot be faulted for pushing up standards through wide scale investment. He fundamentally believed that education is the key to social mobility. New Labour policy was to improve both failing and performing schools with real on the ground action and investment. They invested in teacher training, increased teacher numbers, rebuilt schools, reduced class sizes and massively invested in class room assistants: real actions the coalition are now looking to reverse, whilst the best idea the Tories can come up with are managerial and structural tinkering.

In addition to reform in the welfare state, New Labour had promised constitutional reform. Reform came through devolution and The Freedom of Information Act. The Freedom of Information Act (2000) allows citizens to make requests to public bodies or private sector organisations doing public sector work, and in an average year 120,000 requests are made. The act complements the Data Protection Act (1998), which protected personal information, held by any organisation. Tony Blair later regretted the Freedom of Information Act but it made government at all levels more transparent. Freedom of information has been used to hold the government to account and is synonymous with the MPs' expenses scandal. Labour also promised devolution referenda in Scotland and Wales. The government of Wales Act (1998) was supported by 51% of the Welsh people, just a difference of 6721 voters. The Act gave Wales the right to an executive, an ombudsman, a national assembly and the right to make decisions over policies such as education. In Scotland, the overwhelming majority supported the creation of a Parliament with tax powers. It gave Scotland the right to change policy in areas such as education, health, agriculture and justice. A watered down version of devolution was created in London but rejected by the North East, rendering the further extension of federalism of devolution dead in the water. But the effect on the lives of the people in Scotland, Wales and London has been great. People have more influence over the way their tax is spent and services are tailored to the communities they serve. These three areas did well under the economic boom from 1998-2007 and this is in part due to devolution. Devolution was also a key to the peace process in Northern Ireland.

Away from the reform agenda, Blair had several other milestones during the first government, which included peace in Northern Ireland through the Good Friday Agreement, the death of Princess Diana, civil unrest, a foot and mouth outbreak, and the political sleaze mentioned at the end of the previous chapter. On August 31st 1997, Diana, Princes of Wales was fatally injured in a car crash in the Pont de l'Alma road tunnel in Paris along with her friend Dodi Fayed and their driver Henry Paul. In his memoirs, Blair gives an articulate account of the week following the crash. Let us remember that since divorcing Prince Charles, although parts of media where questioning parts of her lifestyle the public held Princes Diana in high regard and with great affection. Her death saw an incredible outpouring of grief from the public, the likes of which has never been seen before or since, and which left a divide between the public and the Royal Family. Tony Blair's management of the week of Princess Diana's funeral saw his approval ratings surge to 93%. On the morning on of the 31st Blair famously called Diana "*The people's princess*" which summed up the mood at large, and thousands flocked to leave flowers outside Buckingham Palace.

With the Belfast Treaty in 1998 Tony Blair completed arguably his greatest achievement. Credit should also be given to John Major, Bill Clinton, Bertie Ahern, Albert Reynolds and many others. However most premiers tend to make peace in conflict a priority towards the end of their premiership; an example could be Bill Clinton in the Middle East. Blair made peace in Northern Ireland a goal for his first years in office. Like him or loathe him, no one could deny that Tony Blair had an amazing ability to get even the most hostile of people to see things in the way he wanted them to, and even the most ardent of opponents were charmed and cajoled by the Prime Minister into taking decisions they would never have previously countenanced. Blair's talent for reading people, their intentions and telling them what they wanted to hear was perhaps best exemplified by the way that he brought the politicians of that most troublesome part of the UK, Northern Ireland, together in a devolved Power Sharing government. This culminated in the frankly incredible sight of implacably sworn enemies Dr Ian Paisley and Martin McGuiness smiling for the cameras whilst drinking tea together with then outgoing Prime Minister Tony Blair at the Stormont government building outside Belfast in the spring of 2007. It had been a long journey with many twists and turns along the way but Blair had pulled off what most commentators had thought was impossible: a partnership in government between the Republican face of the criminal IRA, and the Democratic Unionist Party who had been seen by many as the ultimate Loyalist stumbling block to any political settlement in Ulster.

Before the 2001 general election, Blair had two further major crises to deal with. In September 2000 there was civil unrest over fuel pump prices. The Blair government was targeted due to the increase in fuel duty, but it was slow to react and it took four days to get the crisis under control. The protesters formed blockades around filling stations, causing panic buying and stopping the emergency services from receiving fuel. Although the protesters were allowing some emergency vehicles through, nurses had to argue face to face with protesters to allow ambulances to pass. After all, even the Tory press asked, who were they to decide if it was an emergency? However the fuel protest slips into insignificance when the 2001 outbreak of Foot and Mouth disease is considered. The outbreak lasted over 3 months and was considered to be one of the worst in history. The result would be to shut down the English countryside and the slaughter of infected herds.

The foot and mouth crisis delayed the start of the 2001 General Election from May to June; however despite the delay the result was not in any doubt. Although the Conservative leader William Hague had brought the Conservative Party back from the brink following the 1997 General Election, he did not develop a clear policy programme to make the Tories electable again. In addition the British people were not willing to trust the Tories with public services and they were divided over Europe, an issue most definitely not a concern to the British public in 2001. The only event of note for the Tories was Shadow Chancellor Oliver Letwin announcing they wanted a programme of £20billion in spending cuts, in doing so losing any hope the Tories had of re-election. For Labour there were only two events which caught the eye, Tony Blair himself getting into a row with a voter over the NHS and Deputy Prime Minister John Prescott punching a man after he threw an egg at him (John Prescott insists he was just following Blair's orders to 'connect with the electorate')[151]. By the time polling day rolled round Labour lost 6 seats whilst the Tories added 1 and the Liberal Democrats under Charles Kennedy added 6. Labour took 10.7 million votes to 8.3 million for the Conservatives and the Liberal Democrats took 4.8 million. Only 29 seats changed hands at the general election.

Blair's judgement in going to the polls was vindicated and he became the first Labour Prime Minister in history to secure two full parliamentary sessions on his own terms. On the face of it the results for Labour were impressive. A thumping commons majority and continued woes for the Tories at the ballot box surely meant that Tony Blair's position was unassailable and he could press on with more radical policies to create and maintain world class public services, and deliver social justice in a 21st century context. However in retrospect the verdict of the UK people in 2001 was pretty damning for the Labour Party as much as it was for the Tories. The election was low key. But when the statistics are analysed a bit closer Labour actually hemorrhaged a massive 2.8 million votes from the 1997 result meaning that Tony Blair had polled fewer votes than Neil Kinnock took in defeat in 1992.

Tony Blair, the bad and the ugly

On the domestic front the 2001-07 agenda consisted of further reforms, an Olympic bid, controversial legislation and a bitter political rivalry. We should also touch on the Hutton inquiry which could have forced Blair from office had it been found there was a case to answer; the day prior to that he could also have been in big trouble over university fees. The latter was controversial because in Labour's 2001 general election manifesto, they had promised not to increase course fees to be paid by students. In 1998, students had begun paying just over £1,000 a year up front, and although this was unfair, it was manageable. The Higher Education Act (2004) meant that students would, through a loan should they wish, pay £3,000 a year increasing with inflation and have access to a further loan to support living whilst at university. Tony Blair had come to the conclusion that universities needed higher amounts of funding to increase participation and the range of research conducted. This was part of the knowledge economy agenda Blair had pushed, the argument being that to compete with the likes of In-

---

151 A one line joke is told by Prescott during speeches

dia, British people needed a high-end education and it went hand in hand with Labour's hands off approach to the economy and the mini education revolution. His argument was supported by leading academic institutions, such as The Russell Group. But it was also felt that Blair lacked the courage to make the argument for increasing Higher Education investment through direct funding by the Treasury. Instead students would have to pay for the privilege of being educated and contributing to the so-called knowledge economy.

This bill was one of the most controversial of his premiership and caused protests on the streets through coordinated opposition from students, including the National Union of Students, and eventually it helped the Liberal Democrats gain record numbers of votes. The Conservatives were in full agreement with the policy and ultimately it was opposition support that pushed the bill through the Commons as Labour backbenchers revolted. There were and are two arguments against what became known as top up fees. Firstly, education should be free to all, people should not be put off by the expense, and such a policy discriminates against the financially poor. It should always be argued that education along with hard work is the key to social mobility. The second argument is the slippery slope argument, that if introduced, as soon as the Tories gain power they will substantially increase the fees paid. Of course this happened; at the time there were counter proposals, including a graduate tax but none of them were taken seriously. By the time the bill came before Parliament for its second reading in January 2004 there had been two large protests in London and opposition from the public, students, including current students who would not have to pay the fees, and the media. The vote itself passed by just 5 votes. It seems totally unfathomable that a successor to Attlee was commoditising higher education? On the slow revolution towards social and economic justice this has to be one of the biggest backward steps. The long-term effect of this policy will leave UK citizens in a position of high debt and society lacking advanced knowledge and social mobility. This is the legacy for the under 30's in the UK. Being charged through the nose to better themselves by a Labour government. Why would any graduate in their right minds vote Labour ever again?

Tony Blair faced similar protests over the fox hunting ban. Labour had long promised to ban the sport. However as Blair later acknowledged the ban, which was more about regulation of cruelty, was divisive and alienated many parts of the rural community. The Hunting Act (2004) banned the use of hunting with hounds, and the controversial bill again caused large protests. However it is interesting to note that the bill was not passed through the House of Lords and was only made law because The Parliament Act was used, which allows the House of Commons to push through new legislation regardless of the House of Lords. It is often seen as a poor example of where The Parliament Act is used. In reality, fox hunting continues to thrive today, and much of the controversy over the issue has died down. Although the ban is not liked by pro or anti fox hunters the Conservatives made an election pledge to overturn the ban and it is likely that the first Conservative majority government will do this. The Labour Party membership is genuinely divided over this issue. Many see the sport as cruel whilst others became frustrated over the "class warfare" feel of the legislation. By pushing this through Parliament some wondered if this made one side look as bad as the other. In addition the bill took seven hundred hours to take through Parliament whilst the Iraq war was debated for just seven. Defence Secretary Geoff Hoon cited not losing the element of surprise as the reason. Pure satire.

The social reform agenda took further shape between 2001 & 2007. Tony Blair became more convinced that outcomes were more important than the manner in which they were delivered and funded by privatising of service delivery. This went to the heart of the New Labour agenda. As in the previous parliament, the government focussed on education and health. Tony Blair introduced foundation hospitals, which allowed top ranking hospitals to break free from local control, enabling them to self-govern and buy in some services themselves; they would have the ability to borrow against their own assets. In a similar vein, academy schools allowed under performing schools to cede from local authorities, often backed by the private sector or philanthropists. The schools which became known as academies, would be given freedom over the curriculum, the way they were run and the purchasing of services. Many academies were sponsored by organisations who built new buildings and bought the students new uniforms, and there was to be an expansion of this policy under the Conservatives. By late 2005, 400 schools free from local authority control were in place.

When it came to social reform, Tony Blair found Parliament and the Civil Service a problem, and in 1999 he launched a thinly veiled attack, accusing the Old School Tie brigade of officials of holding him back: *These forces of conservatism chain us not only to an out-dated view of our people's potential but of our nation's potential. What threatens the nation-state today is not change, but the refusal to change in a world opening up, becoming ever more interdependent. The old air of superiority based on past glory must give way to the ambition to succeed".*[152] But well known BBC historian Professor Ian Kershaw, when evaluating Blair's premiership in 2007, was not surprised. *"In reality, the deep-seated structural problems of the health system, education, transport, crime, juvenile disorder, urban decay, and inner-city deprivation were never going to be overcome, whatever the colour of the government, within a decade or so."*[153]

Did Blair get bored of public sector reform and find it too difficult to execute via the traditional methods of Parliament and the Civil Service? There is an argument that this was the case. As mentioned previously, Frank Dobson was ditched as Health Secretary and his replacement, Alan Milburn launched the government down the PFI route, fighting for Foundation Hospitals which would be free from central control. In addition he got rid of his Education Secretary Estelle Morris in order to pursue the academy school system. You will struggle very hard to find Labour Party members who are teachers that ever supported this approach to school organisation and governance. Blair's efforts to do things the accepted way may have resulted from the only ministerial office he ever held was that of Prime Minister, therefore he was not party to how things worked in Whitehall, or practised in the art of horse trading around the cabinet table, in cabinet committees, or indeed in Parliament.

No matter how thoroughly you analyse New Labour, you can only come to the conclusion that for all the work done domestically to reform the welfare state and develop economic growth, the project will always be over shadowed by the spectre of armed conflict. New Labour promised an ethical dimension to its foreign policy, to no longer stand idly by watching when humanitarian crises were occurring. This chapter will now look at the impact of 9/11 and then Iraq and Kosovo.

Tony Blair's greatest overseas triumph came in 1999 when he finally persuaded US President Bill Clinton that affirmative action, which meant a military commitment, was the only option left to protect the people of Kosovo from the aggression on offer from their neighbours in the Balkans, Serbia led by the belligerent Slobodan Milošević. The civil war in the Balkans had

---

152 *Speech by Tony Blair in September 1999- available from http://news.bbc.co.uk/1/hi/uk_politics/460009.stm*

153 *How will History judge Blair? Produced by BBC from http://news.bbc.co.uk/1/hi/uk_politics/6636091. stm in June 2007*

taken many twists and turns since Yugoslavia had started to break up in bitter religious and political acrimony in 1991. Bosnia had become a byword for tit for tat sectarian massacres culminating in the 1995 slaughter of some 8,000 Bosnian men and boys by Serb backed militia in the town of Sbrenica. The UN was largely paralysed by the inaction of the permanent Security Council members including the UK and America, the latter still scarred by the memories of Vietnam. Major and his Foreign Secretary Malcolm Rifkind were beset by internal battles over Europe and, presiding over a wafer thin Commons majority, Major chose the path of least resistance, doing nothing controversial or that would involve UK troops in anything other than peacekeeping. Even then troops were instructed to withdraw and not return or open fire, no matter who the aggressors were.

Tony Blair took a totally different view to Major; he believed that it was in the interests of the democracies to intervene where human rights were under threat. Speaking in 1999 he set out his ideas in possibly the most important speech a UK Prime Minister has given on foreign policy since Winston Churchill. His Chicago speech began, *"We cannot turn our backs on conflicts and the violation of human rights within other countries if we want still to be secure".*[154]

He went on to put meat on the bones of what this actually meant going into a new century:

"We need to focus in a serious and sustained way on the principles of the doctrine of international community and on the institutions that deliver them. We have to establish a new framework. If we can establish and spread the values of liberty, the rule of law, human rights and an open society then that is in our national interests. The spread of our values makes us safer. Noninterference has long been considered an important principle of international order [but] on the basis of a practical assessment of the situation, are there military operations we can sensibly and prudently undertake?"[155]

This was a game-changing view for the UK, and the western powers' role in international affairs, basically making the case for "liberal intervention" in the cause of spreading the idea that the democratic system of government was the most effective way of organising nation states right across the world. Whilst

154 *Tony Blair Chicago Speech, Reported here by PBS http://www.pbs.org/newshour/bb/internationaljan-june99-blair_doctrine4-23/ 2009*

155 *Tony Blair Chicago Speech, Reported here by PBS http://www.pbs.org/newshour/bb/internationaljan-june99-blair_doctrine4-23/ 2009*

recognising the role of the UN, Blair called for *"A reconsideration of the role, workings and decision-making process of the UN, and in particular the UN Security Council"*[156] which puts into context his willingness to go to war in Iraq without a specific UN mandate. Had he decided that the UN was useful for rubber stamping interventions and helping to clear up the mess, but if the Security Council refused to ratify future plans, and then it would be acceptable to ignore their opinion. Whichever way the speech is viewed, Blair had prepared the ground in his own mind that the UN had little to offer when it came to making crunch decisions. Kosovo may have sealed Blair's view. Operations which began with air strikes against Serb strategic targets had to be ratified by NATO's political structures as Russia, for historical reasons, could not be put in the position of having to decide to support action against Serbia, therefore a policy of Russia giving tacit permission to NATO was pursued and the UN was side-lined. NATO operations were a success and by summer 1999 the Serbs had withdrawn from the region leaving NATO, now under UN blessing, to move in and help reconstruct the battered area and protect them from further Serb aggression. Blair had led, and for once the USA was happy to support the UK taking the lead politically to help solve a major crisis.

Then came 9/11 and Blair told the Labour Party Conference that fateful September, *"This is a moment to seize. The Kaleidoscope has been shaken. The pieces are in flux. Soon they will settle again. Before they do, let us re-order this world around us."*[157] In hindsight there are two interpretations that you can put on this statement and what the Prime Minister really meant. One school of thought says that Tony Blair saw the aftermath of 9/11 as a real opportunity to tackle issues surrounding world poverty, and he clearly made the link between grievances in the Middle East, Asia and Africa as having a real impact on why a sizeable number of people held serious grudges against the west. Blair and Brown delivered regarding overseas aid and development, leading the way on debt cancellation as in 2004 Brown accepted the principle that the current arrangements were inadequate to help developing nations get on their feet. The 2005 G8 Gleneagles Summit in Scotland proved that the Blair/ Brown feud had been put on hold when it came to development due to both men's passion to succeed. Buoyed by the momentum generated by the Live8 global music festival, which was allied to the Make Poverty History Campaign, Blair put the squeeze on his G8 colleagues and they signed up to an unprecedented programme of

156 *Tony Blair Chicago Speech, Reported here by PBS http://www.pbs.org/newshour/bb/international-jan-june99-blair_doctrine4-23/ 2009*

157 *Tony Blair Speech from 2001 Labour Party Conference*

doubling aid for development to $50 billion by 2010, the lion's share which would go to Africa. Blair had changed the zeitgeist in the UK regarding overseas aid.

However there is a darker and more cynical interpretation regarding Blair's *"re ordering"* statement. In this scenario we see Blair agreeing with US President George Bush that 9/11 provided an opportunity to deal with Iraq. Saddam had nothing to do with 9/11, but right away the US government, although not directly linking Saddam with what unfolded on 9/11, did nothing to stop talk of such a link and by 2003 a Gallup opinion poll revealed that 70% of those Americans questioned believed the Iraqi dictator had a role in the attacks. Bush compounded matters by stating in 2003:

"For America, there will be no going back to the era before 11 September 2001. We are fighting that enemy in Iraq and Afghanistan today so that we do not meet him again on our own streets, in our own cities."[158]

Thus the whole thrust of US Foreign Policy backed by the British government post 9/11 was to get rid of Saddam, control the oil fields and send a clear message that the US was *the* superpower of the 21st century and would intervene no matter where if it served American interests. This led to a fatal yoking of Anglo/ American priorities and committed Tony Blair to the tragedy of Iraq. The only question was how to convince people that Iraq was the right war at the right time. There is considerable dispute about whether or not Tony Blair had given the Americans the green light to invade Iraq prior to the late 2002 resumption of weapons inspections in Iraq, and we will probably never know the truth, but Tony Blair seemed utterly determined to prove the case for war, and in September 2002 he produced an intelligence report which he claimed showed, *"Iraq had sought significant quantities of uranium from Africa",*[159] the implication being that Saddam had serious intent to develop an atomic weapon, and Blair went on to state, *"The document discloses that his military planning allows for some of the WMD to be ready within 45 minutes of an order to use them."*[160] The document was prepared by the UK Joint Intelligence Committee, and sources were not revealed, it was said, to protect identities. It was later uncovered

158 Speech by GW Bush, September 2003- reported by the BBC from http://news.bbc.co.uk/1/hi/world/americas/3088936.stm

159 See 'September dossier' and also 'Iraq Dossier' with forwards by T Blair published by The Guardian http://www.theguardian.com/world/2002/sep/24/iraq.speeches

160 Full text of Tony Blair's foreword to the dossier on Iraq published by The Guardian http://www.theguardian.com/world/2002/sep/24/iraq.speeches 2002

that the claims regarding Saddam's willingness to procure uranium were based on a PhD study which was ten years old.

The 45-minute accusation became hotly contested, resulting in BBC radio reporter Andrew Gilligan accusing Number Ten press secretary Alastair Campbell of *"sexing up"* the document to make the case for war incontrovertible.[161] Gilligan claimed he had this information from a source very close to the intelligence community. The finger was pointed at Dr. David Kelly, who took his own life as a result of the media circus that ensued. Guardian journalist Andrew Sparrow laid the claim in 2009 that the 45-minute statement came from *"a taxi driver on the Iraqi-Jordanian border, who had remembered an overheard conversation in the back of his cab a full two years earlier"*.[162] The subsequent Hutton inquiry largely exonerated the government over the incident, but it tarnished the reputation of the government and put Alistair Campbell, Number 10 Communications director into the public spotlight and under huge personal pressure, arguably more than any civil servant, or private citizen should have to endure. The inquiry found that some words were changed to make the strongest possible case for war but that Gilligan's claims were "unfounded." Campbell was exonerated by Hutton report. The facts remain that no weapons of mass destruction, or materials for nuclear weapons were ever found in Iraq, and that Saddam's regime, for self-preservation purposes had complied fully with UN weapons inspectors led by Dr. Hans Blix, thus vindicating the position of France on the UN Security Council when they went on record saying they would veto any resolution presented after February 2003 calling for an invasion.

Iraq. The four letter word that will forever haunt Tony Blair. There is no running away by anybody connected with the Labour Party from the fact that an apocalyptic slaughter of the innocents occurred in Iraq both under the Saddam regime and in the subsequent conflict. Tony Blair's "end" in Iraq is a laudable, one for all internationally minded Socialists: the ousting from power of Saddam Hussein, a man who persecuted his own people, especially Kurds.

It is the use of language that we find interesting about Tony Blair's Iraq policy. Senior Guardian journalist Bernard Jenkin described Iraq as *"Blair's*

---

161 *Transcript of Radio 4, Today Programme where Andrew Gilligan stated quote published by The Guardian http://www.theguardian.com/media/2003/jul/09/Iraqandthemedia.bbc*

162 *45-minute WMD claim 'may have come from an Iraqi taxi driver Sparrow A, Published by The Guardian accessed from http://www.theguardian.com/politics/2009/dec/08/45-minutes-wmd-taxi-driver 2009*

folly".[163] In June 2011 Gordon Brown was quoted as saying Iraq was a *"mistake"* that he wanted to undo during his Premiership, and Head of the Army during the invasion Sir Richard Dannett called Blair's approach *"naive".[164]* Finally in July 2010 ex Foreign Secretary David Miliband told the Labour Party, *"it is time to move on"[165]* from the Iraq issue. These are sickeningly mendacious banalities that belie the inhuman and relentless suffering of a whole nation. They totally trivialise the cruelty inflicted by the Saddam regime, which was then compounded by a series of sanctions, crippling the population and not the ruling elite who continued unscathed until the 2003 invasion. The price of Saddam's despotism and the western powers' overthrow of the regime was paid by the Iraqi people. By 2002 Iraq was on its knees, the tenth richest country on the planet crippled by what UN Deputy General Secretary Denis Halliday described as "genocidal" sanctions which had cost Iraq a staggering half a million dead children in an eye watering total of 1.5 million deaths since 1991, a figure accepted by the UN as "robust".

New Labour came to power in the hiatus between the end of the Cold War and the upsurge in violence resulting from the new terrorism coming out of the Middle East and parts of Asia. The main international issues were the Balkans civil war, and containment of Saddam Hussein who many, including those on the left, suspected of developing weapons of mass destruction (WMD), either via biological and chemical weapons, or the doomsday scenario of nuclear devices. John Major had proved himself to be the victim of vacillation and indecisiveness when it came to foreign policy. Once the oil fields of Kuwait had been secured during the First Gulf War (1991), Major failed to press US President George H.W. Bush to topple Saddam in order to save the Marsh Arabs and the Kurds. Later in 1995 the British government did the bare minimum regarding the genocide unfolding in Bosnia, a stunning dereliction of duty from a member of the UN Security Council, a leading NATO power and a country with a proud record of standing up to Fascism in Europe. Labour's 1997 Manifesto promised to *"put Human Rights at the heart of Foreign Policy"*, and Robin Cook's first major speech as Foreign Secretary set out clearly what this would mean in practice. On

163 *Blair's folly has left Iraq in chaos Jenkin B, Published in The guardian http://www.theguardian.com/ politics/2003/may/28/society.iraq 28th May 2003*

164 *U.K. Army Boss Wants Troops Out Of Iraq ALFONSO SERRANO Reported by CBS News (USA) http://www.cbsnews.com/news/uk-army-boss-wants-troops-out-of-iraq/ 2006*

165 *David Miliband: Time to move on from Iraq D Batty Published in the Guardian http://www. theguardian.com/politics/2010/may/22/david-miliband-iraq-war-labour-leadership 22nd May 2010*

12th May 1997, less than a fortnight after taking power, Cook stood up in the forebodingly traditional Locano Room in the Foreign Office and stated the clear and ambitious aim that Labour's foreign policy would *"contain an ethical dimension"*.[166] A generation of hindsight on this issue has resulted in Labour being hoisted by its own petard when being judged by these criteria during Blair's stay in Number Ten.

How would Robin Cook start to implement the "Ethical Dimension"? Regarding the arms industry Cook quickly realised that 150,000 UK jobs were directly linked to the weapons trade. By February 2003 it had become crystal clear to everyone that it was only a matter of timing, and it was "when", not "if" the US-led invasion of Iraq began. 15th February saw the biggest ever protest march in British history take place. One million people took to the streets of London, but nothing would deter Tony Blair from doing what he thought was the right course of action for the UK. Blair gambled on the presence of WMD, and lost. If even one phial of chemical weapons had been found then Tony Blair would have been vindicated. The damage done to the Labour Party by Iraq stemmed from the WMD gamble. The voters felt Blair would say or do anything to bolster his arguments politically, leading to a cynical view of him to develop, which in turn rubbed off on the Party as a whole.

When it turned out that the US had used Glasgow Airport as a stopover for transporting bombs to Israel without seeking Blair's approval, BBC Political Editor Nick Robinson coined the phrase the *"poodle factor"*[167] surrounding the relationship between Blair and Bush. At the G8 Summit in St. Petersburg on July 17th, Robinson's quip came to pass with a vengeance. At the end of the morning session, when all the microphones were meant to be turned off, Blair approached Bush, whose greeting was, "*Yo, Blair!*" There was further evidence that the "war on terror" and the UK's involvement with this US policy affected other areas of policy. The policy was used as a reason to erode civil liberties of the UK population, this backed up with Tony Blair's desires to capture the law and order agenda from the Conservatives. During this period Home Secretary David Blunkett tried to introduce the concept of ID cards and subsequent Home Secretaries looked at long-term detention for terror suspects, including 90 days, which caused the government to lose a Commons vote. Under New Labour, there was

---

166 *Robin Cook Speech from May 1997 Published in That Guardian http://www.theguardian.com/ world/1997/may/12/indonesia.ethicalforeignpolicy*

167 *Original Nick Robinson blog no longer available on BBC Website*

a perception of authoritarianism, which in part was caused by stop and search powers and the increase in the number of CCTV cameras. Whilst in September 2011 when documents were found in the wake of the fall of Libyan dictator Mummar Gaddafi which showed that the Labour government of Tony Blair had sent people who were suspects in the so called "war on terror" back to Tripoli in the knowledge that they would be tortured and the information passed back to MI6. The security service's former head, Sir Richard Dearlove said, *"It has always been pretty clear that our governments in the UK have accepted that danger and difficulty and have given political clearance for that sort of co-operation."*[168]

The 9/11 terrorist attacks on America thrust Afghanistan right back onto the centre stage of world politics. Islamic extremists had taken full advantage of the chaos and power vacuum in the country following the withdrawal of Soviet troops in 1989. The USSR had invaded in 1979, at first to support a communist puppet government doing as they liked to the Afghans with far superior technology and weaponry. But soon, with the efforts of Texan politician and Democrat Charlie Wilson and the CIA (note, not the Republican White House) they financed and covertly armed the Mujahedeen. The result was a bloody war that killed 15,000 USSR troops and effectively ended the cold war. For the Afghans tribal structures had broken and education and other infrastructures where non-existent. Life expectancy plummeted amongst men especially during the conflict, making the sight of a man over 35 a rare thing. Rather than the west rebuilding the country, they turned their back, leaving a huge void which was filled by Islamic extremism.

Osama Bin Laden, a Saudi with connections to Arab royalty had been part of the CIA funded Mujahedeen resistance to the Soviet occupation of Afghanistan. Within the umbrella of the fighters was a strain of Muslim fundamentalism, which evolved in to the Taliban. Inspired by Sharia law, the movement took governmental power in the country during 1996 and enacted a brutal regime that perpetrated numerous crimes against the people as well as everyday oppression of women. The west again, turned a blind eye.

When 9/11 happened the effect on the US psyche was totally shattering. Never in the modern era had Americans died on the mainland of the US due to a violent act planned and executed by foreigners. Tony Blair expressed the shock of Britain who lost 67 citizens in the attacks,

168 Former MI6 chief denies UK and Libya were too close Reported by BBC http://www.bbc.co.uk/news/ uk-14935403 2011

"This is not a battle between the United States of America and terrorism but between the free and democratic world and terrorism. We therefore here in Britain stand shoulder to shoulder with our American friends in this hour of tragedy and we like them will not rest until this evil is driven from our world."[169]

Thus the UK was bound inextricably with what followed. The decision to take out the Taliban regime was initially popular in the UK. According to research by the Institute of Democracy and Conflict resolution published in 2011, 65% of the UK public backed Blair's 2001 decision to mobilise UK forces to fight in Afghanistan.[170] However by the tenth anniversary of the conflict the Guardian quoted up to 75% of respondents as wanting UK troops disengaging with 53% supporting the idea of an immediate withdrawal.[171]

March 2014 saw the 448th UK soldier die in Afghanistan. This compared to the 179 casualties suffered by British forces in Iraq. What was more disturbing was that one in six NATO casualties were caused by so called "green on blue" attacks where Afghan recruits turned on their coalition colleagues. This totally compromised the aims of the UK government, which was to train Afghan forces to take over security when most of the foreign combat troops were set to be withdrawn by 2015. The coalition forces had suffered 3,247 deaths by March 2014 but this paled into insignificance when compared to the number of Afghans who had perished since Operation Enduring Freedom had been launched with UN authority in 2001. 2,959 civilians had been killed with 5,656 injured in 2014 alone.[172] The repeated use of drone strikes was a recognition that rule of law of the corrupt regime led President Hamid Karzi did not extend to large parts of the country.

The Afghan war has produced unbearable suffering on all sides, and from a UK point of view the relentless death toll has been exacerbated by the fact that since 2006 no government minister has really given a coherent and be-

169 *Tony Blair Speech Reported by BBC http://news.bbc.co.uk/1/hi/uk_politics/1538551.stm*

170 *The Structure, Causes, and Consequences of Foreign Policy Attitudes: A Cross-National Analysis of Representative Democracies by Thomas Scotow 3rd November 2013 http://www.esrc.ac.uk/my-esrc/grants/RES-061-25-0405/outputs/read/d10edee1-bf3b-405e-87d8-bf76443a1408*

171 *Guardian 12th September 2012 Western support for Afghanistan war collapsing, survey shows. http://www.theguardian.com/world/2012/sep/12/western-support-afghanistan-war-collapsing*

172 *Figures for war are not recorded, these figures suggest 2013 estimates. Afghan civilian deaths up in 2013 as war intensifies: U.N. Reported by Reuters http://www.reuters.com/article/2014/02/08/us-afghanistan-casualties-idUSBREA1706D20140208 2014*

lievable answer to the questions, why are we in Afghanistan and what is the end game? Whilst it could be argued that the war started as an essential and ethical response to terror and overseas oppression, the same old Afghan story appears. No foreign power has ever prevailed there, and this has left soldiers and politicians over the last 150 years wondering what they doing intervening in such a difficult country.

This is not a state that works on recognisable lines, there are no high principles surrounding equality, economics or democracy like in the west. If the western powers in Afghanistan were under any illusions that they would be able to leave behind a stable and peaceful democracy, they were sorely mistaken. The country was an economic basket case. Professor Zaman Stanizai, an Afghan academic based in California told the Huffington Post in March 2014 that, *"only 10% of its GDP of $1 billion comes from legitimate economic activity; of the remainder, 30% comes from the underground narcotics trade and 60% from foreign aid."*[173] Security costs alone amount to $4 billion a year and with no independent income stream it seems obvious that Afghanistan is ripe for the Taliban to come back once the US-led forces leave by the end of 2014 as Barack Obama had promised.

Afghanistan has huge economic potential with an estimated (by Prof. Stanizai and the BBC in June 2010) $3 trillion in mineral resources that the country is sitting on. But the UK can't stay and wait; the fatality cost is too much alone. There has been talk of a UN sponsored security provided by a coalition not of western occupying powers, but manned by fellow Islamic nations. The potential threat of terror and narcotics, (Charity Drugscope predicts 90% of the heroin circulating in the UK comes from Afghanistan),[174] means that there is self interest in being part of future activities. It simply is the moral thing to do.

Tony Blair - A Conclusion

In the overall context of the book we have to find that New Labour played its part in the slow revolution. But ultimately, as the Party of Hardie and At-

---

173 *Can We Afford Another Failed State in Afghanistan? Beyond the 2014 Drawdown Zaman Stanizai Huffington Post* http://www.huffingtonpost.com/zaman-stanizai/can-we-afford-another-fai_b_4863736.html 2014

174 *Recourse from Drugs Charity DrugScope* http://www.drugscope.org.uk/Resources/Drugscope/Documents/PDF/Publications/Media_guide_revised.pdf

tlee, how could it not? As we have examined, the election of Thatcher and neo-liberalism left Britain with the same old British problems. High unemployment, low wages, under-employment and rising inequality. Everything good that the Conservatives did between 1945 and 1975 by going along with consensus politics has been wiped away. The Tories turned the clock back for Britain with two exceptions. Firstly, the collective aspirations provided by the welfare state had raised the standard of living for all between 1945 and 1979, and secondly, the popularity of credit amongst consumers, which allowed us to keep high standards of living through high amounts of debt. Had there been no technological capitalism and no welfare state, Britain under Thatcher would have been in the dark ages.

This return to neo-liberalism would have made any politician who craved social justice a success in late 1990s. Neo-liberalism had left Britain on its knees and all Blair had to do was spend on the welfare state. But did Blair's policy of triangulation work? Ultimately, we have to argue, given the test of time that the answer is no. Blair accepted neo-liberalism and private interests in the public sector. The post Thatcher consensus came to involve allowing capitalism and free markets to get on with business in an unregulated manner, which ultimately resulted in the 2008 financial crash. In Britain that meant throwing the doors open to global economic markets through the EU. It meant UK firms going head to head with cheap labour foreign economies, it meant the acceptance of mass immigration and ultimately it meant the full acceptance of free trade neo liberalism. This lack of economic planning, meant no industrial strategy for Britain and an over reliance on the banking and services sector. The legacy of this policy, which started under Thatcher, is that Britain has been left with a narrow un-diverse economy that doesn't really serve the majority national interests.

New Labour accepted the end of collective responsibility by ending clause 4. By doing this it said that there is now no role for public ownership and therefore there is no reason for it. Markets will always work better and therefore each person in this economy is on their own. There will be no government aim to raise the lot of everyone. New Labour was highly successful in implementing equality legislation, but ensuring equality of opportunity, as important as that is, isn't the same as a government creating long term prosperity for everyone. In the long term, Clause Four and the continuation of the utilities being in private hands was one of the biggest mistakes of both Conservatives and Labour. This policy is a central plank of neo-liberalism and continues today through the privatisation of the Post

Office. It has seen fuel prices go through the roof. This is where Labour should have acted. It was also neo-liberal economic policy that caused the 2008 financial crash and subsequent pseudo depression, a crash where the taxpayer had to bail out the unregulated banks. Once again the monolith banks and energy companies have one thing in common, they don't act in the national interest to provide a vital service, they are moneymaking machines. They are now so big and complicated that politicians can't control them or even understand them. Ultimately the majority of our lazy and moribund MP's can't be bothered to try. It's just too much hassle and may result in them not getting a ticket for the gravy train.

New Labour created a new political position. Allowing capitalism to get on and do its worst but making sure the welfare state picks up the pieces. Ultimately, this will be the position that Liberal Democrats end up in. It is a similar position to what the EU also advocates, trying to keep free market capital and the socially minded happy. But it hasn't worked, ultimately what we have created is a UK where wages are so low for so many that the government has to pick up the tab through tax credits, where unemployment is so high that the government picks up the bill through benefits, where so many have been out of work so long they become idle. New Labour should have shored up Britain's economic position.

But the real test of how New Labour changed the country has come in light of the coalition. Rather than New Labour shore up the position of the slow revolution they merely treaded water, allowing so many of the good things they did to be undone by the coalition. Take for example private interests in schools and hospitals. A process started under New Labour, taken to the extreme under the subsequent coalition government. This is the New Labour position taken advantage of by neo-liberal politicians. The funny thing is, New Labour branded itself as new ideas, but ultimately it's the same old stories, liberal politicians have no interest in the pursuit of social or economic justice, they believe that the market will fix all and therefore the welfare state is to be commoditised.

The New Labour political position failed. Labour now has to wake up and address the challenges facing the UK post financial crash and come up with solutions for them. This book argues that the pursuit of social and economic justice is the way forward. Labour itself is having this debate, quietly there is acceptance that the desire to use markets at every turn was wrong and that an industrial policy should be Labour's top priority. This recently came to a head with a large number of parliamentary candidates publicly

147

calling for public ownership of the rail network.

The biggest sign was that Blair didn't stick around to defend his policies. After stepping down as Prime Minister he called a by-election. Swanning off around the world to take a number of high paid positions in business. He could have stayed on as an MP and taken a future role, given he is now seen as such a foreign policy expert. This is maybe why Blair is being judged badly.

Ultimately, Blair disappointed many in the UK and especially the Labour Party. There are arguably three areas where Blair really let himself, his party and the country down, which overshadow a decade of almost unparalleled achievement. Firstly, it must be argued that in the eyes of Labour members, Blair failed to meet the full potential to bring the social changed he promised in 1997. Whilst great change and improvement was achieved, ultimately by failing to undo the reforms of Thatcher, Blair left a legacy that the UK struggles with to this day. His failure was to turn away from Thatcherism, this comes partly in financial liberalism, which it could be argued was the responsibility of Gordon Brown and will be handled in the next chapter. But Blair failed to take on the business cartels in finance and energy supply created by privatisation under Thatcher. Worse still, Blair used the market to finance and run large parts of the public sector citing reasons such as efficiency and risk. Secondly, whilst it could be argued that Blair's foreign policy conquests where noble and moral, there is little or no doubt that Blair's entry into Iraq was overzealous and close alignment to the USA weakened Britain's standing in international affairs. Blair also placed the UK in a perilous position of trying to make the UK the moral authority of the world, when really it could be argued the UK is anything but in the wake of Iraq. Finally, and probably saddest of all, Blair became associated with the dishonesty of politicians. Partly this was because of the use of spin, the media practice, which in a country of right wing press has to be used for Labour to simply get a fair hearing in the press. But more so because of the scandal that overshadowed his final days in office. The Cash for Honours inquiry. You can read numerous accounts of this scandal in memoirs, including Blair's. Eventually it was found there was no case to answer and it had been largely driven by media interest and political infighting.

The 2005-2010 parliament was broken in two by a change of leader, when Tony Blair left office in June 2007, with a reduced majority of 66 he achieved in 2005. His final two years where dominated by the presidency of the European Union and the Olympic Games bid, which was followed by the 7/7 bombings. Britain's presidency of the EU was over shadowed with the spectre of further European integration through the proposed and defeated European constitution. These proposals were widely rejected, but ultimately became the Lisbon Treaty which set the frame for the debates on the EU we see today. However, it was the week of the 7th July 2005 which was the busiest, best and worst of Blair's 10 years in office. The week started positively with the announcement of the Olympic bid in Singapore. The Olympic governing body had over a hundred delegates, many of whom where personally visited by the Prime Minister with Cherie Blair who at the time was given little or no credit for almost single handedly winning the votes needed. The Olympic bid was led by former athlete and Tory MP, Sebastian Coe, who ran a slick campaign focusing on the long-term legacy for London. Hours later Tony Blair was back in Britain and hosting the G8 summit in Gleneagles, Scotland.

Blair's aims for the G8 were two fold. The first was to bring a new climate change deal together to replace the 1997 Kyoto agreement. Kyoto had been one of Labour's earliest big achievements in government, pulling an un-likely agreement together due to the input of Deputy Prime Minister John Prescott, and it had committed all nations to reduce damaging emissions, especially $CO2$. The second aim of Gleneagles was to bring together a new package of aid and debt relief for African nations. Blair had been optimis-tic in bringing the deals together but by early on the morning of July 7th it looked as though the agreements, if any, would only be small. However at 8.50am the tragic news came through that London had been attacked after three British born suicide bombers entered the London transport system and detonated explosives. At 9:47 a fourth bomb was detonated on a bus in Tavistock Square. The explosions killed 52 commuters that morning and injured hundreds of others. Britain was left in a state of shock and there opened up a new debate as to whether Britain should be involved in armed conflicts in Iraq and Afghanistan. Blair left the summit and returned to London. The events, unfolding on TV in front of the world leaders he had left behind, gave them a new focus on the aims of the G8 summit. On July 8th an agreement was signed to begin the process of negotiations to reduce emissions, including the United States and China who had been against such talks and a new deal for Africa was announced, which in-cluded $50billion in aid to developing nations. 50% of this went to Africa to enable universal access to HIV treatment in Africa by 2010, the remov-al of trade tariffs, debt relief and the beginning of the 0.7% commitment whereby developed nations pledge 0.7% of their government spending to developing nations, a hugely important policy which still stands to this day. Never had a set of polarised events signified Blair's time as premier: great social achievement and continued conflict, which it could be argued resulted from earlier foreign policy decisions.

Chapter 9 - The Politics of the Credit Crunch

The rise of Gordan Brown how he failed to identify decline

The credit crunch will be one of those punctuation marks in modern history. Since 1979 the UK had been sleep walking towards the banking crisis and the lack of reforms that have taken place since have created huge inequality in the UK. The credit crunch and ensuing recession will prove that neo-liberalism, or Thatcherism does not have the answers when running the UK economy. We believe that this punctuation mark could well be the start of a slow move toward a more socially responsible way of running the UK economy, an economy that provides jobs, fair prices, a rejection of speculation which has caused inflation in fuel and house prices, and social mobility. This chapter will look at the greater role that Gordon Brown played in government as Chancellor of the Exchequer under Tony Blair, and then what he did or did not do as Prime Minister. There is an argument that Brown failed to prepare for Downing Street by not making the intellectual journey made by both Mrs Thatcher and Mr Blair before him. Unlike Blair and Thatcher, Brown failed to spot and articulate the challenges facing Britain, something that David Cameron did, allowing him to remove Labour from office in the 2010 General Election. We believe that Gordon Brown will be vindicated by history and whilst at the time the press accused him of being the "*Worst Prime Minister in history*", many a journalist would now privately admit he has already lost that title.

Brown had the interests of both Britain and the Labour Party at heart; he was unfairly portrayed in the media as a man out of touch. Although prone to the odd media gaffe, and doubtless made mistakes by the time he left office, he is now seen as a family man who honestly gave of his best, and history is already proving his decisions made during the financial crash were the correct ones. Let us remember that Gordon Brown inherited an unpopular Labour Party and his first days in office were plagued by floods, terror attacks and the first inklings of financial meltdown. Gordon Brown was like a war Prime Minister from day one, with Britain fighting on two fronts and by this point occupation of Iraq was the most likely catalyst for the continuation of tensions whilst the reality that the Afghanistan conflict may be eternal was settling in the psyche of the British people and servicemen. Others would argue that Brown's premiership was one of the most painful in Labour Party history. The evidence for this includes the 2009 European election results as well as numerous poll rating deficits, by-election defeats and ultimately the 2010 general election, which was one of the Labour Party's worst defeats since the introduction of universal suffrage.

Gordon Brown

You cannot underestimate the importance of the will of the Prime Minister of the day in how the country is run. From 1994 to 2007 Gordon Brown was a competitive rival to Tony Blair. During this period Brown made the Treasury the power centre of the British government. He used a system of bargaining with other secretaries of state, allowing him to set the policy agenda in return for cash. Blair gave Brown unparalleled power and influence in his role as Chancellor. He was supported in this by a network of Labour MPs known simply as *Brownites*. This group of individuals which included Ed Balls and Tom Watson that became revered around the Westminster village as the internal opposition to the Tony Blair project. The Brownites had one aim, to gain full control of the Labour Party and enter Number 10.

However when in 2007 Gordon Brown became Prime Minister, from the outside it appeared that he was unwilling to cooperate or accept the healthy challenge and competition of political rivals such as David Miliband, despite Brown playing the role of competitive rival from as far back as 1994. This along with other decisions such as not calling an election in 2007 gave the impression that Brown put his own grasp of power ahead of the interests of the Labour Party and the UK and for some it quickly became too much. Support for Labour, which was already patchy following Tony Blair's tenure started to dwindle as a separation between grass roots party activists and the Labour Party in Westminster developed.

In chapter 7 we explored the idea that Tony Blair had put considerable thought into the political direction of Britain and New Labour. This chapter will argue that Gordon Brown failed to identify a vision for Britain and

Labour, failed to identify his own brand of politics and failed to identify the contemporary challenges facing Britain in 2007. It's been noted at length that Gordon Brown was one of the most intelligent Prime Ministers this country has ever had. He was one of the youngest graduates at the University of Edinburgh and wrote a Ph.D. on the history of the Labour Party. However, with all this intellect why did Gordon Brown fail to identify his vision?

Part of this problem could be the confused political ideology of Gordon Brown, which over his lifetime has taken many twists and turns. University of Hull academic Dr Simon Lee described his eventual political philosophy as *the British Way*.[175] The British way was an attempt to put clear ground between the prior reform agendas of Thatcher and Blair, specifically an attempt to move away from the governance of Tony Blair's third way. On the day Brown became Prime Minister he said,

"This will be a new government with new priorities. If we realise our potential Britain can be the great global success story. I have heard the need for change in our NHS, schools and change in affordable house and to extend the British way of life, this cannot be achieved with the old politics."[176]

Lee notes that Brown abandoned the socialist routes of the Scottish Labour Party in favour of liberalism inspired by Adam Smith and the Scottish Enlightenment,[177] and that Brown moved from supply side socialism to supply side liberalism. Like Blair, Brown was inspired by the 1992 Clinton victory. He identified that Clinton had won the battle of ideas, rather than detailing policy as well as a focus on the global economy[178]. *"From now on Brown's political philosophy would increasingly adopt a neo-liberal perspective on globalisation, with its advocacy of market liberalisation and deregulation."[179]* With this chopping and changing it's of little surprise that Gordon Brown didn't spend his time prior to entering Downing Street attempting to articulate a vision, and this sets him apart from Thatcher and Blair. Had he spent time identifying this vision he may well have spotted the weakness that caused the economy and the banking system to blow up in such spectacular style. It is likely he would have recognised the economic decline Britain was facing: he could have noted that the personal

175 Boom *and Bust S Lee Published by Oneworld Publications 2009*

176 *Brown is UKs News Prime Minister Reported by BBC* http://news.bbc.co.uk/1/hi/6245682.stm 2007

177 Boom *and Bust S Lee Published by Oneworld Publications 2009*

178 Boom *and Bust S Lee Published by Oneworld Publications 2009 P28/29*

179 Boom *and Bust S Lee Published by Oneworld Publications 2009 P31*

debt of the British people was too high and that we had an economy that was sustained by an over-inflated housing market and debt.

Gordon Brown's Tragedy

Once Gordon Brown was bounced by Tony Blair and others, including Peter Mandelson, into giving Blair a clear run at the Labour leadership following John Smith's death in 1994, he was always going to be on the back foot, and a follower rather than a leader when it came to policy making. Despite being given unprecedented control of the Treasury, it seemed that Brown's job was to sign the cheques to fund Blair's pet spending projects regarding the NHS, education and social policy. Blair wanted to deliver world-class public services, but without raising taxes or increasing the deficit left by John Major: spend but not tax. How was this to be done? Britain funded the massive expansion in the public sector by involving the private sector in delivery of public services via outsourcing, but one of the biggest means of raising capital, which would not show up on government balance sheets, was the much-vaunted Private Finance Initiative (PFI). Previously if the NHS wanted to build a hospital then the money would have to come from the government's budget. Because the Tories were ideologically opposed to so called big government projects, (*i.e. building hospitals- there were very few NHS building projects during the 1980s.*) By the 1990s the NHS stock of buildings was running into chronic disrepair. Barnet Hospital in North London was notorious due to the very poor state of its buildings, some of which were prefabricated and required patients to be wheeled between departments outside, no matter the weather. It wasn't until 2002 that this hospital was able to get rid of inadequate facilities. PFI was described to the author by a future leading cabinet minister as a way of, "*us getting world class facilities whilst the private sector takes all the risks. Perfect*".[180] But with the introduction of private money came a raft of associated problems. The first hospital that was built by PFI under Blair was the Cumberland Hospital Carlisle, which quickly earned the nickname of "*Rail Track on the Wards*" due to the shoddy plumbing where pipe connectors that had been put in using cheap materials burst and caused chaos. Cardiac patients were drenched in water,[181] raw sewage had to be cleaned from op-

180 Private conversation from 1996 by a Cabinet Minister who Served at various points during the New Labour Project

181 Observer Sunday 8th July 2001 Filthy, gloomy and chaotic The reality of how a new NHS flagship really works http://www.theguardian.com/politics/2001/jul/08/health.labour2001to2005

erating theatres,[182] and worst of all waiting times doubled in 2001, the first year it was open.[183] But Blair was seemingly addicted to PFI, and by 2009 a stunning £68 billion worth of debt equating to half the deficit had been run up.[184] However this didn't appear on the balance sheets due to arrangements with the Treasury as no actual cash had been advanced by the government. Instead hospitals were saddled with crippling repayments which had to be met year on year from their budgets. Carlisle's annual repayment was £11 million per annum.[185]

Gordon Brown's socialism had been forged in his Christian upbringing, which emphasised putting the needs of others before one's own but with a strong work ethic and thrift built in. So how did he justify ideologically this massive binge of borrowing? In addition when it came to forcing students to take out loans to pay for tuition fees, it was rumoured that Brown did not step in until the very last minute to prevent a major backbench revolt in the autumn of 2003 which would have derailed the legislation for top up fees to be introduced. Brown decided in 2001 that the budget allocated to the NHS would double by 2008, to bring per head spending on health into line with other European nations. He paid for it by raising National Insurance contributions, classic redistribution of wealth to follow a policy of social justice where everyone in society would benefit, despite the outcry from small and big business alike.

Why then did the Chancellor not act to dampen down the chronic levels of personal debt taken on by UK citizens under his government? In 2007 a shocking fact emerged. Bank of England figures showed that Britain's consumer debt stood at £1,345bn - higher than the size of Britain's annual output of £1,330bn, according to the Office for National Statistics.[186] The Bank went on to say that 7.7% of households were at serious risk of mortgage default, a high not seen since 1996. This "buy now pay later" culture had grown under New Labour, and the government was setting an appalling example with its reliance on PFI. As Chancellor, Gordon Brown was in a

182 Observer Sunday 8th July 2001 Filthy, gloomy and chaotic The reality of how a new NHS flagship really works http://www.theguardian.com/politics/2001/jul/08/health.labour2001to2005

183 Observer Sunday 8th July 2001 Filthy, gloomy and chaotic The reality of how a new NHS flagship really works http://www.theguardian.com/politics/2001/jul/08/health.labour2001to2005

184 Financial Times 24/2/09 "Projects Seeks Partners" by N. Timms

185 BBC News 22nd September 2011 "How One PFI hospital Covers its Costs" http://www.bbc.co.uk/news/uk-15016986

186 Figures published by BBC http://www.bbc.co.uk/news/business-25152556

position to take action. But it seemed that every time he seemed to be ready to take Blair on, he backed down. Brown's almost febrile resentment of Blair led to a breakdown of their relationship, but Brown seemed if anything, less willing to have a political showdown with the Prime Minister and instead of preparing for the Premiership by setting out his own individual ideological vision, he seemed to have simply indulged in briefing and plotting.

The credit crunch, the causes, the government response and what the Tories would have done

For most people reading newspapers the Business and Finance sections have remained a mystery. They appear to be written in some kind of code very few of us seem to understand so we leave the analysis of what's being said to others who we assume to be far more qualified than us to comment on such matters. That is basically the attitude that allowed the monumental crisis that swept across the financial world in 2008 to happen. Although there have already been many books written on the causes of the credit crunch and the on-going global recession we still face nearly a decade on, this chapter will outline the basic premises of deregulation.

Gordon Brown, like so many other international leaders, subscribed to the policy of financial/banking deregulation. This in itself is no crime or no criticism. Britain was deregulated by Mrs Thatcher and the policy has been continued by Major, Blair, Brown, Cameron and as Deputy Prime Minister, Liberal Democrat Nick Clegg

John Maynard Keynes had influenced the policies of British governments from 1945 onwards, urging a larger state involvement in economic affairs. However by the mid-1970s American born economist Milton Friedman had begun to influence a new generation of right wing politicians such Margaret Thatcher and Sir Keith Joseph. These policies were also adopted by the New Right in America and became associated with politicians such as Richard Nixon, Ronald Reagan and George Bush. In '*Free to Choose*' (1980) Friedman argues that countries with free market dogma enjoy high standards of living, productivity, free trade and low taxes.[187] He warns against state interference, trade barriers and government subsidies, as markets are ultimately more efficient than state planning.

187 Free To Choose *M Freidman published on audio by Blackstone Audiobooks; Unabridged edition 2007*

For the UK, the deregulation that set up the system that crashed in 2007/8 was created under Thatcher. It was known as the 'big bang' and saw the end of the old financially cautious cartels with a replacement of self-regulated monolithic financial institutions we see today. In the UK, our lives now revolve around credit ratings, bond markets and financial trading indexes. These where set free and turned our country into a truly capitalist state, which values profit over social justice.

The credit crunch itself started in the United States and our own policies of liberalisation and lack of regulation compounded the problems. It is said that since the crisis started in 2007 seven million Americans have lost their jobs as well as trillions of dollars in investments, pensions and savings.

Some have argued that it was not deregulation that caused the American crash, but government actions. It was contended that capital investors were able to take advantage of deregulation and following the bursting of the dot. com bubble in the spring of 2000, recession took hold of the USA. In reaction to the recession and the 9/11 attacks, the Federal Reserve reduced interest rates to 1.75% in September 2001 and 1% in early 2003. In addition the Federal Reserve bought securities in financial institutions in an attempt to increase borrowing to stimulate the economy, and this, combined with an influx in foreign investment, caused a boom in the US housing market.[188] These were not the causes of the crash and the subsequent banking crises that took place, but they were the conditions that set the domino effect of the crash in place, and ultimately exposed a western financial sector run with a lack of regulation and rotten practices. The conditions of low interest rates, easy money and deregulation were to prove a lethal cocktail that exposed the world to an almost decade long financial crises that has put millions out of work and caused a huge reduction in living standards for millions of the poorest people in Europe and North America.[189] Deregulation had also allowed Wall Street to compete with other lenders for subprime mortgages (high risk mortgages in the USA), leading to higher prices being paid for more risky loans. The bubble was caused by an increase in credit and an increase in prices in tandem fuelled by low interest rates. With GDP and personal income faltering, the effects of a bursting bubble were enough to derail the global financial market.

Subprime mortgages were being offered off the back of record low interest

188 *The US Financial Crises Bolton B in World Financial Crises edited by Kozmenko S & Tetyana First edition, Business Perspectives 2010 P10/11*

189 *A Crises of Politics, Friedman J not Economics published in Critical Review Vol. 21 No. 2 P129*

rates with fixed introductory terms. However, the increase in interest rates caused an increase in repossessions and defaults, which not only affected the lender but other financial institutions that had interests in the loans though the complexity of securitization. The deregulation of the 1980s had allowed lenders to seek new forms of capital. Securitization allowed banks to borrow to lend, spreading the risk around a number of other financial institutions leading to constant inter-bank lending, to the value of about $1.57 trillion.[190] This risky behaviour worked on the premise that house prices would only increase, making the value of the asset more expensive than the value of the loan, and allowing repayment completion more achievable.

Subprime mortgages were being offered to those who could not afford them, often on a fixed introductory interest rate, and the problem came as the low introductory rates came to an end, when many subprime homeowners simply could not afford the repayments. Eventually, such a vast number of mortgage-holders defaulted that the market crashed and price bubble burst. But why were these subprime mortgages sold to people who could not afford them? Lib Dem Treasury spokesperson Vince Cable had noted at the time warning that "no income, no job and no assets" (or 'NINJA') loans were being given too freely and were not practical in the long term.[191] This financial product should never have been sold.

But why is this important? The answer is that neo-liberalism, deregulation or Thatcherism ultimately believe that free markets are efficient, that they will regulate themselves to avoid risk and they will self-correct in time of error. This leaves the question why didn't the free market stop the toxic products from being sold?

There are two key phrases that we must understand before we continue. A subprime mortgage is a mortgage leant to someone who is at high risk and unlikely to be able to make the repayments if the interest rate on the loan increases. The second key phrase is securitization, which is a practice used in the financial sector, where a firm borrows to lend, but instead of lending from one place, they spread the risk around. However in the credit crunch it became clear that companies had lost track of where they had lent or borrowed money, and what of it could not be repaid; hence the phrase 'toxic debt.'

Subprime mortgages are a financial product based on high risk and securi-

190 *The US Financial Crises in World Financial Crises edited Bolton B by Kozmenko S & Tetyana First edition, Business Perspectives 2010 P28*

191 *The Storm by Cable V First edition, Atlantic books, London P34*

tization. It has been argued that overuse of subprime mortgages led to over-priced houses, and to the bubble bursting. This caused borrowers to fall into negative equity (where the loan secured is worth more than the actual property). The use of subprime mortgages to high-risk borrowers through NINJA loans has caused a reduction in house prices - as well as an increase in repossessions - resulting in a lack of confidence to borrow and spend. Cable noted:

"It was the genius of securitization that was also its central weakness, debt was so widely and skilfully diffused it becomes impossible to trace it, no one really owns the loans so financial institutions struggled to identify how much of their own assets backed the subprime market."[192]

To put it simply, the deregulated financial market, and the actors within it, had failed to properly analyse the risks of securitization. The subprime mortgage market was simply the crash that happened to cause the crisis. If it did not occur, then another crash would still have caused the on-going problems we see today. As banks were left exposed by subprime mortgages, this led to volatility on the markets, and in some part along with short term collateralised loans, to liquidity runs which resulted in the downfall of Bear Stearns, Lehman Brothers and Merrill Lynch.

Poor regulation and dodgy accounting practice allowed these banks to cover their lack of cash reserves to investors. Imperfect information added to the problem. Unregulated markets need to have mechanisms to understand risk; Ghilarucci & Co note, *"Regulators assumed that the financial sector was a lot more competent than it was."[193]* The sophisticated models put in place by ratings agencies and internally by the financial institutions failed to recognise the risk attached to subprime securitization, rating many subprime mortgages as low risk.

It is basic free market theory that when governments interfere with markets it can cause distortions in prices. The argument goes that in the US, Freddie Mac and Fannie May were encouraging artificial borrowing as government policy. This contributed to the housing crash in the USA as those who could not afford mortgages got them. It should be noted since from October 2013 the UK coalition has had a policy called NewBuy that replicates some of these principles. By March 2014 there was a housing

192 *The Storm by Cable V First edition, Atlantic books, London P34*

193 *Memorandum on a new Financial Architecture and New Regulations in World Financial Crises Ghilarucci T Nell E Mittnik S Platen E Semmler W Chappe R edited by Kozmenko S & Tetyana First edition, in Business Perspectives 2010 P187*

bubble in parts of London that had seen prices increased at 18%. We query whether artificially inflating an already inflated market to win a few extra votes makes good economic sense.

Of course, you have worked out by now that although this crisis was started in the United States, these problems came quickly to the United Kingdom. The UK banking crisis of 2008 saw a situation where, for the one mad month of October, we faced the real and dangerous prospect of the UK having to close for business as the toxic debt of financial institutions such as RBS threatened to leave the government and the people paralysed. Cash points would have run dry, businesses would be unable to function, and families would face losing all their money in savings and mortgage arrangements if the banks failed.

This was caused by a system deregulated in the 1980s under the Conservatives (using neo-liberalism) and overseen by Gordon Brown, by now Prime Minister, for over a decade. The story of how the UK banking crises unfolded is well documented, as indeed has the remarkable work put in by Labour chancellor Alastair Darling and many others to first of all stabilise the situation, and then manage to restore basic confidence in the financial system so that the UK didn't face the spectre of a thirties style depression. Each bank is required by law to hold a certain amount of assets. When it became apparent in 2007 that the mortgages held by banks were worthless, those most exposed banks were forced to borrow on a daily basis to maintain liquidity. When this source of overnight security became less easy to access, and Banks stopped the practice altogether the collapse of institutions such as US giant Bear Stearns in September 2008 became inevitable. The shock for the Britain's government was monumental. Gordon Brown had always placed a great deal of faith in the financial sector, and banks in particular to deliver sustainable economic growth.

If Chancellor Alastair Darling, and Brown himself had really been in the know, they would have put a stop to RBS's activities there and then. The policy of reckless mortgage lending to people who could never afford it is not only immoral but extremely poor economics. The problem was that RBS gave a green light to financial advisers to sell, sell, and sell thereby racking up profits in arrangement fees and other sundry services such as home insurance. Two factors were needed to sustain this illusion. One was the continuation of house prices rising relentlessly thereby making the properties on RBS's mortgage books seem of value if the consumer defaulted. Secondly the whole thing relied on no-one actually pointing out the unsustainability of a mortgage system based on a no questions asked basis where 130% loans repaid over 30 years were becoming acceptable products. Bradford and Bingley which was broken up with the taxpayer taking on the toxic assets and Santander picking over the profitable mortgages, became notorious for handing out home loans on a self-disclosing of incomes basis.

Once Brown and Darling realised the precarious position in our banking sector they acted quickly and decisively. RBS reported a completely seized up liquidity situation. RBS had no cash and was holding a huge number of toxic loans, which if called in would break the Bank. If this happened then all its investors, savers and customers would be in dire straits. Wages would not be paid, cash points would run dry and in all probability RBS would drag the majority of UK banks down with them as investors would flee and loans would be defaulted on.

The weekend of Friday 10th October 2008 saw the UK government lead intensive all night talks with the leading banks, and on Monday 13th Gordon Brown and his Chancellor Alastair Darling announced an unprecedented government intervention, forcing the banks to accept massive government cash injections in return for virtual nationalisation of the sector. All this was met with a deafening silence from the Tories. What could they say? Their system of unfettered, unregulated capitalism lay in ruins. The last thing that they could criticise Labour for was light touch regulation as this very policy had been Nigel Lawson's mantra in the 1980s. Labour's lead over the Tories regarding economic competence was stretched as 2008 came to a close, and when the G20 including the newly elected Barrack Obama decided at April 2009's London summit to copy Brown's stimulus package on a global scale, Gordon Brown's decisive and radical action was endorsed by all. But instead of forging ahead with real changes to the banking system reforming the financial ethos in this country, Gordon Brown retreated.

The UK government's approach of effective nationalisation of large sections of the Banking system allied to a raft of measures to stimulate the economy via tax cuts and government cash injections became the template for other major economies. The strategy had the effect of slamming the breaks on the crisis, thus preventing mass bankruptcies, foreclosures on mortgages and loans, as well as staving off the threat of immediate and catastrophic mass redundancies followed by sustained social unrest. The long term debt in the UK may be a national problem but without doubt, it was the only course that any responsible government could have taken.

At the height of the recession in 2009 the German economy contracted by 3.7%, whilst the UK suffered a 6% drop. By mid-2010 the German economy was growing at 2.1%. The UK recovery was remarkable considering the mess following the 2008 banking disaster, but only came in at 1.7% when Labour left power. Whilst the Germans continued to forge ahead, even in the midst of the Eurozone crisis of October 2011, the UK found its economy flat lining with the real and present danger of a double dip recession on the cards.

The prospects for the midterm according to the IMF were a period of stalling economic performance akin to the depression of the 1930s, which led Bank of England supremo Mervyn King to warn in January 2011 that UK households *"face the biggest squeeze on living standards since the 1920s"*.[194] This in fact wasn't fantasy. By October 2013 it was confirmed in the Observer that this generation of 15-35 year olds facing being the first one in the post war years that will be poorer that its predecessors.

Conclusion:

Just why is the credit crunch of 2007-2012 so important? On a basic level it proves the same old theory, that economies built on the back of financial liberalism are prone to excess and grotesque failures. In these crashes it is the working people who are most affected through unemployment and declining standards of living. These are the essential issues that face the UK in the coming generation.

The housing bubble is too big to burst in Britain, so many Brits have their investments in properties, and this has caused a shortage which has pushed prices up. If the market were to burst millions of us would lose out on investments, and the mortgages they owed money on would be far bigger than the value of the property. This is called negative equity, and was a damaging factor for many homeowners in the early 90's. Thank goodness we have a generation of young people that are forced to pay exorbitant rents to keep this economic fantasy alive. The gap between the homeowner and the renter is becoming problematic. It is a real source of inequality in the UK, often found along the lines of age. Whether you rent or buy is no longer a matter of how hard you work but how lucky you are. If you are

194 Speech by M King reported in the Daily Mail http://www.dailymail.co.uk/news/article-1350557/ Bank-Englands-Mervyn-King-This-biggest-squeeze-families-1920s.html 2011

a sixties child the chances are you bought when it was affordable. This is building a huge gap between the haves and have-nots. This is the legacy of neo-liberalism that the slow revolution now has to face up to is that Labour stood by and let this happen. House prices are now well in excess of 8 times the national average wage and with mortgages being offered at four times earnings it is clear you either have to marry or come from money. In terms of the slow revolution, where does it leave us?

What about the legacy of the banking crisis? It left the UK with high debt and low economic growth. Evidence from history via the US 1930's New Deal, the 1993 recession and Brown's own bail out show that running Keynesian style deficit budget that invests and get the state to do things, stimulates economies. So it's clear that the choice to cut services under the coalition was an ideological one that puts the future prosperity of the UK under severe threat. The UK is very much in the same position as Japan found itself stuck in following the 1991 economic crash. The similarities between the two are shocking. Japan had a sound economy, which due to international pressure adopted neo liberalism. Then ensued a property bubble which burst. To this day Japan has high personal and government debt, high unemployment and an aging population. The UK is in the same place, if not weaker due to our lack of manufacturing. In Japan they suffered a "lost generation" of young people. If we are to avoid the same mistakes here we must turn our back on neo-liberalism. We must develop an industrial policy that gets Britain working and we must become sceptical of global capitalism in its current neo-liberal format. The signs are there we will make the same mistakes as Japan. We are not producing economic growth, this will keep the debt high and we will lose a generation with no hope of prosperity. Ask someone in their 20s if they will ever get a mortgage, ask why so many graduates work in call centres, ask why rent and utilities are so high and government and personal debt are crippling this country. The answer is neo-liberalism. This is Thatcher's Britain, that was Thatcher's crash and these are the challenges Britain faces going forward. Failure to tackle them will see us going the same way as Japan; we are facing what might just be a terminal decline into mediocrity. All because we adopted neo-liberalism.

Chapter 10 - David Cameron the man who Promised to mend Broken Britain

David Cameron promised that he would be the man to fix Britain's problems. But after four years of government, why has he been such a failure? The world following the 2008 banking crisis is a new world, where the old ways of doing things should be questioned. Enter stage right- David Cameron, a politician, very much of the old world, of the neo-liberal Thatcherite era, a man whose politics, got us into this sorry mess. On the 11th May 2010 David Cameron became the British Prime Minister aged just 43. He entered the Commons as the MP for Witney just nine years before collecting the keys to Number Ten, and shot up through the ranks to become leader of his party in 2005. The question that needs answering is this: *"How did Cameron become the front man of British politics?* We will look at how David Cameron became popular amongst parts of the electorate, explore how he identified and articulated the challenges facing Britain allowing him to seize power, despite in reality having little or no answers to the problems facing Britain.

It should come as no surprise, that given the tone of this book we find David Cameron's premiership to be passive and damaging to the UK as a whole. The man once described as *"the heir to Blair"* is seen by his supporters as a moderniser; articulate, visionary, bright, aesthetically pleasing. To his critics he is right wing, upper class and has the slightest whiff of hubris. Love him or loathe him, David Cameron either managed to capture the trust of enough of the electorate to form a coalition government, or he failed dismally to win an election that seemed there for the taking for the Tory Party.

It could be argued that his policies are weak, he is prone to u-turns and his politics are outdated. He is undecided whether he moves to the right or uses the centre ground; he used environmental issues to win popularity and is now at best indifferent to the green agenda. He promised reform to the financial sector which had been subject to all but the lightest of light touches. Even worse, like many Conservatives he believes that Thatcherism has the answers to all of the nation's problems, causing an indifference to poor economic performance and neglecting the responsibility of creating modern policy for modern times.

He won votes by portraying the Labour government as incompetent with the economy and not to be trusted. This chimed well with some, of the electorate who wanted to hear it as they wanted someone to blame. They were unsure about Gordon Brown and the Labour Party and were open to the idea of change as soon as a credible alternative arrived. But David Cameron spectacularly failed to convince enough of the electorate that the Tories had credible policies to change the UK.

Broken Britain

From October 2005 until May 2010, David Cameron as leader of the opposition had a fair amount of time to think about the kind of government he wanted his to be. Like both Thatcher and Blair before him, Cameron claimed a narrative (true or not) that Britain was in decline. He grasped this decline theory and made it his own. Cameron personalised this theory by calling it *broken Britain*, and the lines along which Britain was said to be broken was remarkably similar to the decline theories of both Thatcher and Blair before him. This said that Britain is in relative decline, social decline and financial decline.

In previous chapters we looked at how Gordon Brown failed to identify the contemporary challenges facing Britain prior to becoming Prime Minister and this means his premiership lacked direction. *Broken Britain* was first used to describe anti-social behaviour in the UK; under the Brown government there had been an increase in low-level crime as well as more serious offences including a rise in knife crime. *Broken Britain* also described those who had unfairly been described in the media as 'chavs.' 'Chavs' are stereotyped as being unemployed benefit claimants, or those who indulge in petty crime. They may be young mothers and are seen as part of the developing underclass. David Cameron became synonymous with the term "hug a hoodie". Although he never said this, he appeared happy to be associated with the sentiment. He was trying to articulate that society needed to reconnect with those at the bottom. David Cameron subscribed to the Conservative point of view that social Britain was broken because under

Labour the government extended its reach and took responsibility from the individual, and called for a "responsibility revolution." In Glasgow in 2008, Cameron made a speech on broken Britain:

"Whether it is knife crime or any other symptom of our broken society, we will repair the damage by treating not just the symptoms but the causes too. I want the strength of our commitment to inspire faith.... faith to replace the disbelief we feel as it dawns on us that we are living in a country where being stabbed is no longer the dark make-believe of crime fiction but the dreadful reality of our children's daily lives... The knife crime. The worklessness. The ill health.... Above all, the wasted lives ...The thread that links it all together passes, yes, through family breakdown, welfare dependency, debt, drugs, poverty, poor policing, inadequate housing, and failing schools but it is a thread that goes deeper, as we see a society that is in danger of losing its sense of personal responsibility, social responsibility, common decency and, yes, even public morality. We will focus on the radical social reform required to deal with these problems. How we're going to be uncompromising in taking on any vested interests or establishment cultural attitudes that stand in our way, and how we won't pretend that politicians, politics and policy alone can do the job."[195]

By saying this, David Cameron articulated that he blamed the Labour government for many of the problems in society but directly stated that governments alone could not fix many of these problems. This speech harks back to the conservative viewpoint that individuals do not just have the right to self-improvement but they also have a responsibility to it.

Cameron also espouses traditional views on the family. He had toyed with the idea of giving tax breaks to married couples and wants to end the rules that allow couples to claim more benefits if they live apart. Whilst New Labour believed that education was the key to social mobility, the Conservatives promised to improve school discipline and introduce a supply side element to education by allowing parents to start educational establishments which would be free from government control and have freedom over the curriculum.

Implying that there is social decline can be a vote winner, but in 2010 it wasn't enough to deliver a parliamentary majority for the Tories. Cameron didn't just play on people's fears; he identified a legitimate problem and

195 Speech by David Cameron, published by Conservative Party 2008 http://www.conservatives.com/News/Speeches/2008/07/David_Cameron_Fixing_our_Broken_Society.aspx

gave a vision of how he would fix it. By saying *"We see a society that is in danger of losing its sense of personal responsibility, social responsibility, common decency and public morality."[196]* He appeals directly to the core conservative vote and those who work hard and witness or who are affected by crime. This line is also attractive to those who are sceptical of benefits and the unemployed.

While the Conservative response to the crisis was muddled, Cameron used the crash to blame Labour and attempt to regain public trust in Conservative economic management for the first time in over a generation. The financial crisis thrust Cameron to the front of British politics and he tried to capitalise by repeating, time and time again: "Labour's incompetence." It was important to portray Labour's economic incompetence for several reasons. Firstly the last big economic crash Britain had faced prior to the credit crunch was Black Wednesday in 1992, in which a young David Cameron was directly connected, serving as an advisor to then-Chancellor Norman Lamont. Secondly, until the credit crunch, the UK economy had seen 13 years of continuous growth, and the recovery following the 2008 crash was under way as GDP figures grew by 1.7% as the election was called.

The people had trusted Labour and they believed the boast of Gordon Brown when he said that he had "done away with boom and bust economics." But this promise lay in ruins in the wake of the banking crisis, and in fact Cameron taunted Brown with the phrase. For Cameron, Labour's economic incompetence had several lines of attack; firstly Labour's Keynesian economic strategy included a huge economic stimulus, pumping government cash into the economy to keep it moving in tough times. This left a huge deficit, and Cameron's tack was to convince the voters that this debt was caused by overspending by Labour. Whilst both parties acknowledged there would have to be spending cuts, he told the voters that he was the only man who would actually make them. George Osborne spoke on how Britain had to stop living beyond its means, whilst David Cameron promised to continue spending in areas such as the NHS. This was ironic, given that to this day the government debt is increasing and there have been huge cuts in NHS spending since the election.

But most importantly, using the line of economic incompetence allowed David Cameron to make the cuts he ideologically wanted to make but oth-

196 Speech by David Cameron, published by Conservative Party 2008 http://www.conservatives.com/ News/Speeches/2008/07/David_Cameron_Fixing_our_Broken_Society.aspx

erwise would not get an electoral mandate for. By suggesting the government deficit was a Labour mistake and not an intended strategy he tried to sell the idea of a smaller state and spending cuts. This could be called the "constitutional debt", as it forces the UK government to make cuts that are in line with neo-liberal or Conservative Party ideology. In short the coalition has no incentive to reduce the deficit, because failure to do so means Labour has no choice but to also make cuts producing the smaller state Conservatives crave.

Finally, David Cameron identified the international decline Britain was facing. Whilst Thatcher had to contend with the USSR and Blair with globalisation, Britain in 2010 was facing the spectre of an on-going armed conflict in Afghanistan and a war on terror. As leader of the opposition, Cameron had been quick to side with the armed forces over equipment shortages and to play on how stretched Britain's armed forces were between Iraq and Afghanistan. The UK's foreign decline in 2010 took a number of guises. Firstly, the UK was in the grip of global recession, with our overall economic position going backwards relatively to China and Brazil. Secondly, the UK was stuck in two expensive foreign conflicts when Cameron became leader of the Tory Party. By 2014 the UK would have completely withdrawn from Iraq and Afghanistan. The former had been an embarrassing retreat, what would our exit from Afghanistan be like? Cameron's additional problem lay with his right wing backbenchers and their obsession with the European Union.

"As our parties have worked together it has become increasingly clear to us that although there are differences there is also common ground. We share a conviction that the days of big government are over; that centralisation and top-down control have proved a failure." Coalition Agreement 2010.[197]

We believe the country is at a cross roads regarding political policy. The aim of this chapter is to assess the major political challenges this country faces in a post financial crisis world and to understand the policies of the coalition and the motives behind the politicians running the country. This chapter will argue that the coalition, instead of tackling the problems this country faces, is in fact compounding them.

197 *2010-2015 Coalition Agreement published by the Cabinet Office* https://www.gov.uk/government/uploads/system/uploads/attachment_data/file/78977/coalition_programme_for_government.pdf

CHAPTER 11 - DAVID CAMERON

In the last chapter we looked at the idea that David Cameron managed to articulate the challenges facing Britain. This section will argue that his government hasn't tackled the any of these problems despite the promises made in the run up to the election and the commitments made in the coalition agreement. When he entered Downing Street David Cameron was portrayed as the man of the moment with the chance to restore the voters faith in the political system. By 2014 his shine had worn off, with the government out of ideas and the UK hopelessly heading towards economic stagnation. Cameron tried to embody the aspiration of middle England whilst his mastery of communication and privileged education ensured his place in the political elite of Britain. But now we are asking, where has the fizz gone, why has he lost momentum and where has it all gone wrong?

Cameron, an Old Etonian gained a first from Brasenose College, Oxford in Politics, Philosophy and Economics (PPE). His antics at Oxford University were well noted, this is where he met Boris Johnson as they were both members of the notorious Bullingdon Club. David Cameron almost fulfils the criteria of many peoples most hated kind of politician, the career politician, but not quite. David Cameron did manage a period of work outside of politics, in the media. The problem with career politicians is they simply lack the life experience required to ensure politics makes a difference. Prior to entering Parliament in 2001 aged 34 there were two parts to Cameron's career, the first as a special advisor to John Major's cabinet ministers Norman Lamont and Michael Howard. In this period Cameron gained a reputation for an incredible work ethic and as a man of intellect. The second was as a director of Carlton Television where he was head of Corporate Affairs, a role which he left in 2001 to become a parliamentarian. Cameron came to some prominence nearly a decade before entering public life when his finger prints where on the aforementioned Black Wednesday ERM fiasco in 1992 when he worked as special advisor to chancellor Norman Lamont.

We can presume that this period, both in the Conservative research department under the leadership of Thatcher and Major and then acting as a special advisor to Norman Lamont and Michael Howard is where David Cameron developed his Thatcherite political views. This is supported by the description attributed to him whilst at Brasenose College as a "moderate and sensible Conservative" by Professor Vernon Bogdanor. [198]

By 2001 David Cameron would find a safe seat in Parliament, at the fourth time of trying, in Whitney, Oxfordshire, where he would secure a 7,000 majority in 2001. After entering the Commons in 2001 Cameron was quickly promoted in 2003 to a post as a Shadow Minister to the Privy Council, allowing him access to the political elite that is the Privy Council (although he did not formally join until 2006.) In the two years leading up to that point Cameron had been a loyal MP only going against the wishes of the whip once. This was regarding gay adoption, which Cameron supported. In doing so he joined a number of MPs who destabilised the leadership of Iain Duncan-Smith, which arguably hastened his own rise to Downing Street.

In opposition David Cameron became known as an image specialist. This was displayed as he posed with huskies and appeared to embrace a moderate, centre ground agenda. Perhaps he was just telling the voters what they wanted to hear. This is one of the huge challenges facing the Conservatives today, that there is a gap between the attitudes of the public and the core of the Conservative party (and their donors). This issue affects the political right in both the UK and America, as politicians such as Blair and Clinton did good jobs proving that economic management and social reform could coexist as part of a government agenda. governments of the right had told the public this wasn't achievable, with politicians saying that the pursuit of social justice would lead to the end of liberty and free enterprise, New Labour and the New Democrats proved this was false by offering over a decade of prosperity coupled with social justice. The problem has got worse for the Conservatives, whose commitment to financial neo-liberalism is now being linked to many of the issues in society, such as increased prices, housing issues, increased inequality and economic under performance. This has developed as part of the growing scepticism towards banks and the energy companies in the UK. But whether the public has recognised the link to Thatcherism and David Cameron remains to be seen.

198 The David Cameron story B wheeler published by the BBC http://news.bbc.co.uk/1/hi/uk_politics/4502656.stm 2005

Cameron knew that middle classes wanted a more compassionate, loving, and caring Conservatism. It could be said that they wanted a 'Blue New Labour', with a smaller welfare state, less taxes and no Tony Blair. We saw the same thing happen with GW Bush in 2000 during his presidential election, he offered a kinder conservatism with a smaller state and lower taxes but essentially the same as what Clinton has offered. But Cameron, like Bush would promise one thing but deliver a much more right wing agenda when entering government, thus proving that there is a huge gap between the electorate and the Conservatives core values, as the UK population have become more socially conscious.

This problem is part of a growing pattern amongst conservatives in the USA and the UK; that their policy base simply has not developed since neo-liberalism became the mainstream thinking of the right. Ultimately, the Tories have failed to regenerate new polices; this process has led to stagnation. This problem is exacerbated around economic and welfare policy where they desire less government and more market. This has forced leaders of neo conservative parties to offer catch all or populist polices, regardless of their intention to follow through with them. For example, Cameron championed the environment and promised to protect the NHS but has delivered neither. This problem comes in part because of the conflicting interests between wealthy donors and the mass electorate.

Steve Hilton as one Cameron's political guru's has helped the government bridge some of the gap between the interests of elites and the middle classes by pushing the Tory party from a stuffy right wing brigade to a modern thinking party with a green agenda and such ideas as the big society. However since Hilton has taken a sabbatical in the USA many of these agendas have been dropped. The progressive Hilton could be seen as out of kilter with Tory back bench MPs and donors when the highly controversial Australian political strategist Lynton Crosby was announced as the go to guy for the Conservative re-election bid in 2015. Crosby ran the 2005 General Election campaign for the Tory party with slogans such as "are you think what we're thinking" (used by the far right in France to hint at immigration fears). The Tories were stuffed in this election and the Crosby brand of right wing cynicism was seen as only fit for the fisticuffs of Australian politics. However the 2008 London victory for Boris Johnson which Crosby oversaw restored his reputation.

Crosby already started a "clear the barnacles" approach to Tory politics in

2013,[199] and we predict that the Tories will fight the election in this way. They will not focus on any policy area that distracts or does damage to them, they will chicken out of tough decisions and they will focus all their efforts on blaming Labour for the current situation due to enormity of the 2008 crash. Their policies will be divisive, focusing on benefits and immigration. They are likely to offer tax cuts as an incentive to voters. Essentially, there are no new policies for the Tories, just more Thatcherism at a time when Britain needs to move beyond this discredited and out of date ideology. For a party that promises social mobility, there doesn't seem to be much of it in the upper echelons of the Tory party. Nadine Dorries, the outspoken Tory MP for Mid Bedfordshire stated that Prime Minister David Cameroon and Chancellor of the Exchequer George Osborne were:

"Two arrogant posh boys who don't know the price of milk - who show no remorse, no contrition and no passion to want to understand the lives of others"[200] after having previously attacked Cameron and Clegg directly saying *"The problem is that policy is being run by two public schoolboys who don't know what it's like to go to the supermarket and have to put things back on the shelves because they can't afford it for their children's lunch boxes. What's worse, they don't care, either."*[201]

These statements from a leading political figure prove that it isn't just Labour who believes Cameron and company are out of touch; it's the Tory party as well. Finally, the former Archbishop of Canterbury, Rowan Williams wrote on the government's reforms in the New Statesman, claiming that:

"With remarkable speed, we are being committed to radical, long-term policies for which no one voted. At the very least, there is an understandable anxiety about what democracy means in such a context."

"Does [the] government [ensure that policies are in place] to make sure that, even in a straitened financial climate, there is a continuing investment in the long term, a continuing response to what most would see as root issues: child

199 Telegraph blog by J Kirkup which is about the "get the barnacles of the boat" strategy http://blogs. telegraph.co.uk/news/jameskirkup/100214874/get-the-barnacles-off-the-boat-lynton-crosbys-advice-to-david-cameron-is-pure-west-wing/

200 MP Dorries calls PM and chancellor 'arrogant posh boys' Published by BBC http://www.bbc.co.uk/news/uk-politics-17815769 2012

201 Quote Reported in The Guardian http://www.theguardian.com/theobserver/2012/nov/11/profile-nadine-dorries

poverty, poor literacy, the deficit in access to educational excellence, sustainable infrastructure in poorer communities (rural as well as urban), and so on?"

"government badly needs to hear just how much plain fear there is around such questions [of inflation, services, cuts, economy in general] at present. It isn't enough to respond with what sounds like a mixture of, "This is the last government's legacy," and, "We'd like to do more, but just wait until the economy recovers a bit." To acknowledge the reality of fear is not necessarily to collude with it. But not to recognise how pervasive it is risks making it worse. Equally, the task of opposition is not to collude in it, either, but to define some achievable alternatives. And, for that to happen, we need sharp-edged statements of where the disagreements lie."[202]

These are simply chilling words and what makes them more powerful is that Williams, a religious leader was the first person to identify these issues with such clarity.

The 'Big Society'- The BS

Just what is 'the Big Society' we hear you ask? The Big Society (BS) is a political theory linked to Conservatism and developed by David Cameron in advance of the 2010 general election. His aims were the devolving of power to groups of citizens in local communities, devolving power from central to local government, and supporting social enterprise and voluntary groups to carry out these actions, financed by the state. Furthermore the BS was designed to focus on voluntary and community groups and indicates that there is an important role for charity. The aim of this policy for the 2010 General Election was to play to Conservative core values of community leadership and personal responsibility. In theory it reduces the role of the state, which is also in line with Tory political dogma.

David Cameron developed the BS as he felt it articulated a narrative of British social decline. During the Labour years Cameron argued that there were high levels of anti-social behaviour and growing concerns over the size of the welfare state. At first the BS held no sway with the British community at large, until some actually began to like and accept the idea. But just as there seemed to be some progress Cameron, for some untold reason dropped the idea. This was one of the strangest political decisions, just as

202 Williams R published in NewStatesman 2011

people had come to terms with running community projects and taking responsibility, especially in the aftermath of the London riots, the policy idea slipped from government communication.

The idea itself was an attempt to update and introduce a political theory to challenge the political agenda. However whilst David Cameron should be commended for the values the scheme held, it had some major flaws, and his own rejection of the idea only holds water to the claims that his intentions were not as pure as the words he spoke.

To fully understand The BS we must fully comprehend the context in which the policy was set. The BS was discussed in a period where the UK government had a £1trillion debt. Due to the political ideology of the Tory government and its backers, the coalition government has committed to reducing the deficit through tax cuts and spending cuts rather than direct tax rises. The Big Society can be interpreted as a cynical ploy to save money for the UK government by passing government projects with reduced funding to groups of volunteers or the private sector, ultimately reducing the size of the state. Cabinet Office Minister Francis Maude told the Guardian newspaper in February 2011 that, *"the UK government plans to unlock £78bn in charitable assets for the big society and hand over up to 25% of public service contracts to private and voluntary sector."*[203] This means that the BS was part of the Tory privatisation agenda, the agenda that requires less taxes and less government. Furthermore this was part of a deeper and more sinister ploy, which we like to call *'constitutional debt.'* The idea behind it goes a bit like this: David Cameron was elected to reduce the deficit but in reality he has no intention of doing so, forcing his government and all future government to reduce spending and the size of the state in line with conservative thinking. This reduction in the state was intended to leave a space for the big society to fill.

Charities seemed set to play a big role in the Big Society. All well and good but how were charities meant to be thrust centre stage when many faced the biggest funding crisis in a generation due to less donations as the economy stalled, their assets being rendered useless as interest rates were at 0.5% and a falloff in volunteers as people struggled to keep themselves afloat through these tough times? The Big Society in reality would have seen the UK become more and more divided between wealthy areas where there is the money and time for volunteering, and poor areas where the well is dry.

203 *Francis Maude vows to unlock £78bn in charitable assets for big society Published in that Guardian*
http://www.theguardian.com/society/2011/feb/11/big-society-boost-charitable-assets 2011

However we must accept that this was a policy which attempted to intellectually push UK political debate forward, and although the country was sceptical at first, parts of what Cameron says did ring true. As a country we have become inward facing, we do need to enrich our sense of community. Of course the biggest irony is it was a famous conservative that said "there's no such thing as society". Nearly 30 years after Mrs Thatcher said it, Mr Cameron was trying to undo the damage this attitude has caused to our social fabric. But, if we were to look where this idea goes in the slow revolution we would have to argue Cameron is undoing the destruction of collective aspiration that came about under Thatcherism, trying to rebuild the community spirit the greed destroyed. A greed driven by government policy, there was one final and fatal flaw in the plan

We believe that the BS already exists. In every community people give up their time, unpaid to take part in a number of community organisations that contribute to British life. Whilst many taxpayers have argued that they are relieved of enough money by the government as it is and in return want professionals to run services. But this policy is the only ideological initiative made by the Conservative Party since the late 1970s under Thatcher, so maybe on these grounds alone, David Cameron should be commended. It could be argued that Labour missed an opportunity to open a cross-party discussion on the role of community, and should have presented the concept of mutualisation as a way to deliver effective, but locally accountable public services.

CHAPTER 12 - COALITION GOVERNMENT

The coalition government of 2010-2015 is one of the worst in the history of this country. For all the promises made, never have so many been abandoned. Never has a government run out of ideas so fast. Never have a set of politicians failed to identify problems in the manner of this coalition.

You would think, given the mess that Britain is in, that identifying the problems and finding solutions would be easy. Not for the coalition. The fact is, never has there been such an untalented team running government. They really do symbolise everything what is wrong with the career driven, neo liberal political elite we suffer in Westminster. They promised they would sort the debt, they promised solid economic growth and well-paid jobs, and they promised they would reform the banking sector. A failed set of promises. What we have seen is more of the same. We have seen low-paid jobs created, we have seen little or no growth, we have seen inflation, a prices crisis, and we have seen an increase in poverty and the use of food banks. Just what is this country coming to? The legacy of Thatcherism and neo-liberalism is coming home to roost.

The coalition was formed after 6 days of negotiations following the inconclusive result of the 6th May general election. On 11th May 2010 David Cameron and Nick Clegg agreed they would form a government. We believe that the sole reason that the UK elected a national government was to address the economic challenges facing the UK. The two parties agreed and tore up their manifestos and formed a coalition with new policies to address this mandate. We will argue that the coalition failed to meet the economic challenges but also failed to meet many of the pledges from the coalition agreement.

Social mobility has become one of the key outcomes of this book. We have found that, as university fees have now increased to a level above the national average annual salary and that underemployment and poor economic performance away from London have suppressed social mobility for the young. Then when the cost of housing and transport is added in, it can be understood why huge inequalities, which this government have exacerbated, have led to a decline in social mobility and a cost of living crisis.

The coalition agreement starts with pledges to reform and regulate the banking sector. There are regulations designed to prevent the repeat of the financial crash such as tackling banking bonuses, introducing a banking levy and ending the predatory nature of banking toward UK business. As for business there were promises to cut red tape, and regulation as well as simplification of tax returns. There was a commitment to retain the Post Office in public ownership, there was a commitment to seeing more small businesses pick up government tenders, a focus on research and development (R&D) and high end exports, introducing corporate social responsibility as part of the tax system and support for tourism. To put it simply, none of this happened. Was this the Tories tipping their hat to the Liberal Democrats, only to snatch promises away when the chips were down? On deficit reduction there was a commitment to eliminate the deficit in one parliament by cutting spending and not by increasing direct taxes. There have been two important tax reforms. One was to increase the personal allowance to £10,000 before income tax kicked in, and the other saw a tax reduction from 50% to 45% on all earnings over £150,000. Whilst at the same time there have been two indirect tax increases. VAT went from 15% under Labour to 20% and the failure to undertake the business rate re-evaluation in 2013 as planned by Labour when in government has seen an effective tax increase on business.

Local government has taken a huge hit under the coalition, especially in poorer northern cities, and many local services have been slashed. The coalition promised to devolve responsibility to local government; this has not been the case. There were promises of localisation including the Big Society Bank, a commitment to tackling the chronic housing problem, a commitment to allow communities to run closing services, and curbs against the use of bailiffs as well as a ban on excessive interest rates on store and credit cards. None of this has appeared but we have seen swingeing cuts and an ending of local authority run services. Spending per head by local government has fallen by on average £61 per annum, but in poorer cities the figure is as much as £230.[204]

Before entering government Cameron and Clegg promised to protect the NHS, and the coalition agreement described it as an *"expression of our national values."* There were pledges to increase spending and not to make any

204 According to Deputy Leader of the Hull City Council Darren Hale, has endured a cut of £228.36.

top-down reorganisations. There were promises to give spending powers to family doctors and to increase the democratisation of how the NHS is monitored. The coalition pledged to clean up politics, scrutinise lobbying and political donations, and the Lib Dems got their wish of a referendum on electoral system reform. There were promises over House of Lords reform, the power to recall MPs, as well as government-funded party selections.

On policing and crime the coalition adopted the community policing agenda created under Labour, but with the additional aim of cutting police bureaucracy whilst increasing statistical availability to keep the public informed. The bi-party agreement called for the introduction of elected police commissioners. There was a commitment towards rehabilitation for prisoners, suggestions for curbing binge drinking and implementing temporary bans on legal highs. Then there was a pledge to curb immigration from non and new EU member states, plus commitments to the creation of a border force and an FBI style serious crime agency. The coalition pledged to a 'rehabilitation revolution' through independent providers, as well as a review of sentencing. There was also a pledge to cut legal aid.

On the environment there were commitments to stimulate the green economy and to reduce emissions whilst encouraging renewables through a green investment bank. Also included were commitments to have no new runways around London, fair competition in the energy market, a global climate deal, a commitment to improve flood defences and reform of the water industry. The coalition did agree to the pledge created under Labour for the world's wealthiest nations to commit 0.7% on government spending overseas, as well as a commitment to the millennium development goals.

On jobs and welfare, the coalition committed to the creation of a single welfare to work scheme, ensuring those that can work should work, plus a reassessment of incapacity benefit. They promised the development of out-of-work clubs and a universal credit system to reform the way social security payments were to be delivered. Whilst benefits for the out of work were hammered, the grey vote had theirs protected via a new triple lock pensions guarantee, benefits such as the winter fuel allowance, free TV licences, free bus travel, and free eye tests and prescriptions. This would mean that those who are young now will be working a lot longer. Education was circled for reform; the coalition was going to open education up to the rigours of the private sector by increasing academies and parent-run so-called 'free schools'. Inspections and exams would be reformed, as well as there being a promise to increase vocational education.

We could examine the coalition agreement at further length, but the document is ultimately a list of policy flops, idea failures, or things that simply didn't happen. The October 2010 Comprehensive Spending Review announced by Chancellor George Osborne and his Lib Dem deputy Danny Alexander slashed government spending whilst also beginning the implementation of reforms, forcing government departments to look at the use of the private sector or making mass reductions in service provision. By 2014 the cuts agenda began to undermine economic performance. Even John Major and Ken Clarke realised during their tenure in government that public sector spending was the best way to keep the UK economy ticking along. Even the gold-plated pledge not to cut NHS spending was in doubt, especially when the policy was framed against a huge top-down reorganisation and rising healthcare costs due to new technology and drug innovations. Local government and the Department of Transport experienced cuts of over 25%. The Departments of Business, Justice, Energy, Environmental and Rural affairs, Culture, Media and Sport, as well as the Home Office all had budget reductions of over 20%. The coalition agreement and the spending review help us understand the direction of the 2010-15 government. The rest of this chapter will be dedicated to analysing the people at the top of politics and the decisions they have made, so we can understand the key challenges facing the UK and any future government.

The Liberal Democrats and Education

When considering the Liberal Democrat leadership and Nick Clegg we find a party that has endorsed some of the most damaging education reforms in generations. Nick Clegg is the son of a wealthy banker, privately educated and the speaker of many languages. His mother is Dutch and his wife Spanish. He attended Robinson College, Cambridge where he read Archaeology and Anthropology. Despite one incident where he brutally destroyed Germany's largest cacti collection in a drunken arson attack,[205] he was an outstanding student destined for a career in international finance. Clegg gained a scholarship to attend the University of Minnesota, before moving to New York write for the 'The Nation Magazine', an outstanding American publication with a long and colourful history. He moved from journalism

205 Clegg 'not proud' of conviction Reported by BBC News. 19 September 2007. http://news.bbc.co.uk/1/hi/uk_politics/7003100.stm

in America to the European Commission in Brussels and worked inside the World Trade Organisation. In 1999 Clegg was elected to the European Parliament, representing the East Midlands and serving only one term before joining a lobbying firm as a partner. He became the MP for Sheffield Hallam in 2005, a seat which contains a large university population. Clegg was only an MP for two years before becoming the leader of the Liberal Democrats in 2007 and had only been an MP for five years before becoming the Deputy Prime Minister, one of the quickest moves up the ranks known in British political history.

Nick Clegg called his party the "true progressive party in UK politics." However, most politicians would argue that their own brand of politics is fair and progressive, whether they are on the left or the right. Clegg also adopted a strong stance over corruption in Parliament, which came to a head in 2009. He called for wholesale reforms of Parliament including a shakeup in the way MPs expenses were dealt with, the use of the AV electoral system, Lords reform, the reduction of executive power and party funding. Clegg was in favour of fixed-term parliaments, which have forced us to put up with this government, or any future government for a fixed 5 years, regardless of the national interest. In opposition Clegg called for tax cuts, NHS choice through privatisation, an end to the Trident Missile system and wanted to extend the Labour government's green agenda. He gained popularity by supporting the campaign to recognise the right to stay in the UK for Gurkha soldiers, an episode which demonstrated how out of touch Gordon Brown and his parliamentary party were with the British public. But the policy that Clegg has found infamy for is his U-turn on higher education tuition fees. In the run up to the 2010 election, he committed the Lib Dems to abolishing fees and the creation of a graduate tax. This was just one of the policies the Liberal Democrats were forced to re-think in power. If nothing else, their time in power should show the Liberal Democrats that in the future they will only be able to make pledges that they can keep in government. This incident confirmed a lack of policy maturity. Clegg tried to gain popularity by trying to out flank Labour with a desire to fight single issues alongside social justice, wanting democratic reform and the protection of civil liberties whilst also indulging in financial liberalism. As a party they face a choice: do they become more neo-liberal whilst using the state, (and especially the European Union) to temper the ills, inequalities and social injustices produced by a laissez faire stance? Or, do they remain a party that tries to be all things to all people? In addition, as the Liberal Democrats have no traditional link to public ownership, they are more likely to engage private firms to run the functions of the state, using state finance, essentially giving taxes to private firms to make profits. Previous chapters have discussed why we feel it is important to keep services of public importance away from private hands.

The Liberal Democrats are best known for their desire to see democratic reform. A deal was done via the coalition agreement which would see a referendum on AV, House of Lords reform, and a reduction in the number of MPs, which was wanted by the Tories. The AV referendum was rushed through by the coalition and it was held after just one year of government. However, the public where not interested. The country had elected the coalition to sort the economy out, not to change the way we vote in MPs. The move appeared mistimed and self-indulgent. The British public rejected AV by a margin of 68% to 32%. Essentially, no reform would take place during the coalition years, a widely predicted move because of the entrenched anti-reform views of the Conservative Party.

The Liberal Democrats also held electoral popularity on policies regarding education, specifically the pupil premium and university tuition fees. The pupil premium was introduced in 2010, a long-term policy to direct additional government funding to the poorest pupils in the school system. The fund directed £7 billion over 5 years into funding to the poorest preschool children as well as up to £2.5 billion for the poorest students in schools, each child is worth £600 to a school and the school is free to spend it as they wish. Premium funding was found as part of the comprehensive spending review and was active from October 2010, however it was unclear how many of the children benefitted from the premium with OFSTED actively scrutinising how schools use the cash.[206]

However it was the U-turn on the Liberal Democrat policy on tuition fees which damaged, perhaps fatally, the reputation of both Nick Clegg as an individual, and the Lib Dems credibility as a party. The reason for this is the vast amount of political capital made on this policy alone, by Clegg's critics. With top-up fees, Labour had moved to a policy that alienated voters, selling out a principle that access to higher education should not depend on family income. Whilst this position may not be feasible, the Lib Dems claimed that the Labour position of £3,000 a year was excessive, instead trading on a policy of a tax on income as the graduate moved up the earning scale. Instead the Liberal Democrats have given us a policy that triples

206 *Pupil Premium R Adams Published in the guardian http://www.theguardian.com/education/2013/jul/02/pupil-premium-schools-funds-children 2013*

fees from £3,000 to £9,000 meaning a degree will cost £27,000 before living expenses are considered. The policy has seen increases in social exclusion and reduction in application and enrolment numbers.

Looking to the student vote Clegg decided on a cast iron and unbreakable promise that the Liberal Democrats would make to students. They would not raise fees; they would not even freeze fees. The Lib Dems pledged to abolish tuition fees for students in English Universities and they aggressively pursued this policy. On 3rd November 2010 Tory Universities Minister David Willets announced that from 2012 Universities would be able to raise fees to a maximum of £9,000. He told the BBC that the hike would provide, *"greater choice for students with a stronger focus on high quality teaching".*[207] The National Union of Students response was swift and decisive. Within a week they mobilised 52,000 demonstrators who marched down Whitehall.

The parliamentary vote in December of that year seriously damaged Nick Clegg, as two of his junior ministers quit and 23 backbenchers joined them in the 'No' lobby. Those MPs had taken stock and realised that voting with the government would be signing their own electoral suicide note. Labour strongly believed that to reach a full economic potential every person should be educated and skilled to the best of their ability. A key policy to achieve this under Labour, not mentioned elsewhere, was the Building Schools for the Future (BSF) programme. BSF was a big-spend scheme to rebuild schools whilst also putting unemployed builders back to work as part of an economic stimulus plan. BSF was cancelled under the coalition and in the years since there have been errors and U-turns associated with every under-thought and populist policy from the coalition which has created a huge drop in morale amongst the teaching profession.

Michael Gove, a native of Aberdeen, gained a 2:1 from Lady Margaret Hall, Oxford in 1988 where he was also president of the Oxford Union. He applied to the Conservative research department where he would have met David Cameron had he not been turned town and turned his hand to journalism. In his role as Education Secretary he subscribed to his Party's long held view, claiming that state schools were poor and standards were low, despite the lack of evidence for this and a credible alternative being proposed by the Tories. However, Gove begun to implement a set of radical proposals that aimed to overhaul the education system. This policy agenda

207 *Students in Tuition fee Rise S Coughlan reported by BBC* http://www.bbc.co.uk/news/education-11677862 *2010*

has included the extension of academies thereby encouraging schools to move from local authority control. This policy of allowing procurement of services and freedom from the state, a policy which has proved highly popular with some head teachers and governors. Next came the questionable creation of free schools. Neither of which will be flagship success stories in the 2015 general election. Rather than making the hard decisions that needed making, Gove changed management and not the way we do education. There were more inspections and tinkering than ever from Whitehall, despite promises that the coalition would refrain from practices they had accused New Labour of doing.

In opposition Gove had focused of lot of his energy into saying exams are too easy. His proposed reforms have been described as Dickensian and likened to and equated to values used to create the Victorian education system. The first of such reforms would be a focus on classical texts when teaching English, and punishing those with weaker spelling, punctuation and grammar skills by giving them lower grades. There was also to be a re-focus on learning times tables, languages and improving science teaching. Gove attacked the GCSE system as part of an "anti-knowledge culture"[208] and was caught tinkering with exam boundaries in 2012. Proposed post 2017 GCSE reforms were dropped after the policy was seen as unworkable, a policy that wasted time and money. The lack of reform and the backward steps taken by the coalition mean that any future government would have to prioritise education as the back bone to economic policy. Gove's confrontational style led to poor relations between the Secretary of State and teachers. So much so that Cameron removed the Scotsman and replaced him with the more conciliatory Nicky Morgan in his July 2014 pre election reshuffle.

Economics and business since 2010

If education has to be central to future government policy then economics and business does as well. The sole reason this government was elected was to get the economy moving and the citizens of the UK would have accepted reforms needed to meet this objective. The key objectives of this government economic strategy were to eliminate the deficit in one parliament, to create jobs and reduce unemployment, to create quality sustainable growth and to reform the banking sector.

208 M Gove: *Schools Failing to Promote Classics by G Paton in The Telegraph http://www.telegraph. co.uk/education/educationnews/8419770/Michael-Gove-schools-failing-to-promote-the-classics.html 2011*

The first part of this strategy was the comprehensive spending review (CSR), which had some support amongst the electorate as a "whatever it takes attitude" hit the UK. The CSR started on a controversial note as an £80 million investment in Sheffield Forgemasters was cancelled along with other government spending proposed by Labour in its 2010 Budget. The investment was part of a £200-300bn pound economic stimulus designed to deliver economic growth, it did- one report suggest that the package- equivalent to 14% of UK GDP was responsible for as much as 2% of UK growth per quarter. The knock on effect of the coalition ditching this policy when they came to power has been to starve small and start-up businesses of the funding they need to grow and expand.

As we have already mentioned the coalition was not only committed to not increasing income tax but also to eliminating the deficit via spending cuts. This was not enough however as VAT was increased from 15% to 20% and Capital Gains Tax was increased from 18% to 28%. VAT penalises the poor- est most as high earners pay 1p on every 20p on VAT whilst low earners pay 1p in every 5p on VAT. This tax is a regressive that hinders economic growth. VAT means from every £10,000 you spend on VAT-able items at 15% (Labour's rate) you pay £1304 in VAT whilst now, under the coali- tion's 20% rate you pay £1666 on every £10,000 you spend. A real terms tax increase of around £362 for every £10,000 you spend under the coalition.

Ultimately the CSR would result in a minimum of a 19% cut on average to department budgets, with cuts as high as 40% to follow. At the same time the top rate of tax (ie on earnings over £150,000) was reduced from 50%to 45% despite suggestions from HMRC that the higher rate introduced by Labour in the wake of the crash had seen a surge in tax revenues of more than £100 million. government evidence to counter this point is at best shaky. The result of spending cuts, top end tax cuts and the abolition of the economic stimulus was poor economic growth, high unemployment and worse still under employment. Prices have gone up and social mobility has all but come to an end.

David Cameron was quick to blame the UK's sluggish economic growth on the Eurozone crisis. This is in part true, however as David Cameron refused to recognise the global nature of the recession whilst in opposition claim- ing it was the fault of Brown, this argument is limited. Cameron entered government without a strategy for economic prosperity and growth. In 2011 Cameron gave the game away when he admitted that austerity would not, as promised, take one parliament to achieve this. Austerity would be a decade long affair, regardless of the effects of economic growth. Under Cameron's watch the deficit is heading from £120 billion and increasing it to £158 billion by 2015, not bad for the man who threatened that the UK was heading for bankruptcy. In 2012 the national debt passed the £1 trillion mark or 84% of GDP, when the Tories took over from Labour the debt was 67%.

Since the coalition took power, figures have been released on 14 economic quarters. They started well, as Labour's policies produced growth; yet of the remaining 12, four have been in negative growth, including a recession at the start of 2012 and never a quarter of growth higher than 0.8%. Most of which has come from London. Whilst this government now blames the Eurozone, our counterparts in the United States with their continued economic stimulus are now seeing sustained economic growth.

In August 2012 the UK trade deficit stood at £4 billion.[209] In the same period, manufacturing production fell for the 17th month in a row. So much for the "manufacturing based export led" recovery we were promised. [210] Our narrow economy, focused on London and around the services sector is leaving us vulnerable to a long-term debt crisis exacerbated by current economic policy. It is instructive to compare our economy now with Japan's in 1980s. After a boom built on credit they suffered a huge recession and to this day, still have debts of over 220% of GDP. Instead of turning away from the neo-liberal policies that got them into the mess they are in, successive conservative style government have failed to tackle the problems. Japan now has huge under-employment, low social mobility and an aging population - just like us. This despite having some of biggest companies in the world. Will we be like Japan and stick with neo-liberalism or are we going for growth in a different and more diverse way?

The Conservative Party's lack of ideas comes at a time when unemployment stands at a 17 year high, where youth unemployment is out of control, and where the government is failing to incentivise the private sector to grow, yet is cutting over 1 million jobs from the public sector. The UK is in a no growth, no go scenario whilst living standards are declining, and it's likely we will be here for decades. This ultimately means that not only are the talents of those people going to waste; it also means that the longer they

209 *UK trade deficit widens sharply in August Reported by the BBC http://www.bbc.co.uk/news/business-19881656 2012*

210 *George Osborne has continually talked of a "manufacturing and export lead recovery*

are out of work the less chance they will get back into it, and the more it will cost the government to retrain them. This causes more social security expense, and all the while our young people aren't earning and are therefore are not producing taxation revenues.

The EURO crisis

In 2012 the Eurozone crisis was the single biggest danger to the future prosperity of the UK economy and the survival of the EU project. The Euro crisis is essentially a debt crisis: the worry that states cannot prop up their huge debts as credit rating agencies downgrade their creditworthiness. The irony being that we the tax payers remain at the mercy of the credit ratings agencies which failed to spot the weaknesses in the banks that caused the crisis and who are now calling into question the ability of states to repay their national debts.

The Eurozone crisis has re-ignited the old debates over EU membership in the Tory Party. The Tories have never managed to play nicely together over the European Union, ever since John Major signed the Maastricht Treaty in 1992. The Treaty effectively moved the Common Market away from its basis as a trading group into a fledgling state. Many in the Labour Party saw the Treaty as socialism through the back door, as the Working Time directive provided new and unassailable rights for all workers including part timers. In addition strict Health and Safety legislation was included. But crucially the single currency was never adopted. In one sense this provided a firewall for the UK when the banking disaster and recession erupted, and this allowed the UK not to get sucked into the epicentre of Eurozone crises.

The Euro crisis which resulted in the PIGS (Portugal, Ireland, Greece and Spain) getting in to severe financial straits as the 2008 monetary disaster spread across the world, was the main economic headline facing the Continent. However, the story of the PIGS seemed to have fallen of the radar by 2013. The Economist magazine accused German Chancellor Angela Merkel of deliberately quashing high-level discussion of the next stage of bailouts for the moribund PIG economies until after the German election that September.[211] The magazine predicted that only Ireland would be able

---

211 Change it to: (New Statesman 20/6/12 "Angela Merkel's mania for austerity is destroying Europe" http://www.newstatesman.com/politics/politics/2012/06/angela-merkels-mania-austerity-destroying-europe

to keep on track by the end of 2013, with the other economies requiring more remedial aid.

This poses a lot of tough questions for Labour in opposition. In his last act as Chancellor Alastair Darling committed the UK government to underwriting a bailout for Greece even though Britain was not part of the single currency. The Queen's Speech later that month pulled the UK out of that process and signalled to the rest of the European Union that the UK was not coming out to play. Labour must make a clear and unequivocal decision over Europe to lay down a definitive alternative to the Tory position. Either Ed Miliband must commit to full participation (without joining the Euro) with all its implications, or he must declare the EU as not in the UK's best interests and get out. Both have their dangers and their advantages. If the UK reforms and modernises its economy, which is highly unlikely, the argument for a 'Norway-like' free trade agreement whilst not being a member would be overwhelming. But let's remember the Norwegian economy is essentially a left wing, collectivist one, whilst the UK economy has been a neo-liberal one for over 30 years.

The NHS and welfare reform

Jeremy Hunt may come to symbolise this government. A(nother) privately-educated Oxbridge graduate, a member of the Oxford Union Conservative Association who was elected to the Commons in 2005. Within 6 months he became a shadow minister and by 2007 a shadow cabinet minister for Culture, Media and Sport - a role he continued once the Tory party entered government. He replaced Andrew Lansley who over saw huge NHS reforms with the potential to see the terminal decline of the NHS.

Hunt's elevation to the Health portfolio came as a major surprise when David Cameron announced his cabinet reshuffle in September 2012. Given Hunt's public utterances that the NHS was a *"sixty year mistake"*,[212] his appointment hardly reinforced Cameron's 2010 election promise to *"cut the deficit, not the NHS"*.

212 *We are unsure as to whether or not Hunt actually used the or wrote the quote, the story was reported in the Telegraph 4th Sept 2012 "Jeremy Hunt is controversial appointment as Health Secretary" - http://www.telegraph.co.uk/news/politics/conservative/9520269/Jeremy-Hunt-is-controversial-appointment-as-Health-Secretary.html it is understood there are other titles such as "Direct Democracy" and "The Plan" which have disparaging remarks about the NHS.*

The Health and Social Care Act (2012)

"The problems won't surface in the first one or two years. What will happen is that the process of commissioning care will overwhelm GPs. We are not trained in this, nor are we accountants, so we will be forced to buy in management companies to help us, and they are driven by profit. The care decisions will be far removed from the people on the ground, and I won't be able to give people what they need in the way that I can now". [213]

Hackney GP Dr. Deborah Colvin was explaining her assessment of the impact of the Health and Social Care Bill to Sky News on Monday 19th March 2012, as quiet protests across the UK took place against a piece of legislation that did not appear in any manifesto. The government was deaf to the protests. A YouGov poll taken that fateful week in the spring of 2012 showed just 14% of respondents wanted the Bill to succeed and astonishingly two-thirds of health workers were of the opinion that this top-down reorganisation would make things worse for the NHS.

At the 2010 General Election David Cameron had promised, *"I will cut the deficit, not the NHS"*. This was in addition to promising that, *"We will stop the top-down reorganisation of the NHS."* Yet barely was the ink dry on the Coalition Agreement - which included the following statement, *"We will stop the top-down reorganisations of the NHS that have got in the way of patient care"*[214] - when Tory Health Secretary Andrew Lansley published a White Paper *"Equity and Excellence: Liberating the NHS"*,[215] proposing the biggest shake up to the NHS since its foundation in 1948. Satisfaction levels with the NHS hit record highs just as Labour left office with the British Social Attitudes survey showing this astonishing statistic: in 1997, 35% of respondents said they were satisfied with the NHS; in 2010 70% were satisfied. This led the highly respected medical think tank the King's Fund to ask, *"Can satisfaction with the NHS get any higher?"*[216]

Then came the announcement of Lansley's bill in July 2011. The Bill caused consternation for a number of reasons. The overriding aim of the bill was to devolve responsibility for care right back down to family doctors. This

213 *Interview My Dr Colvin, broadcast by Sky News 2012*

214 *2010-2015 Coalition Agreement published by the Cabinet Office https://www.gov.uk/government/uploads/system/uploads/attachment_data/file/78977/coalition_programme_for_government.pdf*

215 *White Paper published by the Department of Health*

216 *Blog by The Kings Fund from http://www.kingsfund.org.uk/blog/2011/12/can-satisfaction-nhs-get-any-higher*

was to be achieved by abolishing the Primary Care Trusts, whose job it was to oversee the targeting of Department of Health. Cameron and Lansley sold it as GPs and patients taking control, but instead the Royal College of GPs said that the Bill was, "*a damaging, unnecessary and expensive reorganisation which, in our view, risks leaving the poorest and most vulnerable in society to bear the brunt.*"[217]

The Tories idea was to have the rigours of the market come into the NHS to provide value for money. Private companies would be able to bid for services such as physiotherapy, provision of equipment including wheelchairs, and specialisms such as cardiac care. But the part of the Bill that caused shudders across patient and professional groups alike was the clause that talked about "*any willing provider*"[218]being able to bid for contracts. The use of language was telling for many. Not "*qualified*" but "*willing*" seemed to sum up the Tories cavalier attitude to who was going to be allowed to get involved. We have talked through this book of the importance of keeping agents of public importance away from private hands and the high long-term failure rate.

Perhaps the most graphic signal that the Bill aimed to dismantle the principle of the "National" in the NHS was the dropping of the legal responsibility of the Secretary of State for Health to ensure everyone in the UK had access to free healthcare at the point of use. Instead the bill gave this responsibility to the new Clinical Commissioning Groups (CCG's) who were to operate at a local level. The wording talked about "appropriate" levels of healthcare, a phrase wide open to interpretation. For example this could in theory allow the CCG's to say that wheelchair provision falls beyond the remit of providing "healthcare" thus allowing charging to be introduced.

Mark Britnell was a former Head of Commissioning for the NHS that Cameron had brought in to advise the government as the bill stalled. Britnell was attending a conference in the USA when he was heard to say the following at a seminar where private health companies were represented; "*In future, the NHS will be a state insurance provider, not a state deliverer*".[219] Any pretence that the Bill was to be implemented for the good of patients

217 *NHS reform- published by BBC http://www.bbc.co.uk/news/mobile/health-16861672 - 2012*

218 *Any Willing Provider. Source Memorandum submitted by the Royal College of Psychiatrists "We would like to see clarification on how far Any Willing Provider will apply" 11th February 2011 http:// www.publications.parliament.uk/pa/cm201011/cmpublic/health/memo/m24.htm*

219 *David Cameron's adviser says health reform is a chance to make big profits published by http://www. theguardian.com/politics/2011/may/14/david-cameron-adviser-health-reform The Guardian 2011*

was comprehensively blown out of the water. This was the final nail in the coffin of the post war consensus regarding the NHS and in doing so the biggest victory for the slow revolution has been lost. Despite this, media coverage has been appalling. The BBC is especially guilty, with what seems like a media blackout on the subject. The voters simply don't know what has happened to the NHS.

Whilst the NHS was undergoing huge transformations so was the benefits and welfare system, a core Conservative dog whistle policy. By the same token we have seen welfare come under a sustained assault. Iain Duncan-Smith (IDS) has managed to divide the country over the moral position on by making an affordability argument. IDS told the BBC in 2013:

"What we are saying [to welfare recipients] is there are taxpayers who go out to work pay the money for your benefits and in fairness to them you should not be out of work or living in places, for example where rents are £50 to £100k a year, when most taxpayers can't, and commute huge distances to get to work". [220] When pressed by interviewer John Humphrys on whether or not he was, "punishing people", IDS reverted to lazy stereotype of claimants *"languishing on benefits and actively avoiding work... and your children grow up believing that work is not part of what you do in life."*[221]

Humphrys pressed on and challenged IDS over the numbers of people affected by the benefit cap and work. Bearing in mind Duncan Smith had been rapped over the knuckles by the UK Statistical authority for misleading the public on the numbers back in work due to the cap, the presenter cited examples from Haringey, one of the pilot local authorities, IDS's reaction was instructive, *"What you're doing, as always happens with the BBC is seeking lots of little cases that are politically motivated".*[222] Then IDS made an extraordinary claim when the interviewer asked him about "facts". The whole argument in May over statistical evidence revolved around the Secretary of State's avowed claim that 8,000 people had found work in the trial areas because of the benefit cap. The Authority said the claims were *"not substantive or robust... (and could be construed as) misleading".*[223]

"By the way, you can't disprove what I said either. I believe this (the 8,000 back

220 BBC Radio Four's Today Programme on 15th July 2013

221 BBC Radio Four's Today Programme on 15th July 2013

222 BBC Radio Four's Today Programme on 15th July 2013

223 BBC Radio Four's Today Programme on 15th July 2013

at work figure disputed by the National Statistical Authority) to be right".[224] Never mind the facts. Never mind the evidence. The Tories were making massive and potentially damaging and irreversible policy choices based on a gut feeling, and flying in the face of hard evidence.

The interview raises some pretty important questions about the coalition's attitude to welfare. The tone in which the debate is framed is interesting. IDS chose the tack of appealing to workers to condemn those out of work and in receipt of benefits. The "fairness" argument is a brilliant distraction tactic. Instead of laying the blame for wage freezes, a decline in living standards or economic strategy issues IDS encouraged those in work to castigate their fellow travellers in life for what ailed them. This tone sets the underlying ethos towards the issue of welfare reform. The Conservatives pledged to reform welfare through the adoption of universal credits and the reduction of certain benefits, notably housing benefits to those under 25. IDS framed the debate around the idea that 5 million people were being supported by the state not to work including 1.4 million under 25 who are not in training or work. IDS has addressed the idea that those who are under employed should stop having "top ups" from the state though benefits such as housing allowance, despite the fact there is a chronic shortage of jobs and quality diverse employment in this country. IDS led the push for a £26,000 a year benefits cap which passed through the Commons in March 2013. This language and policy agenda set a clear tone that IDS is going to attack those on welfare without taking responsibility for the larger unemployment problems the economy has.

The return of the 'Nasty Party'?

Have we seen the return of the 'Nasty Party'? Despite Cameron spending years trying to clean up the image of the Tories, the old agenda which saw those on the edge of society marginalised has returned. In 2002 the then Conservative Party Chairman Theresa May noted that: *"There's a lot we need to do in this party of ours. Our base is too narrow and so, occasionally, are our sympathies, you know what some people call us: the nasty party".*[225] Michael Howard's elevation to the leadership was a return to the right wing comfort zone for the Conservatives. Leading Tory Anne Widdecombe had

224 BBC Radio Four's Today Programme on 15th July 2013

225 Nasty Party Warning to Tories M White A Perkins Reported in The Guardian http://www. theguardian.com/politics/2002/oct/08/uk.conservatives2002 2002

once observed that Howard had *"something of the night"* about him,[226] and this may have summed up how the nation envisaged a Tory government during the 2005 election campaign. The bizarre and slightly disturbing tag line for their campaign of *"Are you thinking what we're thinking?"* just confirmed the toxicity of the Tory brand to many undecided voters.

Cameron was desperate to take the poison out of the way the Tories were perceived, but this has been hampered by increasing unemployment, sluggish economic performance away from the Tory voting south east, increasing inequality, privatisation and divisive welfare cuts. The nasty edge to the Tory Party really emerged when the ATOS scandal came to light.

Labour's Work and Pensions Secretary Harriet Harman was responsible in 1998 for awarding French company ATOS the contract for carrying out medical assessments for benefit claimants seeking support for not being able to carry on working due to ill health. But it was under Iain Duncan Smith's tenure at the DWP that the whole system of assessment was thrown into the spotlight. On coming to power in May 2010 the coalition announced that between October 2010 and May 2014 all claimants for out of work health related benefits were to be re assessed. This tallied with the aims outlined by George Osborne in September 2009 during the Tory Conference when he told delegates that he planned to slash £600 million from the welfare budget in one Parliament by putting the *"worst offenders"* i.e. those who were deemed to be cheating the system, back to work. In addition he promised to save an additional £300 million by cutting £25 a week from those on the top rate of Incapacity Benefit, those with the most serious illnesses. The reassessment process has been an epic PR disaster. Numerous cases of cruel treatment and totally inappropriate behaviour by ATOS were confirmed in a special report conducted by the Daily Record newspaper in September 2012.[227]

The paper revealed that a report prepared for IDS showed that more than half of those deemed fit for work by ATOS had their benefits restored on appeal. But their benefits were stopped in the meantime causing tremendous suffering. The Daily Record went on to publish a series of heart rend-

226 Ann Widdecombe tested Michael Howard putdown before using it Published in the Telegraph http://www.telegraph.co.uk/news/politics/conservative/6913175/Ann-Widdecombe-tested-Michael-Howard-putdown-before-using-it.html 2009

227 Benefits bullies Atos driving Scots to brink of suicide, shock survey reveals D Clegg Published in the Daily Record http://www.dailyrecord.co.uk/news/scottish-news/benefits-bullies-atos-are-driving-scots-1342594 2012

ing examples where claimants had been seriously mistreated, affirming what many campaigners had been saying anecdotally, but backed up with evidence. Perhaps the worst aspect of this sorry tale proved to be the revelation from ATOS assessors that they had been pressurised into making wholly inappropriate rulings against the most vulnerable claimants.

Joyce Drummond told the Daily Record that an ATOS manager had warned her that as an assessor she was being *"too nice"* to the claimants she was interviewing. Drummond stated that ATOS staff were told to stop the benefits of those who could sign their own name, turned up for assessment smartly dressed, with a toddler in tow or who could self-mobilise to the appointment.

The coalition has been divisive and damaging for the long-term prosperity of the UK. But worse, this has been a do-nothing government, doing as little as possible to address the challenges this country faces. Putting all its bets on buying the electorate off with what amounts to an £800 a year tax cut to those earning under £100,000 and what amounts to an £85,000 tax cut for those earning £1 million. This has been another neo-liberal government that has failed to tackle the economic and social challenges facing the UK.

Chapter 13 - Labour and Ed Miliband

In the previous two chapters we identified some of the big challenges facing the country. The aim of this chapter will be to argue that Labour should be best placed to meet these challenges but must take a leap in faith to move away from the Blairite agenda. In this book we have taken the view that there are dire challenges facing the UK, that the UK is in decline and that our quality of life is under genuine threat because of generations of excess and poor government policy. This is the setting in which Labour and its leaders have to walk a tight rope. On one hand they have to create policies to meet the challenges we face whilst not scaring away those with aspiration into voting Conservative, an argument peddled by an unsympathetic press.

The Labour Party does have three big advantages. Firstly, they have an articulate leader who could, with the right attitude and policies, break the mould of Cameron and Blair. He comes across as sensible and approachable and has the potential to deliver change. Secondly, the Conservatives are out of ideas and solutions, having failed to move beyond Thatcherism, and thirdly, the UK population as a whole is more socially, if less politically minded. Miliband is starting to unravel some of the arguments required when articulating the challenges facing the UK. For example, under the current system of government thinking, no one has actually stepped up to challenge the energy companies, Miliband has. But does he have the courage to go with UK public who want nationalisation? Another example would be growing inequality between the rich and poorest, the cost of living and aggressive legal loan sharking. Is Miliband just another political leader hungry for power or is he a man of courage, who is grasping a chance to potentially change the way the country is run? The forthcoming election campaign will go a long way to answering these questions.

In previous chapters we have covered the journey of the Labour Party, born out of the union movement, and its first tentative steps into Parliament, before forming governments that genuinely radicalised the way the UK is run. This chapter will attempt to understand the direction Labour is now heading in, and argue that Labour is the Party that can meet the policy challenges facing the UK.

Red Ed

Now Labour is in a unique position: in opposition as the coalition falters. We hope that Labour has come to terms with the reason it was cast from office. We hope that they understand that Labour lost touch, Labour got carried away and there was an element of economic mismanagement. But the coalition parties have not performed to anywhere near the standard of the last Labour government.

Let's make no mistake: Labour's finger prints are on the economic crisis facing the UK, but the DNA of the economic crisis lies within the Conservative Party. What's more, prior to the election both Nick Clegg and David Cameron were highly disingenuous while campaigning on this subject. Firstly, Cameron was especially unwilling to accept the role of deregulation, which had been introduced by the Thatcher government, in causing the crisis. Neither Cameron nor Clegg have suggested or introduced adequate regulation to prevent a repeat whilst in government. Secondly, they argued that the debt and deficit were caused by economic incompetence. In fact an economic stimulus package had to be implemented by Labour to stop a total collapse of the banking system caused by neo-liberal non-regulation. This was why we had a deficit. Thirdly, whilst in opposition, Cameron repeatedly blamed the crisis on Labour, refusing to accept that it was a global crisis, but whilst in government, this has been reversed to claims that this actually is a global crisis.

Labour has tried to use its time in opposition to gather its thoughts, take stock and reflect about what happened when they were in government. Labour has attempted to regain touch with its core values and wants to reconnect with its natural support base, and regain energy and self-belief. Not just the belief that the party argues for what's right, but also the self-belief that the party is ready to govern. This is essential at a time when the Conservatives and the Liberal Democrats are faltering badly in government. This attempted transformation is down to one man: Labour's leader. But the question is being asked as the election approaches: has it worked?

The Labour membership took a huge risk by electing Ed Miliband as its
198

leader. His politics are fundamentally different from Blair and Brown, or his key leadership challengers Ed Balls and his older brother David. Both were senior cabinet ministers who it could be argued are closer to the New Labour way of thinking. Upon Ed Miliband's election as Labour leader, the press tried to make him out to be "Red Ed", a man who would crush aspiration by indulging in tax hikes and anti-business rhetoric. However, this didn't faze him, nor did it change his political direction as he threw the Labour party into a full-scale review. Miliband wanted the leadership of the party to get in touch with its membership, its values but most importantly the way that British people were feeling.

But just who is Ed Miliband? Ed Miliband, born 24th December 1969, was the son of left-wing philosopher Ralph Miliband. He is younger brother of former foreign secretary David. His parents were London-based Polish Jewish evacuees. Ed had an adventurous childhood, partly spent in New England (and importantly away from the south of England) with some in Leeds. Miliband gained entry to Corpus Christi College Oxford with less than perfect A-level results. Having gained a 2.1 in the politicians' staple degree of PPE, Miliband soon found himself as a special advisor in the Labour Party. During this period he gained an MA in economics from LSE. He served as Brown's special advisor from 1997-2005, whilst also teaching at Harvard University. In 2005 he was elected to Parliament, representing Doncaster North, and quickly entering government in 2006 as Charities Minister. He was promoted to the cabinet in 2007 and in 2008 Miliband became Secretary of State for Energy and Climate Change.

The 2010 Labour Party leadership election itself was an interesting period in politics. The UK was coming to terms with a new government, which would be enforcing radical government cuts, university fees and the ending of the economic stimulus. Simultaneously, the Labour Party was coming to terms with the end of New Labour. No longer was Labour in a position of being forced to defend its track record in government. Instead there was an opportunity to renew polices and desires to take the UK forward. Many Labour members rejoiced at the end of New Labour, especially in the north where the failures of market economics had seen a huge reduction in the quality of living. These were the challenges that the Labour leadership election had to understand and face. Did the Labour Party continue along New Labour lines, using the free market, and create economic growth whilst using the ever-expensive welfare state to pick up the resulting toxic outcomes, or did the party move towards more socially driven policies, even if this meant economic and fiscal reform?

The test of time and the heat of an election will prove whether Labour really has made a move to the socially driven policies that Ed Miliband espoused in his leadership campaign. In 2010 politicians and voters could have been forgiven for thinking the economic performance of the UK was merely a recession that will pass, as opposed to a grave set of problems relating to UK decline that could see the fall of living standards become entrenched. The three alternative visions for Labour where set out by 5 leadership candidates. Two of them (David Miliband and Ed Balls) offered an agenda that was close to New Labour, with Balls maybe a little to the left. Ed Miliband offered a traditional Labour Party platform, with social democratic principles, with Andy Burnham just to the left of this. Diane Abbott offered a left-leaning agenda for the party. The Labour membership had to get this choice correct: failure to do so would likely see the election of the Tories for a 5 year term in 2015, this time governing in their own right.

Each candidate had his or her own unique advantages. Take David Miliband, a serious intellect with degrees from Oxford and Massachusetts Institute of Technology, a former advisor to Tony Blair and long standing MP. He had 5 years government experience and served in the cabinet. However by 2013, following his defeat to his brother he quit politics all together. Ed Balls was another big intellect but from a public school background with degrees from Harvard and Oxford. A journalist turned political advisor, he also had government experience, and had been instrumental in the building schools for the future programme. Andy Burnham, although the only genuine working class candidate, had followed a similar Oxbridge route to politics via a period as a special advisor. He had also spent time in government. Burnham's more considered approach had been lost amongst the big characters around him. Finally, entering the leadership race from a position of late night TV popularity was Diane Abbott. Abbot, who had remained a backbencher since election to Parliament in 1987, had attended grammar school and was a Cambridge graduate. She had worked at the Home Office and the National Council for Civil Liberties before joining Thames Television in 1980, and then went onto roles at TVAM before becoming head of communications at Lambeth Council until elected to the Commons in 1987. Abbot gained her reputation as a councillor on Westminster City Council, where her involvement in 1980s race relations bought her to national prominence. Upon her election in 1987 she broke an almost 100 year all-white stranglehold on the House of

Commons and she was elected alongside four other candidates including Keith Vaz, Bernie Grant and Paul Boating. Abbott is considered to be to the left of the Labour Party, having voted against the whip on numerous occasions, including the Iraq war.

The leadership election itself went with little fuss. Like the Tory leadership contest five years earlier, the Labour Party managed to stage the event to signify renewal. It offered the Labour membership a real opportunity to select the direction of the party. It was of no surprise that that the favourite, David Miliband, failed to garner enough support; especially after Ed, who sat in the middle of the political debate, was backed by the unions. This saw a departure from New Labour, which despite its many achievements had become stale. Ed's election as leader, winning on a run off against his brother allowed the party to leave the chains of the financial crisis behind and enter a period of reflection. He appointed all his rivals to senior positions with only his brother David declining, and this went some way to uniting the Labour Party.

But what were the themes of Ed's election and why did they resonate with the membership? To answer this question we can point to two passages. The first is Ed's election statement, which recognised the values of the party and that we must re-focus on them, as well as listening to the public over their concerns:

"Our party is defined by our values and our determination to transform those values into change that improves the lives of the British people. But at the last election, the voters decided that they did not want us to continue pursuing that mission in government. To win back their trust we need to do two things. First, we must focus on people's priorities. For all the good we did in the last 13 years, by the end of our time in power we weren't listening closely enough to peoples' concerns whether they were about bankers' bonuses or the benefits system. Second, we must rediscover our sense of moral purpose. The Labour party is most effective when we understand that we are a movement dedicated to transforming our country. We should be proud of our values of equality, opportunity and responsibility and we should fight for them. That means a leader who will match realism with idealism when it comes to making decisions for our party and our country. That is the direction I believe will lead us to victory."[228]

Ed hints that he is interested on focusing on the worries of the lower middle

---

228 *Speech by Ed Miliband- Can be viewed from BBC http://www.bbc.co.uk/news/uk-poliitics-11412289*

and the working class, that he will reconsider policy positions on benefits and perhaps immigration, the relationship with the EU as well as bankers' bonuses and the increased inequality in the UK. Secondly, he hints that the party must rediscover its core values, which it could be argued it began to lose towards the end of the New Labour government.

By the two year mark of his leadership, Ed had carried out a comprehensive review of the Party entitled "Re-founding Labour" and had managed to build his 2010 ideas in the basics of a policy framework which he outlined at his 2012 Party Conference speech. The "One Nation" speech was a social democratic speech that focused on the idea that nothing that was wrong with Britain could not be fixed by what is great about it as well:

"It was a vision of Britain. A vision of a Britain where patriotism, loyalty, dedication to the common cause courses through the veins of all and nobody feels left out. It was a vision of Britain coming together to overcome the challenges we faced. Disraeli called it "One Nation". "One Nation". We heard the phrase again as the country came together to defeat fascism. And we heard it again as Clement Attlee's Labour government rebuilt Britain after the war. Now what does it mean to the Labour Party to be One Nation? It means we can't go back to Old Labour. We must be the party of the private sector just as much as the party of the public sector. As much the party of the small business struggling against the odds, as the home help struggling against the cuts. We must be the party of the south just as much as the party of the north. And we must be the party as much of the squeezed middle as those in poverty. There is no future for this party as the party of one sectional interest of our country."[229]

This is the sentiment that many in the Labour Party feel about Britain. Whilst the Tory Party is seen as the party of the Union Jack and patriotism, many Labour members feel that it is the potential of our people, our attitudes, our actions and our work ethic that have built this country from the bottom up. We have overcome a number of crises before, and we can rise again. From this language it is interesting to note that Ed Miliband is taking the intellectual journey that Blair and Thatcher took, but that Brown didn't. He is identifying the challenges facing Britain and outlining solutions to face these problems. Ed isn't simply a cheerleader for a set of ideas; he is demonstrating himself to be a compassionate thinker. Ed clearly picks out two big issues facing people under the current economic system: unemployment and credit to small business. Ed and his leadership team have

229 *Speech by Ed Miliband at the 2012 Labour Party Conference http://www.labour.org.uk/ed-miliband-speech-conf-2012*

also pledged reforms polarising coalition policies surrounding benefits and the NHS. Ed Miliband's agenda also focuses on youth and general unemployment, a scourge which is now affecting millions, through unemployment and under employment:

"You know I think of the young woman I met at a youth centre in London earlier this year. She was brimming with hopes and ambitions for the future. She was full of life. She was full of desire to get on and do the best for herself. And then she told me her story. She'd sent off her CV to 137 employers and she'd not had a reply from any of them. Many of you in this audience will know people in the same position. Just think how that crushes the hopes of a generation. I want to talk to her, to a whole generation of young people who feel that Britain under this government is not offering them a future."[230]

This speech shows that he believes that there is a role for government in ensuring unemployment is reduced by making sure quality work is available. He is arguing that the economic policies of the coalition have failed by arguing that unemployment should be a high priority:

"If you stop an economy growing, then it leaves more people out of work claiming benefits, not paying taxes. Businesses struggle so they're not paying taxes. And as a result borrowing goes up. Borrowing not to invest in schools, in hospitals, transport and education. But borrowing to keep people idle. So the next time you hear a Conservative say to you Labour would increase borrowing, just remember it is this government that is increasing borrowing this year. So what have we seen? We've seen recession, higher unemployment, higher borrowing. I don't think that's what people were promised."[231]

Ed has developed an articulate theme surrounding the cost of living called the "squeezed middle". This effectively identified those in work whose quality of life is in decline. This is not just because of poor economic performance but also because of growing inequalities and the policies of Thatcherism. This is articulated by noting increased fuel and transport bills. Whilst utility bills have increased, so have the profits of the privatised utilities. Ed is pointing the finger directly at the policies of Thatcherism and is indicating a genuine desire for change in direction.

230 Speech by Ed Miliband at the 2012 Labour Party Conference http://www.labour.org.uk/ed-miliband-speech-conf-2012

231 Speech by Ed Miliband at the 2012 Labour Party Conference http://www.labour.org.uk/ed-miliband-speech-conf-2012

"I want to talk to all of the people of this country who always thought of them-selves as comfortably off, but who now find themselves struggling to make ends meet. They ask: Why is it that when oil prices go up, the petrol price goes up. But when the oil price comes down, the petrol price just stays the same? They ask: Why is it that the gas and electricity bills just go up and up and up? And they ask: Why is it that the privatised train companies can make hun-dreds of millions of pounds in profit at the same time as train fares are going up by 10% a year? They think the system just doesn't work for them. And you know what? They're right. It doesn't."[232]

Ed has also indicated education and health service pledges. In the last chapter we highlighted the coalition's NHS reforms and in the next two chapters we will look at the need for lifelong education and training being part of a successful modern economy:

"For a long time our party has been focused on getting 50% of young people into university. I believe that was right. But now it's time to put our focus on the forgotten 50% who do not go to university. [we need] courses that engage them and are relevant to them. Work experience with employers. And then culminating at the age of 18 with a new gold standard qualification so they know when they are taking that exam they have a gold standard vocational qualification, a new Technical Baccalaureate. A qualification to be proud of. You know, we've got to change the culture of this country friends. We can't be a country where vocational qualifications are seen as second class."[233]

"Let me tell what I hate about this reorganisation; let me tell you what I hate. I hate the waste, I hate the waste of billions of pounds at a time the NHS has its worst settlement, I hate the fact that there are 5,500 fewer nurses than when David Cameron came to power. Think of what he could have done if he hadn't spent billions of pounds on that top-down reorganisation and had used the money to employ nurses, rather than sacking them. But here's what I hate most of all. It's that the whole way they designed this NHS reorganisation was based on the model of competition that there was in the privatised utility industry, gas, energy and water. What does that tell you about these Tories? What does that tell you about the way they don't understand the values of the NHS? The NHS isn't like the gas, electricity and water industries. The NHS is the pride of Britain. The NHS is based on a whole different set of values for

232 Speech by Ed Miliband at the 2012 Labour Party Conference http://www.labour.org.uk/ed-miliband-speech-conf-2012

233 Speech by Ed Miliband at the 2012 Labour Party Conference http://www.labour.org.uk/ed-miliband-speech-conf-2012

our country. So let me be clear, let me be clear, the next Labour government will end the free market experiment, it will put the right principles back at the heart of the NHS and it will repeal the NHS Bill."[234]

This is the clearest statement that Ed will not only protect the health service but will move away from Thatcherism. From these extracts we have seen the emergence of a policy agenda, this agenda is in tune with the membership but can it be articulated to the electorate effectively. These are the key points:

That Labour must rebuild trust and morality;

That Labour must move away from market driven polices and towards socially driven ones;

That the state should re-assert its authority over big business;

That economic policy needs serious reform, away from neo-liberal dogma;

That unemployment is too high and has come about as a result of the same neo-liberal dogma;

That the role of government should be to reduce inequalities brought about by neo-liberalism, (this could be done by tackling transport and energy cartels to reduce the prices of both);

That there needs to be genuine support for small business to stimulate growth and employment;

And committing to investment in education, health and transport by supporting the 50%+ of school leavers who do not go to university and reversing the market-based NHS reforms.

Whom does Ed hope to represent

Miliband was elected by the party membership to create a sense of purpose and vibrancy within the Party, and to provide strong but collegiate leadership to take the fight to the Tories. Harold Wilson summed up what the Labour Party means to many with his statement, *"The Labour Party is a moral crusade, or it is nothing"*. We spoke to grass roots members of the Labour

234 Speech by Ed Miliband at the 2012 Labour Party Conference http://www.labour.org.uk/ed-miliband-speech-conf-2012

party whilst writing this book. All agree that they joined Labour to fight social injustice and see the state as a potential force for good in society. They believe that the state can work to ensure that poverty is eradicated, that universal health care and education ensure everyone gets a fair crack at the whip. Most also believe that strong, state led economic policy and a fair tax system will work and aspiration whilst at the same time reducing financial inequality and protecting the vulnerable.

Ed Miliband won because he gave a clear voice on these values and was seen by the members as moving away from the New Labour ethos, which although espousing similar values on injustice, failed to end the excesses of Thatcherism because of a core belief that market discipline had the answer. Members up and down the UK want Labour to be talking about how to get the economy moving again and creating well paid full time jobs, make sure children can attend successful schools, address the scandals of rent costs and affordable housing. They want Labour to nourish the NHS whilst also cleaning up the financial and utilities sector.

But these policies cost money. In January 2012 the press finally started asking questions of Labour. Which cuts would Labour keep, and which ones would they reverse? This scrutiny has made it clear that Ed can't just do what Cameron did prior to election by saying as little as possible. Ed's policies have to be costed and workable.

With finance in mind, we could do with looking further at the values of Ed Miliband. To do this we can analyse come of things he said during the 2010 leadership contest to try and understand what type of government Ed might run and which voters it may attract. At a speech in Scunthorpe, in August 2010 he began by stating: *"New Labour solutions won't see us get back into power, we became managers in government rather than people who were there with a real passion and opportunity to change society for the better."*[235] This is a huge admission, stating that Labour lost its way, ultimately resulting in its losing the ability to think freely about policy, and using market ideology to solve most problems. This is evidence that Ed in government will aspire to challenge the status quo. Miliband continued: *"We must not end up taking decisions because we are scared of the press, because this erodes people's faith in the ability of politics, and politicians to effect real change in Society."*[236] This is something that resonated with many in the Party who felt that the enormous goodwill and trust that the British people had given

235 *Ed Miliband speaking at an internal party meeting Scunthorpe 2010- attended by Rathbone*

236 *Miliband speaking at an internal party meeting Scunthorpe 2010- attended by Rathbone*

Labour in 1997 had been wasted by an obsession with pleasing the media, meaning that Labour had not been radical enough about reforming the UK. This also resonates with one of this book's key themes: that politicians are absolving themselves of responsibility and the public have picked up on this. This gives us an insight that Ed wanted to be a strong leader when he set out on his journey.

But then why has he been so quiet in opposition on some occasions? When he has been bold Miliband has been at his best. He found a voice for his views on the media when he came out very strongly against the Murdoch dominated press during the hacking scandal of 2011. In July that year he told the Observer newspaper that the Murdoch empire must be broken up. *"I think it's unhealthy because that amount of power in one person's hands has clearly led to abuses of power within his organisation. If you want to minimise the abuses of power then that kind of concentration of power is frankly quite dangerous."[237]* Ed also stood up to the utility companies on prices, the press following smears on his father and reformed the party constitution regarding union links to funding. Maybe it could be argued that if Miliband overplays his hand by being radical whilst in opposition it might deflect from the terrible job the coalition is doing.

But ultimately it is Miliband's moral position on wealth that has genuinely had to break the mould, with Labour committing to a top-rate tax of 50%. New Labour's cosiness with big business was exemplified by Peter Mandelson's infamous statement that he was, "intensely relaxed about people getting filthy rich".[238] This was now the biggest charge that Labour faced; that they had moved from a party of social conscience to a party that managed the excess of capitalism. Miliband was openly critical of the excesses going on in UK boardrooms and the way in which capitalism was operating. He asked, *"Are you on the side of the wealth creators or the asset strippers? The producers or the predators?"[239]* This was a direct questioning of the values at the heart of 21st century business in the UK which had allowed a company like Southern

237 *Rupert Murdoch's empire must be dismantled – Ed Miliband Doward J, reported in The Guardian*
http://www.theguardian.com/politics/2011/jul/16/rupert-murdoch-ed-miliband-phone-hacking   2011
Ed Miliband speech to Labour conference 2011 http://www.labour.org.uk/ed-milibands-speech-to-labour-party-conference
238 *Peter Mandelson gets nervous about people getting 'filthy rich' in The Guardian by Malik S, from*
http://www.theguardian.com/politics/2012/jan/26/mandelson-people-getting-filthy-rich January 2012
239 *Speech by Ed Miliband at the 2012 Labour Party Conference http://www.labour.org.uk/ed-miliband-speech-conf-2012*

Cross to asset strip the care home system,[240] *"They may not have sold their own grandmothers for a fast buck. But they certainly sold yours. They aren't the values of British business. It must change."[241]* Ed Miliband could not have been more unequivocal about his attitude to the rip off culture and growing financial inequalities that have come about because of the post 1979 reforms. Whilst those on the street, in the party and community leaders agree that it's time for a change in attitudes, the press has been more hostile

Thirteen Years in Power: Owning Up to mistakes

Not everything Labour did in power was right; of course every administration has to make tough decisions and many of these will make the government unpopular. However the aim of this section is to identify areas where Labour went wrong in a manner that should never be repeated. These mistakes are ones that lost sight of the core aim of the Labour Party: to pursue social and economic justice. These policies should be considered immoral and should not be repeated by any socially responsible government.

Gambling

In January 2007, just as Tony Blair was about to leave office, Channel 4's Anthony Barnett revealed the full scale of Britain's gambling revolution after obtaining secret minutes which showed that the Labour government wanted to build the equivalent of 10 super-casinos in England and Wales.[242] When a senior Labour cabinet minister, Tessa Jowell, was stating that she wanted to make gaming a mainstream activity,[243] questions about the moral compass of those involved are inevitably raised. Not only is gambling highly addictive: it has the power to ruin people's lives. Every available report demonstrates the link between promotion of gambling and increases in addiction, which inevitably leads to domestic breakdown and all the fallout

240 *Southern Cross, a care home provider closed in 2011, a report from the BBC http://www.bbc.co.uk/news/business-14102750*

241 *Ed Miliband speech to Labour conference 2011 http://www.labour.org.uk/ed-milibands-speech-to-labour-party-conference*

242 *Observer 21st January Revealed: march of the new casinos by Antony Barnett http://www.theguardian.com/uk/2007/jan/21/gambling.immigrationpolicy*

243 *"Dispatches: Labour's Gambling Addiction" Monday 22nd January 2007. Interview with Antony Barnett.*

associated with that scenario.

The gaming legislation passed by Labour in 2005, which came into force in September 2007, has seen an explosion of gaming via new technologies. Gambling is now seen as a pastime, not the corrosive, dangerous, money grabbing habit that it once was seen as. Internet gambling, due to the very nature of how its done, makes regulation impossible. How can an Internet provider be sure that gamblers are not intoxicated beyond reasonable levels, that they aren't under 18, that they aren't recidivist problem gamblers, or, for example, have learning difficulties? A 2006 survey quoted by Channel 4 showed 97% of the British public had never set foot in a casino.[244] So why bother trying to introduce them into mainstream life? More to the point, why Labour? It just seemed so much at odds with the party's core values regarding the protection of vulnerable people from exploitation.

Tuition Fees

This policy, introduced under Labour, is corrosive to economic policy and social mobility. In 2009 we spoke to a nurse at the Royal London Hospital whose story highlights the mistakes made by this policy. The nurse - let's call him David - is making his way in a profession he is totally committed to, admitting to us that he finds the cynicism of his colleagues quite depressing, but he ploughs along regardless. David is hoping to enhance his degree so that he can be a nurse practitioner, which entails a lot of extra responsibility. It is clear to us that he loves his job and puts the kick of helping people above financial reward.

But the facts were simply this: David has spent £24,000, which he still owed with interest, on bettering himself; with the end aim of helping people. That's a policy that a socially driven party introduced. Of course, Royal London Hospital is in rather close proximity to the City, leading him to say: "£24K. That's what I owe. To better myself. To put something back and to help people. Whilst the government are letting their mates down the road (we are a mile from the City and the HQ of RBS) party on and on and on."[245] David's story isn't a one off; millions will soon have debts of well in excess of £40,000 by the age of 22. Students have now started asking, 'Is it worth it, can I afford it?'

David himself went to a comprehensive school and is the son of a lorry driver and a school cleaner. Just the sort of person that Labour is meant

---

244 David, named changed. Conversation during treatment for one of the authors.

245 David, named changed. Conversation during treatment for one of the authors.

to represent. His hard work and talent have been nurtured through state education, with the end result of his being able to move into the professions. Now the university system is penalising him financially for having the steely determination to study hard and succeed. This policy will not only damage the economy but is killing social mobility. The top up fees legislation means it's no longer how hard you work or your talent, but how much cash your parents give you, or whether or not you want to take a huge financial risk.

PFI

The Private Finance Initiative (PFI) was a tool created under the Major government and used by New Labour to allow the private sector to finance and build public sector projects. The public sector would pay for rent and maintenance on completion. Sounds great, especially when you consider the badly needed investment following the under-investment of the 1980's. But the contracts involved were often badly put together and not in the public interest. On 2nd December 2011 the London Evening Standard ran a damning piece, which revealed that no less than five leading orthopaedic surgeons had quit working at the Royal London Hospital in Whitechapel due to "*dangerous*" practices which put "*patients at risk*."[246] This insinuated that PFI had put financial pressure on the hospital forcing a decline in standards. Once again we saw a market-based policy coming unstuck. On the 4th April 2011 a Freedom of Information request was made to the hospital trust asking specific questions regarding how much the Trust had to allocate per annum in repayments and how this would affect the number of beds. The response was staggering:

 "Please be advised that we do not hold the information you require. Most of the information that we provide in response to Freedom of Information Act 2000 requests will be subject to copyright protection."[247]

Essentially is doesn't matter that it's public money; the company involved is private so the FOI legislation doesn't count. In early 2010, the British Medical Association produced a report which contains this information on the repayments:

---

246 *London Evening Standard 2nd December 2011 Five surgeons quit top hospital over patient care fears* http://www.standard.co.uk/news/five-surgeons-quit-top-hospital-over-patient-care-fears-6374464.html

247 *Muhammed Iqbal FOI request https://www.whatdotheyknow.com/request/royal_london_hospital_ beds_figur*

"The new Royal London Hospital in Whitechapel scheme is costing £1 billion and the 35 years of index-linked payments will start at £96m in 2013".[248] *"Non-acute services to reduce staff utilisation by 66%, appointment times (GP consultations) by 33% and prescribing costs by 10-15%"*.[249] *"Decommission 7% of elective procedures, 30% of outpatient appointments, 10% of A&E activity and 10-15% of diagnostics"*.[250]

This means that the Trust will repay *six times* the value of the work done, whilst care outcomes are falling. Add this to the £5bn cuts faced by NHS London and the conditions for a permanent financial crisis are in place. Cases like this are not uncommon in hospitals across the UK.

24 Hour drinking

The Labour Party liberalised alcohol licensing laws when it was questionable if there was a need to do so. Rather than reform the legislation to allow staggered or moving closing times, a system was developed that now allows applications for 24-hour drinking. Alcohol and the British have always had a pretty strange relationship. Beer was credited for making the UK a world power. In the early modern era, ale contained enough alcohol to kill the germs that caused debilitating illnesses and tapeworms, but was not strong enough to make us permanently drunk. It makes for a good explanation as to why we became the major world power in the 18th Century whilst the decision-making of the French and the Italians may have been impaired by their wine being too strong. The concept of the relationship between the feckless and alcohol is not a new one. "Gin Lane" was the painter Hogarth's contribution to the debate around alcohol. Produced in 1751 it portrayed a working class district where everyone from young nursing mothers to the elderly lived in a lifelong gin-fuelled haze.

Francis Place, a leading social reformer of the day reflected that the working classes and the poor only really had two ways to dull the pain of their existence, sex and gin, and that *"...drunkenness is by far the most desired..."*

248 *The state of London's hospitals: full data By Denis Campbell 20th January 2010* http://www.theguardian.com/news/datablog/2010/jan/20/london-hospitals-nhs-data

249 *The state of London's hospitals: full data By Denis Campbell 20th January 2010* http://www.theguardian.com/news/datablog/2010/jan/20/london-hospitals-nhs-data

250 *The state of London's hospitals: full data By Denis Campbell 20th January 2010* http://www.theguardian.com/news/datablog/2010/jan/20/london-hospitals-nhs-data

as it is *"cheaper and its effects more enduring".*[251] Victorian Prime Minister William Gladstone had strong views on the evils of alcohol, and sought to legislate to restrict pub opening hours in response to Salvation Army founder William Booth's observations regarding the British and booze in 1891: "*A population sodden with drink, steeped in vice, eaten up by every social and physical malady, these are the denizens of Darkest England amidst whom my life has been spent.*"[252]

Eventually the government was forced to act to restrict pub opening hours due to the need for munitions workers not to be drunk in charge of ordinance. The new opening hours were 12.00 to 2.30 and 6.00 to 9.30, and remained in force for most of the 20th Century. The Tories relaxed the laws in 1987, allowing pubs to remain open all day, closing at 11pm.

Any light reading around the university education of the Prime Minister and Mayor of London will demonstrate the link between alcohol and disorder simply isn't one restricted to class. The issue is clear: alcohol and public order on Friday nights across the UK is an historical problem and something that the general population are worried about. If you travel abroad there is just not the same seemingly nihilistic approach to going out and getting absolutely hammered. So we have to ask - why is the state liberalising consumption to aid our drink culture, as opposed to leaving the system be?

Take a tour of a UK city centre on an average Friday night and you will come across people in dangerous situations caused by alcohol. From Olympic-standard vomiting to aggressive interaction with other people and inanimate objects such as the nearest wall, drink is at the root of serious issues. Never mind the knock-on effect to the NHS and ambulance services - is life in Britain that bad that the only way to "have a good time" is to completely forget yourself?

Marxists would say that the drinking culture is a classic extrapolation of the principle of alienation; working people are subjected to mind-numbingly boring jobs and live for their weekend escape from reality. Middle class problem drinking is a relatively new phenomenon, but it is the binge drinking, associated with working class British culture, that grabs the headlines when the drinking laws are debated.

---

251 *"Beer Street and Gin Lane Paulson, Ronald (1992) Hogarth: High Art and Low, 1732–50*

Vol 2. Lutterworth Press ISB 0-7188-2855-0.

252 *Eternal Answers to Life's Toughest Questions By Paul C. Rostek (2002) ISBN-10:1591603773*

In September 2013 the Association of Chief Police Officers branded the legislation as a *"disaster"*.[253] The warnings from the police and industry insiders could not have been clearer. The relaxation of drinking laws had led to an increase in alcohol-related violence, poorer health outcomes and increased costs to the taxpayer. ACPOS's 2013 critique of drinking hours was not just a dig at New Labour. The police chiefs were also concerned that the coalition had done nothing to address the problems that had arisen either. *"The impact on the streets of our towns now at three and six o'clock in the morning is very significant and I don't think that is correct and we need to change that."*[254]

This isn't just about offering all-night drinking in big cities, where exceptions can and should be made. Take a more residential and less busy environment such as Farnham, the commuter belt market town in Surrey. Traditionally quieter pubs shut at 11pm pre 2005. If people wanted to keep later hours they went to nearby Guildford or Aldershot. Post-2005 has seen a dramatic rise in post-11pm opening, and associated noise and anti-social behaviour.

As we stated, the problem is in part down to the drinking culture in this country. Drinking and youth culture make the problem worse because it becomes highly attractive for younger teenagers keen to appear grown up. This leads to unmonitored drinking in unsafe environments with no context; these habits lead to a habit of binge drinking, not just having too much every now and then. Regular intoxication comes in many forms, not just high-tax expensive alcohol, but also drugs.

253 *24-hour drink law disaster , J slack, Published in the Daily Mail http://www.dailymail.co.uk/news/ article-2424718/24-hour-drink-law-disaster-Police-chiefs-brand-round-clock-pubs-terrible-mistakes-drunk-tanks-cope-late-night-mayhem.html 2013*
254 *24-hour drink law disaster , J slack, Published in the Daily Mail http://www.dailymail.co.uk/news/ article-2424718/24-hour-drink-law-disaster-Police-chiefs-brand-round-clock-pubs-terrible-mistakes-drunk-tanks-cope-late-night-mayhem.html 2013*

Chapter 14 - What might Labour's Policies be?

As the 2015 general election looms, there is a feeling within the Labour Party that the route to victory must be a radical one. That if Labour produces a timid manifesto it will not identify or stand up to the real challenges facing Britain. The aim of this chapter is to try and identify some of the policies Labour will run with in the 2015 election. There is an issue for Labour: there is a huge disconnect between the Parliamentary Labour Party (PLP) and the membership. This gap is exaggerated in the north of the UK, where the economic policies of the coalition have hit harder than in the metropolitan southeast. This came about when, after the 2010 general election, Ed Miliband rightly set about an exercise called 're-founding Labour'. During this period Labour members were asked to soul search post-New Labour. They did, and in light of the savage coalition government cuts and lack of economic prosperity, they re-found socialism. However, there are questions as to whether or not the PLP re-found their socialist roots, or whether they believed that the trappings of power which New Labour bought was the best way in which to run the country.

Take for example Labour's somewhat divisive shadow chancellor Ed Balls. In opposition, Ed Balls has a strong hand to play, as due to Osborne's bungling and the lack of economic growth, the coalition will fail miserably with its aim to eliminate the deficit in one parliament. Then there is the backdrop of high unemployment, declining living standards and low economic performance. The coalition has made the economic situation worse for the UK. Instead of taking advantage of the situation Ed Balls said to the Guardian, ""*My starting point is, I am afraid, we are going to have keep all these cuts.*"[255] And then the Shadow Chancellor went on to say that he was in favour of extending the public sector pay freeze. This isn't the legacy of

255 *Ed Balls risks union anger in push to bolster Labour's economic credibility P Wintour reported in The Guardian http://www.theguardian.com/politics/2012/jan/13/ed-balls-labour-party-economic-redibility 2012*

the crash: this is the legacy of the coalition. But the reality is that a well-run deficit budget is the only way to create the catch up growth the UK craves, but it's bad politics and the voters won't like it. Especially as borrowing without reform away from neo-liberalism will lead us to a Japanese-style long-term debt crisis.

However, Balls promising this left the party in no man's land. What was the point in Labour? This was at a point when Labour was struggling for momentum. This presented the Labour front bench Treasury team with a clear problem. The economy is in such an unpredictable period that any government opposition would find it hard to display an accurate alternative unless they were prepared to take a leap of faith and move away from supply side economics, which relies solely on growth to pay for social justice.

Labour had two choices: to ignore the problem, or to start electioneering by beginning to voice an alternative plan. This started when Balls on the Andrew Marr Show in mid June 2011 said: *"The government must reverse the VAT rise now and use that money to boost spending in the economy. I said that he should do that temporarily until growth is restored".*[256] Finally a policy - a strong one - a VAT tax cut. Let us not forget that VAT is a tax that hits the poorest hardest, and the coalition raised it from 15% to 20%. The coalition's VAT increase added £362 onto the tax bill for every £10,000 spent on VAT-able items.[257] Here was a clear policy, and one that was costed but without the need to get into the minutiae four years out from an election. Ed Balls went on with his attempt to begin the road to rebuilding the economic policy of the Labour Party by developing the five-point plan. The five-point plan gives definition to Labour's economic strategy and can described as thus:

Labour would bring forward long-term infrastructure projects;

There would be a 25% VAT cut - from 20% to 15% - to stimulate spending;

There would be a 75% VAT cut - from 20% to 5% - on home improvements;

There would be a banking bonus tax;

There would be National Insurance breaks for companies employing new people;

256 Andrew Marr Show, Produced by Jukes, Holleywood and Elgonaid for BBC1

257 For evfery £10,000 you spend- £1666 to reduce VAT from 20% to 15%- to reverse the Tory tax increase amounts to a tax cut of £1304 £362 tax cut

Additional revenues should be used to build homes and address youth unemployment;

And in January 2014, there was a commitment to reinstate the 50% tax bracket on all earnings over £150,000.

But given the dire long-term structural state of the UK economy, this represented an acceptance of the deficit being the main issue in our economy. Yet it could be said that a broken and unfair tax system that targets income - and not assets such as land and vast property portfolios - is the real issue facing us.

Education

Given the ill-thought-out reforms of the coalition it is essential that Labour continues to place education at the centre of its policy for future government. This does not mean tinkering with how schools are run, but by returning to nurturing teachers and students through investment and placing learning first.

Labour started promisingly in opposition when Andy Burnham was Gove's shadow. However matters took a distinct dip under Stephen Twigg, who ended up as one of the few people to be shuffled out of the shadow cabinet by Miliband in October 2013. He was replaced by Tristram Hunt, who became Gove's third opponent in three years. Teachers felt relieved, as Twigg's tenure in the post had seen an endorsement of military academies, and a rejection of the restoration of the Educational Maintenance Allowance, described as: "*not a priority, institutions that can afford to may like to consider it*".[258]

Hunt is another Oxbridge graduate, who found fame through TV, and who is now responsible for what we believe is the most important reform that Labour will have to make if elected in 2015. As far as we can see there are six key areas Hunt has to address:

A full curriculum review to meet the economic and social challenges;

The role of local authorities and if they should be trusted to run schools;

---

258 *Labour Party Education event in Hull, attended by Party members and members of the teaching profession- attended by Rathbone*

That education funding should be the top priority for government;

A full review of inspection criteria and answering the question of where now for OFSTED;

To let teachers teach by ending politician led pet project interventions;

And that there should be a review of the key stages of education.

Tristram Hunt should be focusing on these issues outlined above but in addition he must speak for school staff that are seeing their profession continue to be a political football. Morale is low, while pressure is high with ever-changing goal posts and OFSTED inspections, as well as the trashing of pay and conditions. Labour has rightly pointed out the comparisons between Sweden's failing Free Schools which Gove wants to adopt here, and Finland's amazing success. But to adopt the Finish system we will have to adopt their high tax and spend ethos, which means a high spend on maternity and childcare costs.

In December 2013, just two months into the job, Hunt told the Daily Telegraph that Labour wanted, *"competition between schools... and we'd also, where we need new schools, absolutely think about establishing parent-led academies".*[259] This left members of the teaching profession asking: *"What's the real difference, is this just another politician who doesn't understand that it's not how a school is managed but what goes on in the classroom?"*[260] There were huge developments in education under Labour that should be celebrated. New Labour, for all its faults argued that prosperity and social mobility go hand in hand. Investment in education, its infrastructure and teachers was a break with past and current Conservative policy. What we need now is a radical thinking and a professional lead approach; whilst the Tories supposedly let doctors call the shots, they don't trust teachers to do the same.

Gove confused vision for education, allied to a lack of a radical alternative from Labour led the New Statesman magazine to conclude in October 2013 that, *"parents, most of whom merely want a good local school and are largely uninterested in dogma and ideology, have been left with the impres-*

259 Tristram Hunt: 'White British boys are not getting the education they want' M Riddell, In The Telegraph   http://www.telegraph.co.uk/education/10539284/Tristram-Hunt-White-British-boys-are-not-getting-the-education-they-want.html 2013

260 Private discussion

sion that Labour has little constructive to say about education."[261]

Academies are a failing policy that have not really seen an improvement in standards and have led to a number of cases of financial mismanagement. The situation is the same with free schools or *"Parent-led Academies."* The Local Schools Network produced a report in 2012 that showed categorically that secondary schools academies were lower attaining than traditional Local Authority controlled establishments. This related not to just the bald 5 A* to C grades at GCSE (40% for academies, 60% for LA schools) but also on how much progress students make; the so-called "value added" by the school. 65% made expected progress in academies but in LA schools the figure was 75%.

The evidence that this book is gathering shows that a move away from market led policies is desperately needed. For the sake of education we hope that these challenges are met by the evolution of teacher lead radical thinking on education. Not more of the same market dogma. Schools and educational establishments should not be in competition with each other. The concept is entirely flawed, with demographics, intake, and socio-economic and other factors making "competition" a totally oxymoronic concept. Schools should in fact be working in collaboration to offer our young students the best education.

Welfare & Health Reform

Andy Burnham MP is one of the leading lights of Labour Party, he embodies the values the party. We had the privilege of speaking with him in 2011. A 'comp lad', he went on to attend Fitzwilliam College, Cambridge, gaining a degree in English. Burnham then worked as researcher to Tessa Jowell, for the NHS confederation, the Football Task Force and later as a special advisor at the Department for Culture Media and Sport. He entered Parliament in 2001 as the MP for his hometown Leigh, in Lancashire. Burnham was quickly identified as a high flyer from his work on the Commons Health Select Committee. He initially served as a Parliamentary Private Secretary, (the first rung on the Ministerial ladder), to Work and Pensions Secretary David Blunkett, and then to Education Secretary Ruth Kelly before being made a junior minister at the Home Office following the 2005 General Election. Tony Blair promoted him to the

---

261 Leader: Tristram Hunt could allow Labour to regain control of the education debate Published in New Statesman http://www.newstatesman.com/2013/10/tristram-hunt-well-qualified-take-education-fight-gove 2013

post of Under Secretary at the Health Department in 2006, and when Gordon Brown became Prime Minister in 2007 Burnham entered the cabinet as firstly as Chief Secretary to the Treasury and then he served as Culture Secretary before replacing Alan Johnson at the helm of the NHS in 2009.

The fact that a politician with core socialist values such as Burnham was trusted under New Labour with jobs at the very top says everything about his undoubted talent. Burnham is a man of passion and heart, not some cold, calculated, vote-seeking politician. He really is a lion heart of the Labour Party, and to whom many look to set policy direction alongside Ed Miliband.

Burnham talks about Tony Blair as *"brilliant, a real winner"* and describes what was achieved by the Blair government, especially regarding health and education, with a pride that you cannot fake. But he is the first to admit that, *"we lost our way, a perception grew that we had become managers rather than visionaries".*[262] One thing that you will never hear from Andy Burnham is any statement condemning Labour's time in power, and when trawling back over interviews and speeches it is almost impossible to decide whether Burnham was in the Brown or the Blair camp. This is because Burnham's obvious love for the Labour Party means that the needs and aspirations of the Party to serve the people come before any personal ambitions.

Conversation with Burnham reveals a refreshingly down to earth belief that politics has an almost limitless potential to change society. We discuss where the Labour Party is in Autumn 2011. Regarding the economy, Burnham, as a former Chief Secretary to the Treasury, is fully in tune with Ed Balls' mantra that the Coalition are:

"Cutting too fast and too soon. Whilst President Obama is pursuing a programme of investment in jobs, and tax cuts to stimulate demand, the Coalition have flat lined our economy by a programme of reckless cuts in public spending and a damaging rise in VAT which has been particularly hard on small business, the very sector that the Tories claim will create growth in the economy. We aren't naive. We in the Labour Party realise that the deficit created by the failure of the Banking system needs to be sorted out, but it has to be dealt with in a fair way which comes from a formula of tax rises allied to a well thought out and considered cuts in public spending."[263]

262 Interview between Rathbone and Andy Burnham 2011

263 Interview between Rathbone and Andy Burnham 2011

It is this realism that gives hope that Labour will move away from market-based reforms in health care and towards values-based policies that focus on social justice. But Labour has a tougher battle on welfare. The Labour Party's commitment to social justice through redistribution and welfare remains unquestioned, but the coalition placing this issue high up in politics makes the subject highly divisive. One great policy Labour announced was a jobs guarantee: Labour need to be tough but also need to ensure the state is doing something other than leaving employment to market forces.

"Labour will be tougher than Tories on benefits, promises new welfare chief". The promotion of Rachel Reeves over Liam Byrne in the role of Shadow DWP Secretary was seen as a positive one, with headlines such as: *"Rachel Reeves vows to cut welfare bill and force long-term jobless to take up work offers or lose state support"*. Labour went on a mission to *"explode the "myth" that Labour is soft on benefit costs"*.[264] The challenge for Labour is ensuring that the message on benefits, especially those related to unemployment is a message of hope, and to focus on the government policies that have seen unemployment too high for too long. Our narrow economy, growing population and greed culture don't help. Labour can't be dragged down by the right's constant attacks on the welfare state; reform needs to come through the action of the state, the creation of quality and diverse jobs and a bit of carrot and stick. Labour MPs - most of whom have never been anywhere near a job centre - droning on about being tough on benefits simply allows the Tories to set the agenda in this area, when the real question should be: why are there 3 million unemployed, why are there millions more under-employed, and why is the welfare state picking up the bill? The answer is simple: generations of Thatcherite policies that have failed to produce a diverse range of quality jobs spread around the UK. Instead of dancing to the Tories' drum, Labour should be challenging them.

The welfare state is not just a safety net but also a means to reduce inequality and produce social mobility; not forgetting that it looks after the vulnerable whether they be young, of working age or in retirement. The danger is that welfare is seen as an expense that should be reduced to just the level of a basic safety net, whilst low tax rates and aggressive capitalist policies see inequality widen and quality of life for those at the bottom vastly reduced. The overall result of growing inequality is a more expensive welfare system.

264 *Labour will be tougher than Tories on benefits, promises new welfare chief T Help Published in The Guardian http://www.theguardian.com/politics/2013/oct/12/labour-benefits-tories-labour-rachel-reeves-welfare 2013*

The poorest in society are not forms of entertainment. The poverty-porn culture which sees TV shows such as Channel Four's "Benefits Street" parade the poor for the nation's entertainment points to the fact that this is a national disaster.[265] A disaster caused by generations of economic policy that left high unemployment, low wages and a narrow economy. We don't make or do anything; our service industry is all that Britain has left and it's not suitable for all. This is not just a benefits issue: it's an unemployment issue. Under-employment and unemployment are something we should be angry about. It's easy to vilify and remain passive rather than get to the centre of the problem.

Labour has to turn its back on the bedroom tax. There simply isn't enough social housing out there to make this policy fair. Helen Goodman, Labour MP was quoted as saying *"We've said that the bedroom tax should... apply if people have been offered a smaller place to live and turned it down because, obviously, it is better to use the housing stock more efficiently."*[266] She failed to mention that the problem was a lack of planning, not enough stock and a rented sector that is overpriced. Successive failures in housing policy have led to this situation and it isn't really a welfare issue at all.

Foreign affairs & the Cost of Living

Ed Miliband has excelled in a further two policy areas as leader of the opposition. Firstly, on foreign affairs, and, secondly, by identifying the cost of living crisis.

In the lead up to the Iraq tragedy in 2003, the UK public made it abundantly clear where it stood on the issue of going to war with Saddam's vile regime. On February 15th of that year over one million people took to the streets to beg Tony Blair to pull back and seek another way to deal with the regime in Baghdad. He refused, and the public was proved right when no weapons of mass destruction were discovered, and a catastrophic civil war ensued due to the US/UK-led coalition having no exit strategy whatsoever. There was a danger that a Labour leader might shrink in the face of foreign conflict given the recent experiences of the Party. Such fears, however, were unfounded.

---

265 Benefit Street Love Productions for Channel 4 composed by Matthew Cracknel

266 A copy of this quote was found at http://www.snp.org/media-centre/news/2013/mar/labours-bedroom-tax-hypocrisy-condemned

During the summer of 2013 Syrian government forces, to the disgust of the world community, attacked the nation's own citizens with chemical weapons. US Secretary of State John Kerry, with the support of UK Foreign Secretary William Hague, immediately issued a threat to escalate the already disastrous situation in Syria with the promise of air strikes. The easy option for Ed Miliband would have been to sit back and mutter neutral statements about showing a united Anglo-American front. However, Ed Miliband and his shadow foreign affairs team had actually taken on board the lessons of the Iraq debacle. They decided to front up to Cameron and Hague's bluster and desire to please the US at all costs. When Parliament was recalled in August to approve military action, Miliband was crystal clear in his opposition. The eyes of the world were on the House of Commons and the pressure was on Miliband to deliver:

"I don't think anybody in this House or anybody in the country should be under any illusions about the effect of our relationship to the conflict in Syria if we were to militarily intervene. In our minds should be this simple question, which is upholding international law and legitimacy - how we can make the lives of the Syrian people better?"[267]

In a direct reference to Blair's Iraq disaster, the Labour Leader said: " *This is fundamental to the principles of Britain. A belief in the rule of law. A belief that any military action we take must be justified in terms of the cause and also the potential consequences."*[268]

Miliband had taken a central plank of New Labour's foreign policy and revoked it. It can be argued that this was Ed Miliband's "Clause Four moment", as it positioned his tenure as being totally different to the Blair/Brown era. Miliband appeared statesman like. Quite the opposite to Cameron and Blair's obsession with pleasing the White House.

Miliband continued by exhorting the Tories not to treat the UN as a "*sideshow*", and his passion for internationalism and justice was injected into his conclusion: *"In the end the fundamental test will be this: as we think about the men, women and children who have been subjected to this terrible atrocity, and we think about the prospects for other citizens in Syria, can the international community act in a lawful and legitimate way that will help*

---

267 *Hansard 29th august 2013 http://www.publications.parliament.uk/pa/cm201314/cmhansrd/ cm130829/debtext/130829-0001.htm*

268 *Hansard 29th august 2013 http://www.publications.parliament.uk/pa/cm201314/cmhansrd/ cm130829/debtext/130829-0001.htm*

them, that will prevent further suffering?"[269] Thirty Tories and nine Lib Dem MP's were persuaded, and Cameron lost the vote 285 to 272. Ed Miliband came out of the whole affair emboldened and strong. *"Britain doesn't need reckless and impulsive leadership, it needs calm and measured leadership".*[270]

Another area where Ed Miliband "gets it" in a way that the Tories never will concerns the crippling rise in the cost of living. Most MPs simply don't understand how hard it is on a day-to-day level to pay energy, fuel, housing and food bills. We do not expect our parliamentarians to go around in sackcloth and ashes, but the least they can do is familiarise themselves with the worries that their constituents have about the basics of life: food, heating, and shelter. In 2013 we were appalled to find that Labour MPs were still claiming their heating allowances on expenses. Not many of us can pass this expense on to our employers after all.[271]

We assume Ed Miliband has never had to hunt down the back of the sofa for his bus fare, but by challenging the Tories on the expenses of everyday life he moved to taking not only the moral but also the practical high ground. Miliband perfectly encapsulated this in Labour's cost of living campaigns, which focused on a central pledge to ensure that energy companies freeze prices for 20 months. This is the first time any politician has seriously taken on the inequalities posed by the policies of neo-liberalism, and the Labour leader should be commended.

But there really is a crisis in the cost of living in this country. Let's start off with some basic facts and figures about how the coalition has wrecked living standards for the many, leaving us with increased inequality and trashed services that will never come back. Since the 2010 general election the average family, according to the Labour Party in figures published in January 2014, is £1,600 worse off per annum. That's a whopping £133 a month or £30 a week.

Energy bills are up by nearly £300. The Bedroom Tax has hit 700,000 people. Homecare charges for the elderly and disabled are up by £740 a year on average. By January 2014, prices had out stripped wage increases in 41

269 Speech to commons can be found at https://www.labour.org.uk/statement-in-the-house-of-commons-on-syria,2013-08-29

270 Hansard 29th august 2013 http://www.publications.parliament.uk/pa/cm201314/cmhansrd/cm130829/debtext/130829-0001.htm

271 Accusations of hypocrisy as MPs claim energy bills on expenses published in Hull Daily Mailhttp://www.hulldailymail.co.uk/Accusations-hypocrisy-Hull-MPs-claim-energy-bills/story-20033808-detail/story.html#ixzz2xZJDDnrK 2013

out of the 42 months Cameron had been in Number Ten. We expect our young people to pay to be educated, which is mad in itself, but now we charge them £27,000 in tuition fees with no living costs accounted for. Private renting costs are up by nearly £1000 per annum, with landlords getting subsidised by the taxpayer via housing benefits especially in the South East. Rail fares are up 20%. Millionaires got a £40,000-per-million tax cut. Half a million people have been referred by health and welfare professionals to Food Banks. If you can find work (8 million are unemployed or don't have enough hours to make ends meet) then childcare costs soared by £304 in 2013 alone. The facts speak for themselves; why would Ed Miliband *not* run a campaign on the cost of living?

On the issue of Europe, Ed Miliband has had a mixed performance. We will argue that the Labour Party should support an EU referendum, and outline the advantages that would accrue from having it sooner rather than later. Not only would it be good politics, but also it's time we had a genuine debate about the pros and cons of the EU. This would be the perfect springboard for reform or exit.

In March 2014 Ed had promised that *"The next Labour government will legislate for a new lock – there would be no transfer of powers from the UK to the EU without a referendum on our continued membership of the EU."*[272] Essentially this is a promise of a referendum, but not for one without a concrete reason. There will have to be reform of the EU - as we discover in chapter 12, there are at least 5 key areas that undermine the UK's membership and are putting the Euro project in doubt. But only once reform has been suggested will there be a referendum. This is good politics because it parks the issue, but maybe bad policy because of the need for the UK people to have a say sooner, rather than later.

But Labour has been here before regarding the EU, and it is important that lessons are learned to avoid the charge of not trusting the people with a vote on our relationship with Europe. In 2004 Tony Blair told Parliament that they should debate the new European Union Constitution proposals: *"in detail and decide upon it and then let the people have the final say... Let the issue be put. Let the battle be joined."*[273] Then in the 2005 Labour Party election manifesto the voters were told: *"We will put it [the constitution] to the British people in a referendum and campaign wholeheartedly for a*

272 *Ed Miliband says in/out referendum on Europe is unlikely Published in that Guardian P Wintour* http://www.theguardian.com/politics/2014/mar/11/ed-miliband-referendum-europe 2014

273 *Hansard 20 April 2004; Vol. 420, c. 155-57.*

Yes vote." But the constitution died and the Lisbon Treaty was created in its stead. For the time being, this ends the notion of a European super-state with a joint constitution. There are a number countries with track records of voting 'No' to EU entry, notably Switzerland and Norway, but what would the British people say?

The reason for not playing the referendum card is political. The argument is: does Europe help or hinder working people in the UK? The EU referendum promised by Cameron if he wins an overall majority in 2015 can be an opportunity for the Labour Party to take an argument and present in an optimistic and positive way. If Labour had called Cameron's bluff and backed a referendum to be held at the same time as the European Parliamentary elections in 2014 then it couldn't have lost because of the prime opportunity to showcase its beliefs and values by going head to head with Nigel Farage's UKIP.

Writing in the Daily Mirror, high profile Labour MP Tom Watson said that Farage is a: "*turbo-Tory. He believes in higher taxation for most, a flat tax where a cleaner pays the same income tax as a banker. He's a classic Liberal economist who believes in fewer rights in the workplace and further privatisation of the NHS.*"[274] Yet despite this, UKIP will be challenging a number of northern Labour marginals in 2015, playing on the protest vote as well as the anti-EU vote.

But Labour itself is at a crossroads on EU membership, as the grass roots electorate are not as in favour of the European project as they once were. A socially responsible Party should be exposing just how damaging the EU is to the interests of the working class. The Tories pose as anti-EU, but when it suits them they are happy to hide behind the red tape they claim to despise. Here is a typical example of the two-faced nature of the Conservative Party when it comes to the European question.

The 2013 EU/US trade talks included means by which the NHS, and any other public service body for that matter, may have to be sold off as an example of a state monopoly stymieing the holy grail of neo-liberalism; privatisation. TUC General Secretary Frances O' Grady summed up the fears of NHS campaigners who were vainly trying to persuade Shadow Health Secretary Andy Burnham to rule out future private sector involvement in

---

274 *Why a referendum on Europe could have been a positive opportunity and defeated Nigel Farage T Watson MP Published in The Mirror* http://www.mirror.co.uk/news/uk-news/tom-watson-european-elections-referendum-2980809#ixzz2xZKFnRt6 2014

a Labour run health service when she said in January 2014 that the trade talks, "could thwart attempts by a future government to bring our health service back towards public ownership."[275] Section 75 of the 2013 Health and Social Care Bill states that NHS contracts must be open to "any willing provider" (note not "qualified").[276] This means that the NHS cannot legally give contracts to so called "preferred bidders" ie NHS organisations already providing the service such a physiotherapy, or the provision of aids such as wheelchairs and crutches. If a bidder feels unjustly dealt with, they can sue, which dovetails with the spirit behind the trade talks: that of private interests trumping state provision which is at the heart of Tory values. How ironic that their bête noir, the EU, could be the Trojan Horse to promote their ideology.

Gay Marriage: A Cameron Policy he needed Labour to introduce

As autumn moved into winter 2012, David Cameron felt the icy back blast of anger from the usual Tory back bench Euro Sceptic suspects such as David Davis, Bill Cash and Peter Bone. But worryingly for Cameron's authority, the 2010 intake including Brigg and Goole MP Andrew Percy, and Rochester's Mark Reckless, were in the vanguard of the rebellion. Halloween seemed a somehow appropriate time for the horrors of Europe to come out and haunt David Cameron.

On 31st October 2012, MPs defeated the government line that called for a freeze on the overall European budget. The Tory right, along with their Irish DUP Eurosceptic friends, formed an unlikely alliance with the Labour Party. Ed Balls and Leader Ed Miliband argued that if the Tories were going to force austerity on the UK with spending cuts, then it would be hypocritical for them to vote for a European freeze. Cameron must have felt he was in a re-run of "John Major: The Movie". Beset by a failing economy, the press running his Ministers out of office, a gaffe prone Chancellor, sleaze and now a serious challenge to his authority over Europe.

Cameron desperately needed an issue which he could use to sideline his right flank Eurosceptic MPs. He chose gay marriage. The Prime Minis-

---

275 Quote can be found at http://www.tradeunionfreedom.co.uk/tipp-and-trade-unions/ =

276 British sovereignty 'at risk' N Morris published in The Independent http://www.independent. co.uk/news/uk/politics/british-sovereignty-at-risk-from-euus-trade-deal-uk-in-danger-of-surrendering-judicial-independence-to-multinational-corporations-warn-activists-9057318.html 2014

ter reasoned correctly that Labour would back plans to grant gay people complete marriage equality because, after all, it had been Labour governments who had led the way on gay rights. As we have seen, Wilson's 1964/70 tenure saw many progressive social policies come onto the statute book. The law making love between two men a criminal offence had been lifted in 1967, and the Blair government had introduced Civil Partnerships (which allowed gay people to register their relationship formally) in 2004, so it seemed a natural progression for gay marriage to be the next step.

Cameron thought that he was boxing clever by tabling gay marriage legislation and hoped that he could achieve two things. Firstly, the policy continued his programme of the detoxification of the Conservative brand by reaching out to a minority group previously maligned by the notorious Clause 28 section of the 1988 Local government Bill. Secondly, the move would flush out his opponents on the right. Would they let him suffer the temporary humiliation of relying on Ed Miliband and Labour to pilot through legislation?

As expected the Tory right revolted against their leader's expressed will for the legislation to pass when it reached the Commons in May 2013. Despite it being a non-whipped vote, (conscience issues are traditionally left to the individual), Cameron had made it abundantly clear that he wanted this vote to pass. 133 Conservative MPs - including two cabinet ministers - voted against allowing same sex couples equal marriage rights, and the legislation only passed because of Labour's overwhelming support. For Labour, the real party of social justice this vote was a non-issue. Equality for all regardless of sexuality, race or gender is the only way run a country. It is disingenuous that the history books will credit the Conservatives with securing marriage equality, when it is Labour that has historically done more for gay rights. But it should be trumpeted that without Labour MPs there would have been no gay marriages taking place on March 29th 2014.

This was an example of great policy ending up as bad politics. Cameron had done the progressive thing, but by doing so he had exposed the chasm in his party between the modernisers and the reactionary right. Cameron had ended up with the worst of all worlds: thoroughly disenchanted backbenchers who felt he had blindsided them with gay marriage, and an opposition buoyed by having legislation that they agreed with passed by a weakened Prime Minister. If Cameron fails to win a Commons majority in

2015 he has alienated his parliamentary party and will be forced from the Tory leadership by the very "Nasty Party" strain that he had so desperately wanted to see the back of.

Chapter 15 - Conclusion

Conclusion- Don't stop thinking about tomorrow.

So far we have identified that Labour has been the party of social reform, but also that to be electable Labour must ensure economic competence but not by doing the same things that led to the crash. The long-term policies of neo-liberalism or Thatcherism have opened the door for a new political vision in Britain. A vision which places social responsibility at the heart of the government agenda, moving away from the use of market forces to deliver essential public services and utilities.

It is time to stop taking decisions for today and start thinking about tomorrow. House prices, the cost of living and mass un/under-employment have left a poor legacy for the young of today. The young don't want things given to them; they just want the same chances that previous generations of Britons enjoyed. The same free education, the same NHS and the same chance to get on in life. We are losing a generation who graduated since the financial crash, a generation who not just struggled to get a job, but who find prices a real barrier to settling down and starting a family. Instead of addressing the challenges of economic growth, the government have made things worse.

Ed Miliband has made some sound noises in opposition. If Labour is elected we suspect the state will no longer be passive in tackling the issues facing Britain. Take the cost of living crisis and standing up to the banks and the vested press interests. For the first time in a generation, we have a politician who isn't afraid to stand up and say what's right on these issues. Miliband's challenge is ensuring that his manifesto is imaginative enough to appeal to a wide range of voters, and finding candidates who share his vision. A vision marries social responsibility with efficient and open government.

The use of neo-liberalism is a path of least resistance and it absolves states of responsibility. It allows this coalition to take no responsibility for low employment and economic growth. Labour needs to use the state to solve the very real and significant problems we face. Labour needs to ensure it delivers change that it can be proud of.

As mentioned in chapter one, this book is a twin. Whilst this book has examined the past, the next book is dedicated to future. Its looks at economics, education, welfare, globalisation, the environment, civil liberties, living standards, equality and law and order to argue that there needs to be a bigger role for the state, and that social responsibility is the cornerstone when formulating government strategy.

As we have examined, Britain really is at a crossroads. From 1900, we have travelled a path of a slow revolution. We now have the choice of becoming a neo-liberal state, not dissimilar to Edwardian Britain, where poverty and private interest are held in higher esteem than the pursuit of social and economic justice. This will be the full Americanisation of the UK, the acceptance of capitalism, a dangerous place to be in a country not known for its political radicalism. Made worse by the pure apathy of the British people, who will not fight or get angry over the event of total capitalism in the UK, despite the fact it is highly regressive.

Labour has played a pivotal, if not exclusive role in the social revolution. The crossroads we face present the choice between returning to the battle for social and economic justice in the face of neo liberalism or accepting that the writing is on the wall. Those who accept neo-liberalism, or any watered down version, should accept New Labour - or worse still, the Liberal Democrats. But this ideology won't address the problems Britain faces. It will compound them; financial liberalism always has done, and that's why we have socialism.

In 1994 future Blair biographer Anthony Seldon published a book with co-writer Stuart Bell, *"The Conservative Century".*[277] The book argues that because the Tories were in office for the majority of the 20th century, then it automatically followed that it was their agenda that drove the nation forward. We have argued in this book that actually it was the centre left agenda that came to dominate the century, and that the Tories were forced to tack along with this prevailing ideology in order to remain in government and to win elections. Even the dreaded Mrs Thatcher was forced to accept the sacrosanct position of the NHS in the minds of the UK public. Then, after 18 years in power from 1979, the Tories did not create one single grammar school - despite Thatcher going on the record in 1967 as saying, *""I am a*

277 *OUP Oxford; 1st Edition edition (13 Oct 1994) isbn: 0198202385 13th Oct 1994*

firm believer in our grammar schools. For many years now they have been the ladder from the bottom to the top."[278]

The post-war Labour government nationalised swathes of British industry. Yet the 13-year Conservative government that followed was forced to stick to the idea of the state having a huge stake in, and direct control of, economic and industrial policy. The Heath Administration (1970-74) actually increased the number of nationalised firms when it purchased Rolls Royce on behalf of the taxpayer. It went on to pump government cash into the Clyde shipbuilding yards the following year, to prevent them going to the wall and creating mass unemployment.

The advances made for ordinary people in the 20th century such as paid holiday, rights at work and decent quality housing were all initiatives that came from the left, socialists and the trade union movement. Not for nothing are the Tories called the "Conservative" Party, as all these gains for the working class were made against the gnashing and grinding of teeth from the right. The Tories voted against every bill that the 1945 Labour government proposed to set up the NHS.[279] From the legalisation of homosexuality in 1967 to the Race Relations Act of 1976 the Tories have been on the wrong side of the argument. This is something David Cameron has recognised, and this is why he staked his reputation on legalising gay marriage.

The 20th Century was the Labour century. This is because the party used its periods in power to drive real and lasting change through radical legislative programmes. The first Labour government was short lived, but its legacy after just nine months in power was the 1924 Housing Act. The legislation freed up local authorities to borrow money over a long period to build quality homes for their residents. 508,000 dwellings were built for rent by councils.[280] This policy laid the foundations for the revolution in social housing that saw the decline of the Rackmanite landlords and the rise of well-built public housing that was spacious and included such (then) luxuries such as inside toilets and bathrooms.

We have seen how the 1945 Labour government created the NHS and rolled out the Welfare State via implementation in full of the 1942 Bev-

278 *1967 speech to Barnet Young Conservatives quoted by the Margaret Thatcher Foundation* http://www.margaretthatcher.org/document/101584

279 *BBC "Making Britain Better" 1st July 1998* http://news.bbc.co.uk/1/hi/events/nhs_at_50/special_report/119803.stm)

280 *"Urban Process and Power" (1994) by Peter J Ambrose, page 107 Routledge*

eridge Report. The Wilson years were synonymous with great social reform such as divorce and giving women control over their lives via availability of contraception and access to abortion. As well as the Race Relations Act, the 1974-79 Labour government passed the Sex Discrimination Act which outlawed unequal pay based on gender, and forged a positive relationship with Europe after the 1975 referendum which saw the UK public say "Oui" to the Common Market. Perhaps the most interesting fact about the mid 1970s was that the period of Callaghan's government saw inequality at its narrowest in UK economic history between 1977/79.[281]

When Labour was returned to power in 1997 the NHS was still in existence and free at the point of use. State schools were comprehensive with no selection allowed, and remained overwhelmingly under local authority control. The UK was still part of the European Union, and the welfare state picked up the pieces when individuals and families fell on hard times. Public spending and running a deficit budget to achieve growth (otherwise known as Keynesianism) had been adopted by John Major and his chancellor Ken Clarke to put boosters under the economy in the wake of the 1991-2 recession. All of these policies and means of running the economy had their roots in centre-left ideology and had first been implemented by 20th century Labour governments.

Tony Blair has rightly been heavily criticised for inviting private providers whose sole aim is profit into running parts of the public sector. But his reasoning was that it was a way (now recognised as flawed) of funnelling large amounts of cash into the public services, especially the NHS. The result was a massive improvement in the health service as we have documented in this book. When Labour left office in 2010, satisfaction levels were at a record high and the Tories were forced to promise not to cut NHS funding. Even though Cameron is in the process of breaking up the NHS, the Tories are desperate to hide this from the public by constantly repeating their mantra of 'no NHS cuts'. The facts, however, are different. In June 2014 a report from Monitor, who scrutinise NHS finances, said that 1 in 3 hospital trusts were in deficit compared to just 1 in 10 when Labour left power. The £3 billion top-down reorganisation had seen cash removed from the front line and pumped into reconstituting how care of patients was managed.[282]

281 (note: Guardian "Inequality 'worst since second world war'" Danny Doring 27th June 2012 http://www.theguardian.com/news/datablog/2012/jun/27/century-income-inequality-statistics-uk)

282 The government has lost control of NHS finances" Guardian 18th June 2014 http://www.theguardian.com/society/2014/jun/18/labour-claims-the-government-has-lost-control-of-nhs-finances

Despite the evidence we have discussed regarding the squeeze applied to the NHS budget in England, David Cameron continued telling anyone who would listen, *"This government has increased spending on the NHS".*[283] Yet the BBC reported the very same day that this statement was made that the service was facing a funding gap of 2%, equivalent to £2 billion. BBC health editor Hugh Pym told his readers, *"The NHS has experienced a prolonged budget freeze as part of the government's plan to reduce the UK deficit."*[284]

The Tories, despite Health Secretary Jeremy Hunt's now notorious quip that, *"the NHS is a sixty year mistake"*, realise that the UK public see the NHS as a red line issue. They know that with the last election having been so tight, and that in all probability their chances in 2015 of forming a majority government are slim, it is absolutely vital that the voters do not get a sniff of what is really afoot: cuts and privatisation by the back door. The Conservatives realise the NHS is Labour's ground and are keen to portray themselves as locked into the NHS ethos, whilst painting Labour as incompetent in delivering the service for Wales where the devolved government is run by Labour.

There has been a slow social revolution since 1900 in Britain. We have become a socially minded country. The Tories have been forced to accept it, at least in public. We have become somewhat greedy in the last 20 or so years; we abandoned collective aspiration in pursuit of individual aspiration. The UK must now decide which route it wishes to take, the wealth just for oneself or the wealth and prosperity of all us.

In this book we have painted a picture of how the Labour Party has evolved by placing it in the context of the political story of the UK. There have been many successes, and some low periods. The Party has spent time in the doldrums but has generally come back fighting and ready to address the issues facing the country head on. Its election victories in 1945 and 1997 created a buzz that no Tory victory has ever come close to emulating.

Cameron could only dream of the rapturous reception afforded New Labour and Tony Blair that early summer morning in May 1997. *"A new dawn has broken has it not?",*[285] proclaimed the young Labour Prime Minister

283 (note: PMQ's June 18th 2014 in response to Natacha Engel MP. BBC Parliament).

284 (Note: "NHS 'facing funding gap of up to £2bn' in England" by Hugh Pym 18th June 2014 http://www.bbc.co.uk/news/health-27894551)

285 Quoted by Peter Hennessey Daily Telegraph 13th May 2007 http://www.telegraph.co.uk/news/uknews/1551357/He-spoke-of-a-new-dawn-and-clouds-rolled-in.html)

on the footsteps of Labour's Milbank HQ early on 2nd May. This moment, whilst a part of the quiet social revolution, for many was a let-down, a failure to reach the full potential of a Labour government. A let-down because New Labour became neo-liberal Labour.

Ultimately the difference between Labour and the Conservatives is Labour believed that the UK had a vast untapped potential and that the old days of sleaze and minimum aspiration should be cast aside.

In book two we will argue that very same thing, but set in a modern, 21st century context. We will urge Labour to be bold and grab that spirit of '97, but not by looking back in a literal sense and aping New Labour policies. We mean that the buzz and sense of hope that Blair created around the Labour Party must be recreated in the 2015 campaign. All need not be doom and gloom. We are the seventh richest economy in the world according to the International Monetary Fund, and it is completely unacceptable that 913,138 Britons were forced into the humiliating step of being referred to a Food Bank in 2013, up from 346,992 in the previous year.[286]

This is not poverty; it is 1930s style destitution. We will argue that there is another way for our country, and that Ed Miliband must embrace a new and radical agenda for Labour, starting with the means by which the UK government calculates, raises and spends money raised by taxation.

Ed Miliband, we will contest, has correctly identified what ails the UK. But does he have the policies, and crucially the moral courage to actually deal radically and effectively with these challenges? To find out what these issues are, and what else Labour needs to do in order to win a majority in the general election?

Election 2015 is the most important election since 1945 because if Labour does not win, the slow social revolution will falter and die. But most importantly, if the Labour Party fails in May 2015, the British people will pay a terrible and irreversible price. Labour must not let that happen.

286 Trussell Trust June 2014 http://www.trusselltrust.org/foodbank-figures-top-900000his